DISMANTLING GLOBAL WHITE PRIVILEGE

DISMANTLING GLOBAL WHITE PRIVILEGE

Equity for a Post-Western World

Chandran Nair

Berrett–Koehler Publishers, Inc.

Berrett-Koehler Publishers, Inc.
1333 Broadway, Suite 1000
Oakland, CA 94612-1921
Tel: (510) 817-2277
Fax: (510) 817-2278
www.bkconnection.com

ORDERING INFORMATION
Quantity sales. Special discounts are available on quantity purchases by corporations, associations, and others. For details, contact the "Special Sales Department" at the Berrett-Koehler address above.

Individual sales. Berrett-Koehler publications are available through most bookstores. They can also be ordered directly from Berrett-Koehler: Tel: (800) 929-2929; Fax: (802) 864-7626; www .bkconnection.com.

Orders for college textbook / course adoption use. Please contact Berrett-Koehler: Tel: (800) 929-2929; Fax: (802) 864-7626.

Distributed to the US trade and internationally by Penguin Random House Publisher Services.

Berrett-Koehler and the BK logo are registered trademarks of Berrett-Koehler Publishers, Inc.

Printed in the United States of America

Berrett-Koehler books are printed on long-lasting acid-free paper. When it is available, we choose paper that has been manufactured by environmentally responsible processes. These may include using trees grown in sustainable forests, incorporating recycled paper, minimizing chlorine in bleaching, or recycling the energy produced at the paper mill.

Library of Congress Cataloging-in-Publication Data

Names: Nair, Chandran, author.
Title: Dismantling global white privilege : equity for a post-Western world / Chandran Nair.
Description: First edition. | Oakland, CA : Berrett-Koehler Publishers, Inc., [2022] |
    Includes bibliographical references and index.
Identifiers: LCCN 2021033451 (print) | LCCN 2021033452 (ebook) | ISBN 9781523000005
    (paperback) | ISBN 9781523000012 (adobe pdf) | ISBN 9781523000029 (epub)
Subjects: LCSH: Whites. | Social status. | Race—Social aspects. | Race—
    Economic aspects. | Racism.
Classification: LCC HT1575 .N35 2022 (print) | LCC HT1575 (ebook) | DDC 305.809—dc23
LC record available at https://lccn.loc.gov/2021033451
LC ebook record available at https://lccn.loc.gov/2021033452

First Edition
27 26 25 24 23 22 21   10 9 8 7 6 5 4 3 2 1

Book producer: Susan Geraghty
Text designer: Paula Goldstein/Westchester Publishing
Cover designer: Alvaro Villanueva

This book is dedicated to all those people from around the world who have suffered discrimination because of the color of their skin.

It is also dedicated to those who enjoy White privilege but are honest enough to recognize it and are committed to changing the status quo.

It is dedicated to all those who want to take action within their families, workplaces, and organizations to dismantle White privilege wherever they see it.

It is dedicated to all of these people because they will need the strength, determination, and information to embark on an important journey—which will take at least a generation—as the global community transitions into a fairer, post-Western world.

Finally, it is dedicated to you, the reader.

All proceeds from direct sales of the book by the Global Institute for Tomorrow and from worldwide royalties will be directed toward furthering the cause of dismantling global White privilege.

CONTENTS

Foreword ix

Preface: White Privilege: It's Woven into the Fabric of Globalization xi

Introduction   Black Lives Matter and the Tip of the Iceberg 1

1   Geopolitics of Dominance: The White Knights of Chess 22

2   The Retelling of History: This Version Ain't Mine 39

3   The World of Business: Uneven Playing Fields 55

4   Media and Publishing: Captive Minds 70

5   Education: Schooling and Grooming 83

6   Culture and Entertainment: Gone with the Wind 97

7   Sports: Match Fixing 110

8   Fashion: Little Black Dress 123

9   Environment, Sustainability, and Climate Change:
Zero Carbon and Other Myths 137

Conclusion   How Change Happens: No Whitewash, Please! 154

Discussion Guide 173

Notes 177

Acknowledgments 191

Index 195

About the Author 207

Working on Equity: The Global Institute for Tomorrow 209

C handran Nair's book is, in the best sense, a revolutionary one. A few years back, the title alone would have made that clear, but now, deceptively, the title may lead readers to think it is another of the books about race relations in the West. It is not—is about decolonizing our world.

Thanks in particular to the transformative impact of the Black Lives Matter movement in the US, conversations about White privilege are no longer taboo. Fortune 500 CEOs, newspaper commentators, and even chat shows are all talking about it. As welcome and overdue as those conversations are, they are nevertheless, as Nair points out so powerfully, the tip of the iceberg. White privilege is not a domestic US or European issue alone; it is, rather, a descriptor of a global aspect of dominance. White privilege globally shapes not only economics and politics but even culture, ideas, and both White and non-White people's sense of identity.

Those of us who grew up in the developing world during the generation after decolonization held powerful conversations about challenging the structures of racial dominance. We were clear that although White domination had come with empire, it had not gone away merely with the lowering of European flags and the raising of new independent flags on Africa and Asian soil. The Bandung Conference of 1955; the pan-Africanist movements; the bold challenge made by leaders, from Sankara to Lumumba to Nyerere; the international antiapartheid movement; and the movements in the Frontline States battling the racist South African government all spoke to confronting White privilege and global Western hegemony. We were demanding change and were clear in those conversations, which could be heard not only in parliaments and international conferences but in university halls and street markets by the village water pump; they could be heard, too, in the food halls in the West where young African and Asian diaspora communities met.

With the imposition of neoliberalism across the world, much of that conversation was silenced. Nair's powerful book will help bring it back, in a new frame, for a new generation. Of course, you don't have to agree with everything Nair says—indeed, I think he wouldn't want you to; he enjoys a good argument too much! But I hope that the book will help reignite in you, as it has in me, that spark that can kindle the determination for a truly global shift of power and status so that every person on earth can live in dignity.

Thomas Sankara told us that "we have to work at decolonizing our mentality." Bob Marley told us to "emancipate yourselves from mental slavery / none but ourselves can free our minds." Nair's book is an invitation to do just that. And all of us, because we all deserve to be free, deserve the opportunity to get to read this book.

Winnie Byanyima,
executive director of UNAIDS,
undersecretary-general of the United Nations,
and former executive director of Oxfam

White Privilege: It's Woven into the Fabric of Globalization

> Me only have one ambition, y'know? I only have one thing I really like to see happen. I like to see mankind live together— Black, White, Chinese, everyone—that's all.
>
> —Bob Marley, *Marley*

I have been very fortunate to have had the opportunity to live and work in different parts of the world, thereby experiencing the people and cultures of many countries. I was also lucky to have been born in one of the most racially and religiously diverse countries in the world. This was a most enriching gift and gave me an early sense of living with diversity and not feeling threatened by people of other races and religions. Thus I had little fear of other people and no sense of superiority.

But it might also be the case that because my formative years were spent in a former British colony, I was highly attuned to how White people acquired special status and privileges wherever they went in the non-Western world. I was struck by how they seemed to view themselves as superior to others and leverage this in many subtle ways for their own economic benefit and social privileges. This book is a result of that early awareness and subsequent search for answers.[1]

The impacts of White privilege are much more profound and insidious than commonly understood. White privilege needs to be better studied by the younger generation across the world. Too many people, especially non-Whites, just accept it as the norm and even seek Whiteness, a phenomenon that I will describe in this book. White privilege needs to be understood beyond the descriptions in history books about the horrors of colonization, the nature of imperialism, and the oppression of Black people in the US, and beyond even current-day liberal explanations and theories about Western hegemony. Many books have been written on these topics, and most look back to document events and actions of great injustice that can no longer be denied. But not enough books have entered the mainstream in examining how the past is being actively preserved today through various mechanisms for the same economic objectives that triggered colonization and imperialism. Greater awareness is needed if this process is to be reversed and a more just world created in the coming post-Western world.

Most versions of history have been written by Western historians, and while some have been honest in their pursuit of the truth, the majority have been selective in narrating history, absolving the West of many of the horrors of its past.[2] What is common is the framing of these atrocities as events in the distant past and the active cultivation by Western governments, historians, and the media that the enlightened West of today has now learned its lessons, turning its societies into the most progressive in the world. This book will argue that this is a lie and that the aim of dominating the world remains the principal objective of Western powers, often working in tandem through strategic economic and military alliances. The sharp rise of White supremacy in the United States in the last few years, with links to a wider fear of other nations and races—present in Europe too—should make this crystal clear to anyone in doubt.

There is a need to reject the notion that what we experience and see today with regard to Western superiority is a legacy of history and is on its way out. This too is a lie, as the preservation of White privilege is an active and ongoing process. It is aided and abetted by many, including global corporations, the media, and leading international institutions, despite pronouncements about the fight for a fairer and more just world.

Much of the current discourse on race, Western power, and White supremacy does not in my view fully explain how White privilege works globally. The current discourse in the West in popular literature and media commentary—aside from academia—does not honestly explore how it is actively promoted and is spreading across the world despite all the posturing about fighting White racism.

This book will argue that the people and institutions that support and in fact actively promote White supremacy and privilege are not, as often suggested, delusional—which downplays how mainstream they really are—and they cannot simply be dismissed as racists. White supremacists do not simply have an assumption of superiority; they have an entrenched belief in superiority, intermingled with strongly held religious convictions, honed over centuries, extending to large segments of the global White population even if they publicly reject such labels.

This book seeks to show that White privilege is in fact centuries old, has been reengineered for the modern world, and extends well beyond the confines of the historical and current socioeconomic conditions that catalyzed the creation of the Black Lives Matter movement in the US, which can be viewed as the tip of the iceberg of the often unrecognized and unseen larger-scale features of global White superiority. Why? Because it is now woven into the very fabric of globalization, lurking in its structure. The victims do not see the perpetrators as delusional but instead as those who project power with intent and use it ruthlessly to preserve their economic interests, even through violence.

When living in Africa, I came into close contact with the many facets of White privilege and superiority by witnessing the brutality of the apartheid system in South Africa, and got involved in supporting the struggle against its injustices. It was a turning point in my life and provided a deeper understanding of the economic basis for a racist system of governance, which not only actively deprived the majority of their basic human rights but also sought to strip them of their humanity and dignity. This was much more than simple racism. Through hundreds of conversations with people in the liberation movement—in South Africa, Zimbabwe, Mozambique—I began to understand the economic drivers of enslavement through enforcing racial domination and the instilling of White superiority.[3]

My experiences in living and working across the world made me aware of yet another interesting phenomenon—White people invariably have a free pass to the world and expect it. This pass is out of reach for the Nigerian, Chinese, Egyptian, or Indonesian. From businessmen to journalists, lawyers, bankers, and academics, they demand a special status. There is even a contemporary term that captures that status—*expat*; being an expat immediately confers an elevated status and thus privileges often viewed as rights by White people.[4]

Are Westerners aware of this? And, if so, why do they fake innocence? Then again, why would they admit to race-based privileges? Are they simply inured to their sense of superiority over others and view it as normal? But why do others not only accept and tolerate it as the norm but in fact reinforce it by being subservient and becoming the allies or surrogates of White privilege? It is these questions that sowed the seeds of this book: one that is not about racism and imperialism but about White privilege. The failure to find these issues addressed concisely in the nonacademic literature made me want to write this book.

It is also critically important to remind the reader that this book is not in any way arguing that all race-based injustices in the world are perpetrated by Western powers, White people, and the associated phenomena of White privilege. Neither is it suggesting that equity in a post-Western world is wholly dependent on dismantling global White privilege. That would be absurd and factually incorrect. The book also does not seek to negate the enormous contributions of Western civilization toward human progress.

I am acutely aware that there are numerous other forms of race- and religion-based injustices. Many are abhorrent and must not be tolerated under any guise. Some of them are close to home, such as the caste system in India and the Malay-first policy in my home country, Malaysia, about which I have spoken and written; religious persecution across parts of Asia, Africa, and the Middle East; the discrimination suffered by women in many parts of the non-Western world; the discrimination against dark-skinned people in parts of Asia; the harm being done to indigenous communities in the name of progress; even the racism of Black people toward Whites in different parts of the world.[5]

But this is not a book about global racism and injustices. It is about a phenomenon that has its origins in events starting five hundred years ago, which has persisted in various forms and is still very much part of the world today. And that phenomenon is Western superiority and White privilege. There is no running away from the fact that Western domination of the world over the last few centuries for economic reasons was rooted in racism. It was based on a belief that races who lived in other parts of the world were inferior and could be tricked, cheated, or just exploited. The resultant global economic domination by the West shapes the world we live in today, and so does White racism rooted in superiority toward most people of the world. White racism has not disappeared. It continues to show its intolerance of any threat to its global economic dominance. It has no rival in terms of longevity, global reach, harm done, and continuing subversion of other cultures and societies.

The audiences for a book like this will range from people in business and media to those who work in multilateral agencies, governments, and civil society organizations, and, I hope, students and those in academic institutions. These various audiences will react differently to the arguments, but I hope they will find enough evidence to stop being in denial and take positive action. The starting point is acknowledgment of these issues in all the ways they manifest themselves across the world and as described in this book, but with which so many people are unfamiliar. It will be a first for many to have these topics, ranging from the impact of international business practices to Western pop music and fashion and even the fight against climate change, argued and presented in this way.

Having worked closely with global businesses, multilateral agencies, and NGOs for more than thirty years, I am well versed with their often blinkered understanding of these issues, born out of sheer ignorance or willful denial. Thus a key objective of this book is to address some very inconvenient truths and suggest practical ways forward. New narratives have to be the starting point for raising awareness.

For instance, I have for years cringed at being referred to as a citizen of an "emerging market" or from the "'Global South," especially when these terms seem to refer to people from a range of ill-defined countries. We need to challenge the use of these terms, as they come loaded with many negative connotations. They are part of an archaic and condescending Western narrative about development and growth, very much rooted in a sense of superiority.

Yet these terms are frequently used by economists and development experts. They have no meaning apart from the negative innuendo attached to their use. Emerging from what? Poverty, deprivation, backwardness, incompetence, and drudgery?

And emerging *to* what? A Western standard of prosperity, progress, and modernity achieved through perpetual growth wedded to Western political and value systems? Who decided *Global South* was synonymous with poverty and bad governance, all of which was self-inflicted?

If this idea of emerging has any meaning at all, it might be: "Emerging from centuries of exploitation, plunder, and repression by those who at the same time preach freedom, human rights, and liberty."

If the arguments are objectively received and appreciated as the basis for an overhaul, then business leaders should look at three key areas to begin the process of change. The "how to" is not as difficult as the willingness to accept these issues and act. The three areas are (1) the way their organizations are structured, which helps preserve White privilege locally and globally; (2) an audit of the goods and services they offer, which are based on promoting Whiteness and Western superiority, especially in the non-Western world; and (3) the positions they take worldwide on global issues, which are still rooted in promoting and consolidating Western power.

Each chapter provides enough food for thought and specific areas to tackle if leaders are serious about the issues and committed to shifting mindsets. The final chapter is a call to action in which I outline practical and implementable ideas that can be seized by corporate decision-makers, multilateral agencies, and civil society leaders, drawing on examples from many spheres of globalization. It provides a list of three to five key priorities for each of these players. This list is not comprehensive, but it will identify some priorities so people can make a start.

The book cannot cover every aspect of global White privilege, and there are two areas that I have left out and hope others will take up in the future. These are the role of organized religion and the effect of gender and gender politics. Both are very important topics, and with regard to organized religion, the book does address the issues related to how privilege is institutionalized. I am also aware of how gender dynamics are critical to how we understand culture, cultural power, and change. But those are topics I felt are beyond the scope of this book.

In conclusion, I should point out that I am drawing on my experience of having lived an international life, one that made me fairly well versed in how the modern world works. This is my account, and although I have also done the research to substantiate certain arguments, the thrust of the book draws on my life experience, one that rarely escaped the tentacles of White privilege.

INTRODUCTION
Black Lives Matter and the Tip of the Iceberg

If you are neutral in situations of injustice you have chosen the side of the oppressor.

—Bishop Desmond Tutu

Dominance, Privilege, and the Beat

Music may seem like a rather odd subject to bring up at the beginning of a book on the very serious and uncomfortable topic of global White privilege and how it maintains Western economic dominance across the world.

But music can sometimes be seen as an art form of protest, from folk songs that skewer those in power to how all forms of music are used during times of turmoil to both galvanize people into action and lift spirits when the odds seem insurmountable. Yet Western music in its commercial and popular form, especially during and after the twentieth century, was the trigger for my formative thinking about the harm done by unchecked Westernization, the insidious nature of White privilege, cultural erosion, and how the instruments of Western soft power are used to make non-White people subservient.

Most know me today as the founder and CEO of the Global Institute for Tomorrow, the pan-Asian think tank. Some may remember me as the person who built Asia's largest environmental consulting firm and was its former chairman. They perhaps view me as someone focused on sustainability and economic development, or on a wide range of social issues. They may see me as a policy wonk with no other interests.

What they may not know is that music shaped my life, as have sports. I play the saxophone and was a member of a band when I lived and worked in Africa. The band played an eclectic mix of Black music, ranging from roots reggae to South African township music and some jazz. We even once played to a crowd of thirty thousand in Swaziland supporting the legendary reggae superstar Peter Tosh, widely regarded as Bob Marley's right-hand man in his group the Wailers. Being backstage and watching Tosh and his band belt out classics such as "Get Up, Stand Up" and "Equal Rights" were rainbow moments.

But it is what took me to Africa that has a bearing on this book. It goes back to my childhood and the influence that Western culture and pop music had on me. When I was in my late teens, I began asking some hard questions. Why was it that a young child of migrant parents from South India was so easily led astray, to the point where I rejected my parents' culture and was so keen to embrace anything from the West? How was it that, while being brought up in the unique multicultural society of Malaysia, I was not drawn to the rich traditions of Malay or Chinese culture?[1]

Was it because that, even at a young age, I was being influenced by the belief that embracing White culture would give me access to White privilege and all its associated economic benefits? After all, everything I was taught, everything I read and watched during my childhood, made it clear that White people were superior—from the plantation managers to the missionaries and the people on the movie screen.[2]

What is clear in my mind is that pop and rock music had a strong influence on me and all my friends as teenagers living in a country that at that stage was hardly developed. The latest music from the West was fed to all of us as an essential pathway to joining the modern world. Rejection was not an option. We were all sucked in by the giant vacuum cleaner of global Westernization, and Western music shaped the lives of millions. It seemed to cement our subservience to Western culture.

In my teens, I began to read about and understand the story of Black America and its heroes, such as Malcolm X and Muhammad Ali. Through those two American dissidents, I learned the truth about the war in Vietnam and the various liberation struggles around the world, from Latin America to Africa. That paved the way for discovering Black music and a strong rejection of pop and rock. That led to an acute interest in roots reggae and African music, especially forms steeped in sociopolitical struggles.[3]

It was the start of a never-ending interest in music from all corners of the world, starting with the music of my Indian parents, and expanding to include the flute music of the Sunda Islands, the desert music of the Tuareg of the Sahara, the sounds of the Middle East, the village songs of China, and Choro music from Brazil. It was almost as if, having been force-fed pop and rock music in my early years, I was spending my adult years rebelling and looking for different sounds and melodies from the rich cultures of the world to understand more than what Western influence and education wanted me to know.

The reality was that I was liberating myself from the soft power of Western pop and rock music to remain free. I was trying hard not to allow what I saw as a tool of mind control to colonize my way of thinking. It may appear counterintuitive, but popular Western music can be a powerful tool of subjugation, and I was determined to be open not only to the beats and rhythms of the world but also to its rich cultures, traditions, and knowledge.[4]

This desire not to become captive to Western influences resulted in restlessness. The resulting openness was part of what took me to Africa, where I experienced the liberation struggle and antiapartheid movement in Southern Africa firsthand. It was in Africa where I shed any remaining innocence I had about the motives behind colonization and began to understand the economic nature and sheer scale of its true brutality. In 1986, I had the privilege of conducting an interview with Dr. Oliver Tambo, the leader-in-exile of the ANC. It was the tipping point in my understanding of the nature of the economic drivers of domination, which underpinned the apartheid system.[5]

The journey has brought me to this book—my attempt to describe and explain the insidious nature of White privilege as it persists today, the global chokehold it retains, and how it hinders human progress as well as the search for equity and peace. The book will explain the origins of White privilege, its goals, how it affects the world, the harm it does, how it is preserved, and how it can be dismantled. White privilege is so well packaged in how we discuss modernity and progress that it is rarely identified as a root cause of global injustice. It subtly camouflages an economic and political system built to perpetuate global White supremacy.

Why Talk about Global White Privilege Now?

Readers of this book may have been exposed to such topics as colonialism, imperialism, and globalization, but this book connects how our current globalized world works with race and racial privilege. Now is the time to make this connection crystal clear to a wider global audience. The eyes of the world were locked on the United States as the frequent killing of African Americans by the police made global headlines. Similarly, the world became acutely aware of the sharp rise in racist attacks against Chinese people in the US and other parts of the Western world because of the pandemic and tense US-China relations.[6]

America's conversation about race did not start with the killing of George Floyd or with any of the previous instances of police brutality that sparked and sustained the Black Lives Matter movement in the United States. But the protests of 2020 appear to have shifted the mainstream conversation about discrimination and racism in two particular ways.

First, the 2020 protests appear to have been a turning point for American, and broadly Western, opinion on racial injustice. Many Americans expressed support for the protests and admitted that racial injustice continued to plague the United States. More organizations embraced, at least symbolically, the language of antiracism. Of course, change has not yet come: White privilege remains a powerful political and electoral force, as shown by the presidential elections of 2020 and the unprecedented attack on the Capitol in Washington, DC, by White supremacists.

Second, similar protests in other countries, such as the United Kingdom, France, Australia, and Brazil, were targeted inward, protesting racial injustice and structural discrimination in their own countries.

There is an increasing awareness among the global public that social structures and other norms—from legal and regulatory systems to workplace culture, educational institutions, and popular culture—have helped reinforce the idea of White privilege and grow racist mindsets and behaviors among White communities. These structures and norms have succeeded in entrenching feelings of superiority and at the same time allowed White communities to benefit from a structure that places Whites at the top of an economic, political, and cultural pecking order.

The historical and global linkages that surfaced from what was initially a nationwide response to racism in America quickly expanded into a global recognition of the ubiquitous nature of White privilege as depicted in figure I.1. It shows how the Black Lives Matter movement has helped revive a conversation about race and White privilege that, at least in Western countries, has lain dormant for years. Yet these conversations do not highlight how this privilege operates outside the United States and Europe. Today's global order places White societies at the top, and five centuries of colonization have ensured that White privilege is deeply woven

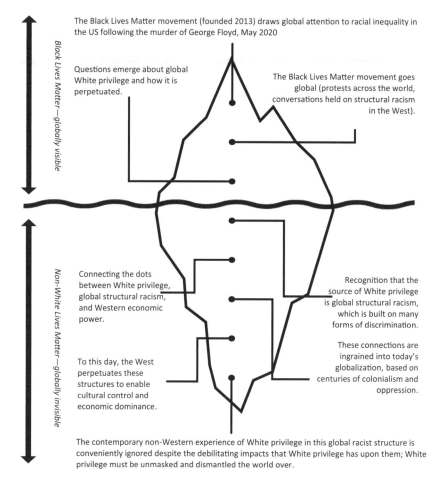

The Black Lives Matter movement (founded 2013) draws global attention to racial inequality in the US following the murder of George Floyd, May 2020

Questions emerge about global White privilege and how it is perpetuated.

The Black Lives Matter movement goes global (protests across the world, conversations held on structural racism in the West).

Connecting the dots between White privilege, global structural racism, and Western economic power.

Recognition that the source of White privilege is global structural racism, which is built on many forms of discrimination.

To this day, the West perpetuates these structures to enable cultural control and economic dominance.

These connections are ingrained into today's globalization, based on centuries of colonialism and oppression.

The contemporary non-Western experience of White privilege in this global racist structure is conveniently ignored despite the debilitating impacts that White privilege has upon them; White privilege must be unmasked and dismantled the world over.

Black Lives Matter—globally visible

Non-White Lives Matter—globally invisible

Figure I.1 Black Lives Matter—The tip of the iceberg
Source: Global Institute for Tomorrow, 2021

into the fabric of globalization. And why? Because of the need to actively maintain and preserve White economic dominance over others, as African Americans know all too well. At the global level it is seen in the actions of the US and its Western allies to contain the rise of other economies such as China.[7]

White privilege elevates, shapes, represses, subjugates, and destroys to seek and preserve economic power. Yet much of the mainstream conversation is focused on the domestic instances of White privilege and the suppression of non-White people in Western countries. While these are important topics, we also need to examine the role of White privilege in modern global society, from geopolitics and international business to sports and fashion.

I hope in this book to bridge the middle ground between how academia and popular discourse talk about race; this understanding is critical if people are to have an understandable framework and be equipped to take action.

The book's thesis is straightforward: **Examining the ideology and complex workings of White privilege is the best way to understand how oppression and dominance by Western cultures operate and are perpetuated globally, within countries and between them, with the key objective of sustaining economic superiority.**

So, while Black Lives Matter is an important and effective way to open people's eyes to the prevalence of White privilege, it is merely one part of the conversation about whom it harms and how it constrains people's lives. Figure I.1 shows how the visible injustices that spark Black Lives Matter should lead us to recognize the invisible injustices that mark global White privilege.

I should note that this is not a book rooted in theory. My life has been international and has been spent in business, policy, and nonprofit work, not in the critical theory or academic discussions on which much of the theoretical work has been based. My hope is to bring these ideas together for the nonacademic Western and non-Western reader, providing arguments and examples in a concise manner to give people a new way of looking at the workings of our globalized world and, I hope, help them look at themselves and reach their own conclusions about global White privilege and its links to Western economic dominance.

Nor is the book an attempt to replace the conversation happening in the United States and elsewhere about racism and racial privilege; instead, it is intended to complement and expand those discussions by bringing in the global dimension from a non-Western perspective.

However, I believe that much of the existing work, whether academic or not, is targeted to a Western audience. Those writing about racism for the layperson hope to explain the mistreatment of minority populations by their own societies. Those theorizing about race, whether on the domestic or international level, are talking to a population of Western-based academics.

With this book, I explain how racism and White privilege persist at the global level, with the intention of including non-Western readers at the same time, whether they are business leaders, policymakers, civil society groups, or concerned citizens. This is a book based on my personal observations and experiences. It is born from my non-Western—not anti-Western—perspective and written to involve and include the non-Western audience. I will not pretend that it covers the whole range of literature that exists, nor that my chosen examples will be relevant to every reader.

But I hope this book serves as a start to illustrate how deeply White privilege pervades the global system, and to encourage everyone—Western and non-Western, White and non-White—to take actions to dismantle it.

Speaking of action—a personal example is the use of the term *White*. The word initially made me uncomfortable, as I had never used it, and it felt awkward, as I believed the term to be rude and even offensive. But why? Because I had not yet fully embraced the idea of dismantling White privilege. White people can call others Black, Yellow, or people of color, and use all sorts of race-based descriptions, but non-Whites cannot refer to Whites by color. I remember being on a panel at a conference in France in 2018 where I shared the platform with two former senior US Republican politicians. Both of them and quite a few of the Americans in the audience felt offended when I said that Donald Trump is very popular because there are many White people who support him. It became clear to me that White people are very uncomfortable being called "White" because it confers a multitude of negative racial generalizations that they do not like applied to them.[8]

Dismantling White Privilege: Tackling a Taboo Subject

White privilege must be dismantled—not just because it is an injustice but because by working to dismantle it, we will be creating a post-Western world that has less conflict, is more united, and is better able to respond to the existential challenges facing all of us.[9]

The first step in dismantling White privilege is to unmask it. White privilege has been carefully masked to avoid scrutiny, even when it resorts to intimidation and force. It must be revealed to show its design, its true features and layers of cosmetic surgery, the contours and lines of control, power, influence, and propaganda.

Donald Trump did the world a favor by showing the true face of White privilege and supremacy, particularly that he does not represent a minority of those with political power in the United States. For the first time, many in the non-Western world have come to terms with the existence of White privilege, its intentions, and its scale, as the mask was taken off when White supremacists attacked the Capitol in Washington, DC, on January 6, 2021. But Donald Trump and his followers are not alone, whether in the US or globally. Under various "shades of White," the Western world believes in its superiority and works together with the US to maintain the status quo over a global majority.

It is time to dismantle White privilege by having a global debate about what has long been a taboo subject in mainstream circles of power and polite company. There are many examples of leaders in business and multilateral bodies providing support for "fighting racism," but the irony is that it is taboo in these leadership echo chambers to talk about how so many of the roles they occupy are disproportionately White. This includes organizations such as the International Monetary Fund (IMF), World Bank, and many global corporations.[10]

Questions of racial privilege and how to counter it are considered awkward, such as when Morgan Stanley fired its global head of diversity for trying to eliminate barriers for Black employees within the company,[11] or when newsrooms were confronted with their own issues involving the coverage of racism.[12] From my own experience, I know that my attempts to bring up these questions have been dismissed in boardrooms and meetings as, at best, a misunderstanding of the situation or, at worst, professional jealousy over others' success.

Westerners should not see the arguments in this book about White privilege and fairness for a post-Western world as an attack on White people, or as something rooted in anti-White or anti-Western sentiments. These are long-overdue arguments about global social justice and fairness. The arguments in this book do not seek to negate the achievements of the West, nor do they call for the West to be relegated to some imagined subservience. Nor do they excuse the bad actions of non-Western nations, nor the ineptitude of those who can't solve issues of injustice in their own countries. It is, however, a global call for a unified and fairer world where the West does not call the shots but is instead a partner with the global majority, and where White privilege is not used to retain economic dominance.

It is also necessary to define what I mean by a post-Western world. The sixty to seventy years after the end of World War II, which also saw the start of the decolonization era, was a period of great human endeavor and progress as the non-Western world began a journey of self-determination after centuries of subjugation. Some countries succeeded more than others, and the West retreated from exercising direct control to carving out a global architecture that would ensure it did not relinquish its power and economic dominance. This ideological belief has been at the center of postwar geopolitics, which has seen the US and Europe work together as partners to maintain this architecture of dominance.

However, at the dawn of the twenty-first century, certain trends began to be established that saw regions formerly impoverished by imperialism become economically stronger. First with the oil-producing states, then Japan, and most recently China, this new confidence and demographic realities challenged archaic structures of Western dominance, which in turn threatened the West as its self-serving rules-based order began to fray.

That was when the notion of a post-Western world was conceived, and we are now at a critical moment regarding the birth of this new world, which, by definition, will be fairer and more democratic. This birth may be delayed or aborted by the resistance of the West to sharing power, but those interested in global justice must help with its painless delivery.

The Expressions of Global White Privilege

Global White privilege is expressed in numerous ways: not merely through military and economic might but also through culture, norms, and "soft power." It influences almost every aspect of contemporary life, including sports, fashion, and even the books we read. White editors and publishers will decide whether this book is worthy of a review and global attention. Global White privilege, as exemplified in social norms, cultural values, economic structures, political systems, and institutional operations, concentrates privilege and power in White communities.

The international order was built during a historical era marked by the unchallenged and unabashed pursuit of White privilege, and a better world cannot be forged without deconstructing and dismantling the contemporary global superstructure that perpetuates White and Western economic and military dominance. Across all the chapters in this book, I will give examples to demonstrate the construction of this superstructure and how it is reinforced via globalization and other mechanisms to retain Western economic primacy. A chapter will be dedicated to laying out how history has been selectively interpreted to help create White privilege at the expense of others.

A global conversation about White privilege does not replace the conversations taking place in the United States or any other country. Instead, it complements and expands these discussions by bringing in the global dimension and vital non-Western experience to help us understand how the world experiences global White privilege. The conversation will help open the eyes of readers and people across the world to the power White privilege holds over the world and that is maintained by design. White privilege is present in both crude and subtle forms, and societies need to recognize those forms and take action as needed. Recognition is key to dismantling White privilege, as centuries of dominance have inured the world to it.

Some readers might rightfully ask whether White privilege is a cause or an effect of global White economic supremacy. This book argues that White economic power is the objective and has been ever since the first colonial adventures. The end of the decolonization process meant that the need to retain global economic power could no longer be furthered simply by force. There was, however, the opportunity to leverage the institutional and soft power of the West that was already in place to actively and subversively colonize the minds of hundreds of millions of former subjects.[13]

So it is best to view global White privilege and its active cultivation in so many forms as a necessary prerequisite to maintaining White Western economic power. The book will show how Western nations today work to actively maintain their current power and their grip by perpetuating and installing White privilege in all spheres of the globalized economy despite pious proclamations about spreading democracy, freedom, and social justice. This dominance is reliant on and feeds off the concept of White privilege, which bestows on White people a special global status.

Understanding Privilege, Race, and Ethnicity

The most critical concept for this book is *White privilege*: founded on, reliant on, and thus also the result of the active creation of institutions, belief systems, norms, and practices that translate into transactions of economic power and influence that in turn preserve and reproduce the barrier between those in society who possess "Whiteness" and those who do not.

Whiteness is more than just skin color; it also includes the economic, social, and political power connoted by White skin. An ethnic Chinese person who speaks fluent English and went to an Ivy League school would possess more Whiteness than an ethnic Chinese person who primarily speaks fluent Mandarin and was educated in Beijing. The Western-educated individual is then ready to be accepted by White organizations keen to use that person and deploy them under the guise of diversity and inclusion, as an agent furthering the cause of spreading Westernization and modernity.

Access to the opportunities of White privilege encourages people to seek admission into these elite circles, which reinforces the sources of White privilege and maintains the economic power that White communities hold over others.

This is why this book will use *White privilege, Western privilege,* and *Western superiority* interchangeably. The power that White privilege confers is primarily held by Western countries and granted by Western institutions. These two manifestations of power cannot be separated.

More broadly, *race* and *ethnicity* are socially constructed divisions between different groups of people. Race tends to be focused on differences in external appearance, such as skin color, whereas ethnicity tends to refer to cultural and linguistic differences. However, societies have often used these distinctions to make sweeping—and untrue—judgments about temperament, intelligence, behavior, and so on.

Racial prejudice would be any judgment of a person or community based on these divisions, where the socially constructed and scientifically unsound assumptions about a particular group are used to reach a conclusion about an individual. *Racial discrimination* refers to any action based on these untrue conclusions, expressed through unequal treatment between different groupings. *Racial privilege* is the inverse—when one community is offered special protection, opportunities, or rights based on their membership in this social group.

When talking about racism and racial discrimination, there are perhaps three different forms that should be discussed: overt racism, implicit racism, and structural racism.

- *Overt racism* concerns much of our popular conception of racism, from the use of racial slurs to race-based legislation.
- *Implicit racism* is in play when certain language, symbols, and portrayals, while not explicitly race based, have connotations of racial superiority or inferiority.
- *Structural racism* exists when legal, economic, and social structures, while nondiscriminatory on their face, end up having unequal consequences for different communities. These often work in tandem with assumptions about particular racial and ethnic groups, and each reinforces the other.

Like most of the current debate about racism, this book is primarily concerned with structural racism and how it is woven into the entire fabric of modern-day globalization. It analyzes how global institutions, cultures, and norms, while not explicitly based on race, end up perpetuating systems of White dominance and lead to unequal outcomes for non-White groups or suppress their expectations. Some discussions about global culture will also deal with implicit racism, where certain language, symbols, and portrayals have unspoken connotations of privilege and inferiority.

From Domestic to Global

Discussions of racism have shifted from treating it as a psychological problem regarding individual mindsets toward understanding it as a structural issue, where discrimination is born from social and legal structures. As early as the 1960s, the civil rights leader Stokely Carmichael (later known as Kwame Ture) observed:

> When a Black family moves into a home in a White neighborhood and is stoned, burned or routed out, they are victims of an overt act of individual racism which most people will condemn. But it is institutional racism that keeps Black people locked in dilapidated slum tenements, subject to the daily prey of exploitative slumlords, merchants, loan sharks and discriminatory real estate agents. The society either pretends it does not know of this latter situation or is in fact incapable of doing anything meaningful about it.[14]

Frantz Fanon is one of the key non-American thinkers on this subject, whose works sparked much of postcolonial studies and critical theory. As early as 1952, Fanon argued that the colonial project left no part of the human person and the human experience untouched.[15] His 1961 magnum opus, *The Wretched of the Earth*, is a full examination of how colonialism affected societies; he describes his taxonomy of the colonized, which includes the "worker," the "colonized intellectual," and the "lumpen proletariat."[16] The colonized intellectual is the middleman between the colonizer and the colonized, trading in the cultural capital of the colonial power without ever getting to be a part of it. An example is that of elites from Asia studying in Ivy League schools and then seeking jobs in the leading Western corporations, especially in investment banking or finance, which are made out to be the most sought-after careers.

Fanon's work sparked further extensions of critical theory throughout the world, with one particular development being the creation of "critical race theory," which applies critical theory to racial issues in the United States. First developed in the mid-1980s, the theory has two particular tenets:

1. Legal systems play a role in preserving and maintaining systems of racial supremacy.
2. The relationship between law and racial power needs to be transformed in order to achieve an antiracist agenda.

However, this is an understanding of race, racism, and structural discrimination that is born out of an American context and its particular history with race and race relations. It does not examine the use on a global scale of White power over centuries to dehumanize and oppress other nations for economic gain.

Race as a concept generally does not feature in mainstream discussions of global governance and international relations. Some theorists try to apply racial dynamics seen on the domestic level to the international sphere—for example, how racial inequality and social unrest affect perceptions of countries overseas and thus impact a country's "soft power." Race is conveniently ignored in providing explanations as to why only an American or European can head up the World Bank or the IMF. That racism defines the way two of the world's most important multilateral agencies are governed is rarely if ever discussed in the open.

Although few theorists use the explicit framing of race to understand how countries and societies interact with each other and how power is exercised, there is far more discussion of how we talk about and understand the way the world reinforces Western privilege.[17] Within the realm of academia, there is some criticism that Western Europe and North America are portrayed as the places "where things happened," whereas the rest of the world merely adopts Western innovations and reacts to developments happening elsewhere.[18]

More broadly, much of postcolonial thought analyzes how colonial domination persists through current global institutions and the global security framework.[19] Such aspects as the global network of American military bases and the global debt structures for developing countries are seen as continuations of colonial and imperial dominance rather than active preservation of Western dominance.

But why has the insight of critical race theory—that laws, social structures, and cultural norms perpetuate White privilege—not been applied on the global level?

One possibility is that global governance and social structures are evolving in the postcolonial era as differences between countries become more obvious and there is no clear consensus yet for a post-Western world. As I noted in my book *The Sustainable State*, global governance and international law often rely on states to do the work for them, meaning that when global and national interests collide, national interests usually win out.[20] This means that the usual analytical focuses used to address structural racism—laws, regulations, and institutions—are less strong on the global level.

In addition, the traits and behaviors of different ethnic groups are often conflated with national governments, which can complicate the search for causal factors. For example: Are assumptions about ethnic Koreans based on assumptions about Koreans as an ethnic group, or motivated by actions of the South Korean national government? This brings in discussions of international relations and national security, which complicate (but do not preclude) any discussion of structural racism.

Finally, another potential reason why critical race theory has not been applied as much outside the West, at least in domestic contexts, is that non-Western countries have often dealt with race and ethnicity more explicitly in legislation, in both positive and negative ways. For example, Malaysia practices affirmative action for the Malay majority, providing privileged access to positions in all areas of the economy as well as in both the civil service and state-run enterprises. There is much analysis about racial politics and racial discrimination in Malaysia, but the explicit use of racial and ethnic categories in legislation means that there is little "need" to uncover more structural and implicit discrimination.

Yet the application of contemporary critical race theory and other insights from the academic discussion of structural discrimination would help to reveal much about how privilege operates on the global level. Why do Western governments and institutions who represent a small minority of the global population have so much say in what happens around the world? Why do those who lead them assume automatically that they have a right to get involved, have a role to play in solutions, and have all the answers? And why are their solutions automatically assumed to be the best?

This book's analysis of global White privilege helps close the gap between critical race theory and postcolonial discussions in a manner suitable to the average reader.

Race and White Power: The Fetish of Economic Dominance

But where do racist ideas, and the structures born from them, come from?

My theory of race starts from economic dominance: whether due to environmental factors or access to resources or technological change, some communities seek to have military and economic power over others. While some, including academics, have argued that this is simply the nature of how human societies have interacted throughout history, European expansion across the world beginning in the sixteenth century was unparalleled in terms of its scale, its plunder and dominance, and its persistence over five centuries.[21] This economic dominance and resulting sense of superiority is now hardwired into the structures and institutions of globalization and thus even part of the ideological basis of the West alliance. This ideology has to be exposed and dismantled by raising awareness through new narratives. This book is a first step in this direction.

Ideas are created to justify these patterns of domination. The ideas help normalize and institutionalize these power differences, among both the dominators and the dominated. These norms and values are then turned into institutions, regulations, and laws, which reinforce this inequality. One example from international history: the nineteenth-century idea of "civilization," which Western states used to determine the rules of international relations. Civilized states—almost entirely Western—would deal with each other on an equal basis. The more a society diverged from the Western norm, the less "civilized" it was, and thus the more unequal relations would be allowed to be. The common reference to the US as the only country with a continuous democracy more than two hundred years old is normalizing a lie: the whole country is built on land expropriated from indigenous populations, and Black people were denied their human and civil rights, including the right to vote, until at least 1963, which is still under threat today.[22]

This ideology and the institutions that back them up allow these structures of privilege and an aura of superiority to persist even as the economic foundations they are built on change or the history is different.

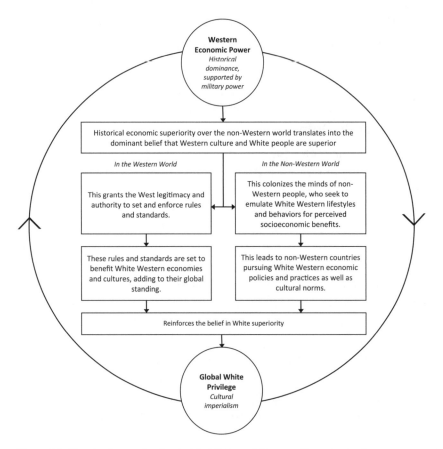

Figure I.2 The circular mechanism behind White privilege and its perpetuation
Source: Global Institute for Tomorrow, 2021

Even as obvious power differentials disappear, the structure preserves the privileges afforded to those in a superior situation. In addition, the structures can even close off potential avenues through which less privileged communities can escape from these structures and become upwardly mobile.

Figure I.2 shows how to think about the pursuit of economic power and its reliance on the creation of structural discrimination, which in turn is key to maintaining global White privilege. White privilege is primarily sustained by subverting minds even via liberal narratives and the so-called soft power of the West.

Figure I.2 demonstrates that the starting point is in creating a dominant belief across the world—installed by historical and contemporary

White Western economic power—reinforcing the view that people, knowledge, products, and services associated with Whiteness are superior in all aspects of human existence. This results in the widespread desire to ape Western culture, which in turn ensures economic and cultural domination by White people.

Therefore, Western White leaders, organizations, and ideas have the legitimacy and moral authority to set and enforce rules and standards, which are also set up in ways to benefit White Western economic dominance and culture. From rules on international finance to the governance of the internet and which vaccine can be trusted, the West seeks to maintain control.

The inherently rigged outcomes of this setting and the active enforcing of the rules and standards works to reinforce the dominant belief that Whiteness is superior. It also colonizes the minds of non-Whites, who now seek to emulate Whiteness for its economic and cultural benefits. Ultimately, this creates global White privilege and cultural imperialism, which aid Western economic power. Thus begins another iteration of this White privilege cycle, further entrenching its dominance.

For example, a Western country that has established economic dominance and has the intention to pursue and preserve that dominance starts to subvert local culture and traditions, trying to replace them with Western-based and Western-derived institutions. The initial push may be to build a local society more suitable to Western economic, political, and military interests, such as revamping the local economy to make it more suitable for an imperialist economic model.

In building these institutions, White societies capture both moral authority through the imposition of a new value system and epistemological authority by promoting Western narratives and controlling the space for education and discourse.

Over time, this capture of authority builds up the perception that Western and Western-derived ways of managing society are superior. Those in non-Western countries try to emulate what they believe is the right and successful way of doing things, resulting in the maintenance of global White privilege.

Finally, global White privilege creates an international structure of institutions, rules, and norms that institutionalize these ideas of global White privilege across the world. Perhaps unsurprisingly, these rules tend to benefit those at the top of the global pecking order: White and Western countries, who see their economic power increase as a result.

Organization of This Book

This book focuses primarily on the global level, though several of the cul tural elements have implications for other levels of change as well. It will examine the manifestations of global White privilege in several critical spheres of global society and culture: economic policies, political systems, cultural priorities, environmental agendas, and social foundations, as illustrated in Figure I.3. Nine key areas will be discussed in individual chapters to exemplify the contemporary process of the perpetuation of White Western economic power, how this has given birth to White privilege, how White privilege causes harm across the world, and therefore why it must be dismantled and how.

Figure I.3 The spheres of discussion in this book and their relationship to global White privilege
Source: Global Institute for Tomorrow, 2021

Chapters One through Three deal with the broadest and most institutionalized expressions of White privilege: geopolitics and world order, the reframing of world history, and international business practices. In these three areas, Western dominance has instituted structures and narratives that severely limit the power of non-Western societies to shape the world. The privilege of writing the rules, whether in terms of security or economics, and to judge others is reserved for the West.

Chapters Four and Five deal with how narratives of White privilege are disseminated and perpetuated across generations through the media and the education system. By positioning White sources as the most objective and truthful sources of knowledge, these social institutions preserve White dominance and, worse, encourage the elite in non-Western countries to adopt the styling of White privilege to increase their own cultural capital.

Chapters Six through Eight deal with the soft-power spheres of White privilege: entertainment, sports, and fashion. In all these areas, White cultural products remain the aspirational standard by which all cultural products are judged. Even when non-White societies see international cultural success, that success is often built on a Western model; it is Western cultural norms, forms, and aspirations that symbolize youth, modernity, and the cultural mainstream.

Chapter Nine deals with a topic close to my heart: environmental protection and sustainability. The conversation about sustainability closely follows a White savior model, whereby technologies and practices built in the West will save the world, while the non-Western world is judged for being underdeveloped, poorly governed, and for sabotaging the global effort to fight climate change. These narratives are counterproductive, blinding the West to its own failings and denying an honest discussion about multilateral solutions to the climate crisis that are based on fairness.

Key Themes

This book covers a vast array of different issues. There are the large topics, such as global geopolitics and business, about which people may think there is "nothing I can do about it." Then are the less threatening areas, such as sports and fashion, about which people may think that they are "surely binding the world together." But sadly, in all these cases, an informed observer can see the same patterns emerge again and again. These patterns reinforce White privilege.

The first pattern is that the "ideal" form of each sphere is modeled after a Western example. Whether regarding structure, actions, beliefs, or any other characteristic, the model is assumed to be a Western one. Why? Geopolitical control and dominance to maintain economic supremacy are paramount and nonnegotiable. Deviations from this norm are dismissed, if not viewed with outright suspicion. Whether we're talking about a peace agreement in the Middle East, an Asian trade pact, a Chinese business believed to be cheating against international rules, or an Indonesian writer struggling to gain traction globally, the standards everyone is being judged against are Western and White in origin. The leaders, guardians, and rule makers are Western; when they are not, they are considered a threat and must be contained or dismissed as usurpers.

The second pattern arises from the emphasis on Western terms of reference and gives rise to the idea of legitimacy—whether something is deemed to be an acceptable expression or activity. At the moment, the only bodies deemed capable of granting this legitimacy are White and Western. A very contemporary example that is playing out right now is the subject of vaccines for the pandemic.

The third pattern is that the institutions that judge an entity's adherence to these standards must preferably be Western and White led. These bodies determine access to the economic, social, and cultural power afforded by global Whiteness. This power looks different depending on what we are analyzing: in geopolitics, the use of military power in pursuit of national interests and the indiscriminate use of sanctions; in education, the accreditation of educational qualifications; in fashion, connections to the "chic" nature of modern high fashion.

A final pattern: only White and Western authorities are allowed to punish those who violate the rules and regulations of the global order. Sometimes this power is mostly reputational: a dismissal of non-Western entities as truly serious examples of the action in question, expressed as dismissing non-Western products as fake, low quality, or lacking in understanding of how things "ought" to be done. However, in other cases, these sanctions can be much more real: ostracism or suppression. This is real, harmful power that is subtle and so woven into international norms that they go unquestioned.

The aforementioned major patterns emerge time and time again, and they are expressed in ways that are common across all the various areas discussed in the next chapters. The reader is invited to look out for these manifestations to appreciate the widespread nature of White privilege and the challenge of dismantling it. These include:

- The deeply held belief that terms of engagement on the international front can only be set by the West, even in areas such as diplomacy
- Double standards, manifested when, for example, countries call for open and free markets, but in practice adhere to protectionism to uphold long-established White privilege in global markets (e.g., EU agriculture policy, US blocking of Chinese tech companies)
- Ignorance of and disrespect for the cultures of other people and their traditions of rule making and standard setting
- The spread and celebration of narratives about White success and the downplaying of the success of non-White people, aided by the global (Western) media
- The fake morality of the White savior complex and its role in furthering White superiority and White moral standing

What Happens Next?

This book is primarily focused on revealing the ways that White privilege pervades global society, in the hopes that people, from policymakers to ordinary members of society, can develop their own ways of dismantling global White privilege in their own societies and contexts.

But some steps can be taken now using ideas in the book and others that the book may now trigger in the reader. Each chapter too will present some ideas about what can be done to start the fight against global White privilege. The conclusion, in turn, will highlight six objectives that the global community can embrace to bring about necessary change, and presents numerous channels where the individual—regardless of origin or race—can start the long fight against global White privilege.

CHAPTER 1

GEOPOLITICS OF DOMINANCE
The White Knights of Chess

> The West won the world not by the superiority of its ideas or values or religion . . . but rather by its superiority in applying organized violence. Westerners often forget this fact; non-Westerners never do.
>
> —Samuel P. Huntington, *The Clash of Civilizations and the Remaking of World Order*

Cold War in Name, Hot Wars for Real

Because I grew up in Southeast Asia, the Vietnam War had a lot to do with how I began to understand geopolitics. Muhammad Ali's famous riposte to questions about his refusal to be drafted for the war—"I ain't got no quarrel with them Vietcong"—was a turning point.

That awakening got me onto the path of better understanding the war and the distortions of the American political and media narrative about the history of the region, then called Indochina. The war shaped many of my fears during my teenage years, as the "domino theory" was used to scare millions into believing that Western imperialism was going to save us from impending catastrophe if the Vietcong and their allies—all people seeking to be free of imperialism—defeated America and its allies. What transpired after the end of the war in 1975 and the reality today of a vibrant and mostly peaceful region have been the complete opposite of what was predicted, exposing the lies of media and politicians alike.

My appreciation and understanding of China and today's US-China tensions began when I moved to Hong Kong in 1990. This period coincided with China's rise and the reshaping of the world order. China fascinated me ever since I read books about the revolution and learned, when I was living in Africa, about the support the various liberation movements there received from China. Since then, I have had a front-row seat to what has been the greatest large-scale transformation of a society in history, including the lifting of hundreds of millions out of abject poverty.

But this great human success story also brought about the geopolitical standoff of our time, as the West, led by the US, comes to terms, for the first time in two to three centuries, with the rise of a non-White civilization that appears capable of surpassing it on many fronts. To this day, I am puzzled by how anti-China the West and its media are, with any reasonable discussion of the changes and challenges presented by this transition overwhelmed by xenophobia and even racism. The truth is that Western governments and media refuse to recognize the historical fact that the rise of China is posing a challenge to centuries of Western dominance and White privilege. India's turn may come next.

The current global tensions arising from the desire of the West to suppress China should make clear that perhaps the grandest forces shaping our lives today are the relationships between countries and the structure of the international order. How countries interact with each other—where they define their interests, where they work together, and where they compete—has huge effects on how those in society live their lives. This runs even deeper in our globalized era: disputes between two powers can have repercussions for someone living on the other side of the world.

Mainstream histories of international relations state that the period since the end of World War II has been a historically unique period of peace. Tensions between the world's two postwar superpowers, the United States and the Soviet Union, may have been severe, but they never erupted into open conflict. The end of the Cold War in 1991 then turned the bipolar world into a unipolar one, with the international order led by the United States.

This peace is also credited as the reason the world is now as prosperous as it is. This international system, established and managed by one superpower, has created rules and institutions that have encouraged stability. Clear rules and norms have allowed nations to thrive, their economies to grow, and their populations to get rich.

One can understand why Western scholars take comfort in this narrative, as it places the West at the center of the international system. Even when they recognize the hugely damaging effects of Western imperialism, they can point to the current liberal world order as a meaningful shift away from that imperialism. The claims of peace and a Western rules–based order also act as a subtle warning to others: if anything were to happen to this Western-led system—perhaps due to the rise of a new non-Western challenger—this peace and prosperity may end.

To the rest of the world, however, the Cold War and post–Cold War eras look very different: this period of superpower peace has been anything but peaceful. Since 1945, there have been over 285 armed conflicts involving state and nonstate actors, with a majority of these occurring in Asia, Africa, and Latin America. Worse is when the conflicts involve one of the great powers: the Vietnam War, the conflicts in Afghanistan, or the illegal invasion of Iraq.[1]

It is true that the world has not faced a global, system-wide conflict on the scale of World War II. But this matters less to the many around the world who still suffer from conflict and oppression—often spurred by the actions of one of the great powers.

White Privilege in Geopolitics

This analytical neglect is part of an international structure that supports and perpetuates the idea of White privilege: an idea that the countries that matter are Western and that the dealings between them should set the norms on how international politics should be managed too. Countries that lie outside this group either need to accept the way things are done or will be classified as a threat and dealt with.

In this chapter, we will focus on the international institutions and organizations that manage the global world order. These are the bodies that discuss important global issues and take actions to resolve them. They are the bodies that set the rules for proper international action, judging who is acting responsible and who threatens international peace and stability. And these are the bodies that, under the pretext of preserving the world order and peace, take punitive actions against those who are deemed to be breaking the rules.

Many examples of these Western alliances to preserve White power exist. One is the Five Eyes Intelligence Alliance, comprising a cabal of five

Anglo-Saxon nations—the United States, the United Kingdom, Canada, Australia, and New Zealand—all bound together by their colonial ties. As Nikolas Kozloff, author of *Revolution! South America and the Rise of the New Left*, notes, the Snowden revelations demonstrated that "some of Britain's former English-speaking colonies have banded together in a crass effort to take advantage of people of color."[2] Despite being an anachronism, Five Eyes has gathered strength in the last few years as its members band together to oppose rising powers such as China. The Five Eyes showcases something unique with regard to White racism and privilege in geopolitics: the existence of a coalition made up solely of the Anglosphere, of which four are White settler communities that created nations through large-scale violence against non-White indigenous populations.

These bodies come together in what is frequently described as the "international rules-based order," which is often credited for the peace, stability, prosperity, and interconnectedness we see today. Join the system and follow its prescriptions, and you will be accepted as a member of the international community. If you are seen as a threat, your country will be ostracized and punished severely.

The issue is that the countries doing the judging tend to be Western and White. White individuals sit in global leadership positions, bringing their own frameworks and biases to discussions of international importance. Challenges from their peers are seen as honest criticism; challenges from those outside the group are seen as dangerous, uninformed, and threatening.

This means that every non-Western country needs to decide how it will operate in a Western- and White-led world. Do you accept their leadership in the hope of getting support for your own national objectives, even if it means reinforcing an unfair system? Do you try to opt out of the system, only to be ignored and neglected in international affairs? Or do you try to challenge the unfairness of the international system, only to risk punishment from those in charge?

Why Geopolitics Matter

Why do the structures of global geopolitics matter in our discussion of global White privilege?

First of all, global geopolitical structures can have significant effects on people's lives. They determine whether people need to worry about conflict. They determine whether they can trade with other regions. They determine whether someone might receive assistance when in trouble. And, perhaps most important, they determine whether someone can live largely free of interference from other countries or whether their country will attract unwanted actions by the West. Play it safe like Singapore and you are left alone; be belligerent like Iran and all hell breaks loose.

Second, geopolitics determines what kind of world we live in: a world marked by fairness and equality or one marked by hierarchy and oppression. These geopolitical outcomes then dictate who gets to develop and who does not. The international system has oscillated between equality and hierarchy at different periods of time, and different parts of the system can often be organized on different principles: for example, when nineteenth-century European countries were preening themselves for their respect for sovereign equality and noninterference, they were rampantly engaging in empire building and plunder elsewhere in the world. France is a good example of this supreme hypocrisy.

Finally, we need to understand how geopolitics is played if we are to avoid war. Those working in the field of international relations often say that their main objective is to prevent another massive global great-power conflict on the scale of World War II. And these great-power conflicts often emerge when a challenger to the existing global system emerges.

As other countries such as China and India rise, they pose a potential threat to the existing system.[3] Such power transitions run the risk of leading to great-power conflict—which will hurt a great many people. Yet an international system riven with White privilege makes this global conflict more likely, as White people try to protect ill-gotten gains and privileges from people on the rise who want their fair share. Only by rooting out this sense of entitlement born out of White privilege will we be able to transition to a more multipolar world while avoiding the death and destruction that characterized the first half of the twentieth century.

Sovereign Equality: Not for the "Uncivilized"

The international system is nominally predicated on the idea of sovereign equality—the idea that every state is equal to each other and should be allowed to conduct its domestic affairs without interference. Also known as the "Westphalian system," these norms supposedly grew out of Europe due to a desire to end the constant religious conflicts among the continent's various kingdoms. This system was not globally applied for several more centuries, as European countries practiced imperialism and oppression overseas while proclaiming equality at home. Following the end of World War II, the success of the decolonization movement in the twentieth century, and the establishment of the United Nations, the idea of sovereign equality—that no country will have dominion over another—was universally applied.

But alongside the idea of sovereign equality is another concept that has had much more pernicious effects on the international system: the idea of the "civilized state." This idea determined who would receive the full set of rights and legal protections afforded to sovereign entities. Those states deemed uncivilized would not be protected: actions against them would not be deemed "beyond the pale."

We can see how this concept worked in the time of empire. Much of the world was deemed uncivilized, and thus could be invaded and conquered by Western countries. Long-standing cultures and societies, such as those in India, Southeast Asia, the Middle East, and Africa, were deemed to be uncivilized because they did not conform to the Western norm, and thus were taken over and plundered in order to build the economies of the West.

Even countries that were considered civilized enough to escape being conquered were not considered to be wholly equal to the mostly European countries that made up the West. The independent countries of Latin America—perhaps due to their former history of European colonization or due to the "protection" of the United States under the Monroe Doctrine—were never included in any of the formal nineteenth-century European empires. Yet all countries were subject to constant political and economic interference from the West—the United States, their erstwhile protector, prime among them throughout the nineteenth and early twentieth centuries.[4]

Japan is an excellent example of the power of the idea of "international civilization." With the defeat of China during the Opium Wars and then Commodore Perry's forced opening of Japan in 1853, the country realized that it needed to quickly model itself after the West if it wanted to be protected from foreign invasion. The country speedily embarked on a "modernization" program, copying Western ideas, cultures, techniques, and even modes of dress. The goal was to be taken seriously as a "civilized" power and thus allowed the full range of actions and protections afforded to European countries.

This drive culminated in war several times. The first was the Russo-Japanese War of 1904–1905, where Japan's victory over Russia led it to be seen as a major power. The second was Japan's involvement in World War I, where its cooperation with the Entente Powers resulted in concessions at the Versailles negotiations (at the expense of China). Finally, and most devastatingly, a drive to secure resources and build its own global empire led to Japan's invasions throughout East Asia in the run-up to and during World War II. The reputation of the Japanese took a beating, and they were dismissed by the Western powers, who ironically were themselves illegal occupants and plunderers of the lands the Japanese foolishly sought to take.

The Civilized State and the Rogue State

The idea of civilized and uncivilized nations was supposed to end with decolonization and the establishment of the United Nations. But the idea persists today, seen in some of the key terms used to describe countries in the international system.

One is the idea of the "rogue state": a country that flouts the rules of the international system and poses a grave threat to international peace and stability. Such a state needs to be controlled and, at worst, put in line, through force if necessary. Several states around the world have been slapped with this label: Iraq, Iran, Venezuela, Cuba, and North Korea, and all by White Western powers. Almost all have been hit with some form of sanctions; some have even been invaded in the name of promoting human rights, democracy, and global peace.

The West has supported military interventions in order to oust leaders it feels are threats to world peace: Iraq, Libya, and Syria are the most recent examples. These interventions have served to create further instability, often making the problem worse. Disingenuous justifications for interventions and even invasions have become part of the Western discourse around the "responsibility to protect": the idea that sovereignty is conditional upon state governments protecting the lives of their citizens. When a state fails in this regard, its sovereignty no longer needs to be respected, and punitive actions can be taken against it.

This is not to deny that the leaders of these countries and other "rogue states" are innocent. All are guilty to various degrees of mistreating their populations and even mismanaging their economies, but much of their woes are also a result of years of Western intervention. Examples include the complex situations in Myanmar, Iran, and Venezuela. But their being deemed beyond the pale ended up encouraging actions against them that have led to demonstrably worse outcomes.

It is also clear that the Western powers are willing to overlook equally terrible measures on the part of countries and leaders who do not upset the status quo. It is common knowledge around the world that the West has not only turned a blind eye to authoritarianism, corruption, and other human rights abuses when conducted by an ostensible ally, but even aided and abetted them when it served Western economic and strategic goals: from anti-Communist dictatorships in Latin America (the military juntas in Guatemala and Argentina, General Pinochet in Chile—all supported by the CIA) and Southeast Asia during the Cold War to states in the Middle East critical to "regional stability."[5]

The inverse of the idea of the rogue state is the "responsible stakeholder": a country that understands its place in the international order and contributes resources to its support. These are the countries that pay their dues to international organizations, that provide forces for peacekeeping, and that play their part in sustaining the international rules-based order. This requires accepting the international system as it is, including which countries lead it.

Being considered a responsible stakeholder can be quite lucrative. Explicit support for the international system might give a country some niche role within it, expanding its influence in the Western countries that run it. That conferred legitimacy, in turn, might be used to serve its own national interests.

This is not hypothetical. Non-Western countries spend millions of dollars on lobbying campaigns in Western capitals to prove that they are truly responsible and thus are integral parts of the existing international system. By flattering the West, they potentially stand to benefit. It reinforces the notion of White Is Right and delivers White privilege across the world. Hong Kong was a friend of the West as long as it was able to walk that tightrope, but that became very difficult once it became a pawn in US-China geopolitics and was therefore punished.

But to be responsible stakeholders, countries also need to contribute to an existing rules-based order that they had no hand in creating, and they have little to no ability to change the rules to account for their interests.

In the end, the countries that set the rules will remain the same: the large Western and White countries.

Yet choosing not to take part leads to lectures about being "irresponsible." This may not come with any material consequences (unlike the designation of being a rogue state), but it means not being invited to sit at the table with the other major powers and being sidelined.

So, rising countries are in a bind: take part in the system in order to be invited to the head table, yet have no influence once you get there; or ignore the system and be neglected.

International Leadership: Who Runs the World?

On October 9, 2020, the Nobel Peace Prize was awarded to the World Food Programme (WFP) of the United Nations "for its efforts to combat hunger, for its contribution to bettering conditions for peace in conflict-affected areas and for acting as a driving force in efforts to prevent the use of hunger as a weapon of war and conflict."[6]

The person accepting the award was WFP's executive director, David Beasley. Before joining WFP, he was perhaps best known for being a one-term governor of South Carolina in the late 1990s and for his (laudable) efforts to remove the Confederate flag from the South Carolina State House. According to his biography, he spent the years since his election defeat in 1996 "working with high-profile leaders and on-the-ground program managers in more than 100 countries, directing projects designed to foster peace, reconciliation and economic progress."

With no offense to Beasley and his likely sincere efforts to help those around the world, one wonders why he was nominated to be executive director. The simplest answer is his connection to the then US ambassador to the United Nations, Nikki Haley, herself a former governor of South Carolina.

Beasley is the latest in a long line of US administrators of WFP. The executive directors have been American since 1992. In fact, only one executive director of WFP since its inception has come from a non-Western country: Francisco Aquino, who served from 1968 to 1976.

There are a number of unwritten rules governing who gets to run these major international institutions. For example, there's the long-standing agreement that the World Bank is run by an American and the IMF is run by a European. Thus, although Christine Lagarde from the IMF is lauded as a champion of women's rights, her activism rings hollow when it is a fact that no non-White woman was even considered for the post. She is a beneficiary of global White privilege.

When International Leadership Means Western Leadership

Major global bodies are often led by Westerners. When they aren't, then the bar is set very high, and they are often the subject of attacks by Western nations and experts, as Tedros Adhanom, who was elected director general of the World Health Organization (WHO) in 2017, has found out in his attempts to grapple with a once-in-a-century pandemic and the constant criticisms of WHO's decisions. Many of the world's most prominent economic groups—such as the Group of 7 (G7) and the Organisation for Economic Co-operation and Development (OECD)—are dominated by Western countries, with only a few non-Western members.

Non-White political leaders, too, are of the subject of ridicule and constant criticism, with hardly any balanced reporting in the Western media. In the past, this included Lee Kuan Yew (the first prime minister of Singapore). Today it includes President Paul Kagame of Rwanda, who transformed a country that experienced genocide into a successful country in the space of two decades. Yet White leaders who have committed international crimes, such as George W. Bush and Tony Blair, are given a free pass and even rehabilitated. This is White privilege at work too.

Membership in organizations like the G7 and OECD were originally justified on the basis of economic development: both were meant to involve the world's largest economies. However, with the rise of other countries, membership is now offered on the basis of "democratic values," justified along Western lines.

When international institutions are set up along Western lines, see the world through Western framings, and are led by Westerners, one should not be surprised if their actions, advice, and prescriptions follow Western framings as well. One should also not be surprised that those who then appear to be the "most qualified" are White, establishing a permanent "ruling class" when it comes to global and elite institutions.

The international bodies that most exemplify this institutional form of discrimination are the World Bank and the IMF. These institutions were set up to manage the global economy, especially in the aftermath of the Great Depression and World War II.

However, these institutions have largely pursued an economic development platform that promotes free markets and deregulation, often at the expense of living conditions on the ground. Developing countries, faced with an economic crisis—oftentimes not of their own making—have been forced to enact sweeping and drastic policy reforms at the insistence of the IMF. These Structural Assistance Programmes were based on the ideas of the Washington Consensus: that economies must be market driven, with reduced public sectors and limited assistance. These reforms were often hugely damaging, destroying standards of living and demolishing trust in political and economic institutions, including in many of the fledgling democracies seen after the fall of the Soviet Union.[7]

Trade agreements—at least those pursued by the West—often include other priorities that are meant to benefit Western companies and business interests. For example, the Trans-Pacific Partnership (TPP) did not just include efforts to reduce barriers to trade but also forced many countries to agree to tighten up their protections for intellectual property, open up their service sectors to foreign firms, and allow Western companies to sue governments in court to overturn regulations they did not like. TPP was not popular in many of the countries involved in negotiations, but in the end, the promise of better access to the United States was enough for them to bite the bullet.

By contrast, the Regional Comprehensive Economic Partnership (RCEP), agreed on by the Association of Southeast Asian Nations, China, Japan, South Korea, Australia, and New Zealand, is a much slimmer document, focusing primarily on reducing trade barriers between the countries involved. It does not involve itself with intellectual property, investor disputes, service sectors, or government support, yet this has now led to the creation of the world's largest trading bloc.[8]

The Rules-Based Order: Sanctions and Military Interventions

The final aspect of the rules-based international order is what happens when a country is deemed to have broken it. The bodies that make those judgments and that ultimately apply the punishment are almost entirely Western.

For example, the UN Security Council remains the pinnacle of the international security apparatus. This body can decide whether or not to take action against any particular member of the international community. Yet it is also a product of the postwar era. Its permanent five members are the victors of World War II: the United States, the United Kingdom, France, Russia, and China. Three out of the five are clearly Western; four out of the five are White. China remains the only non-Western, non-majority-White country on the council. These five member countries have veto rights, and they thus control the debate at the United Nations.

There have been efforts to expand the permanent members of the council. Germany, Japan, India, Brazil, and South Africa have all agreed to support one another's bids for membership, yet for various reasons, none have gone through.

Countries that are deemed to be in violation of the rules can be made subject to a range of punishments. Yet when a UN resolution to call for an end to racism, racial intolerance, and xenophobia (something that most countries are guilty of, to varying degrees) came up at the UN at the end of 2020, only fourteen countries voted no. These included the US, the UK, Australia, and Canada—four members of the Five Eye Alliance—who are typically the first to call out others on human rights and freedoms and even intervene.[9]

The most serious of these punishments is military intervention, which has been implemented throughout the Middle East in much of the twenty-first century. In Iraq, Libya, and Syria, Western countries—often without formal authorization from the United Nations, supposedly the main body to decide these things—went ahead to oust leaders they felt were threatening to the international order. In all of these cases, the intervention served to make matters worse, causing instability, the deaths of hundreds of thousands, and violence that persists today.

Military interventions remain controversial; even within the Western bloc, countries were sharply divided as to whether the interventions were justified. It should be noted, however, that they were not controversial enough to spur Western countries to denounce the United States or the United Kingdom as "rogue states" for their interventions in Iraq or Libya. None called for labeling those interventions as war crimes.

As military interventions have become politically unfeasible internationally and domestically, Western countries have increasingly turned to economic sanctions as their punishment of choice. Western governments and organizations have turned to the reckless use of unilateral sanctions, such as the US sanctions against Iran or the European Union sanctions against Cambodia.

Sanctions are generally seen to be a less violent, yet still punitive, mechanism to enforce international rules. It is important to note, however, that the effectiveness of sanctions is entirely dependent on their ability to inflict pain on a population: the idea is that sanctions will make the operation of society and the economy so painful that a government will be forced to compromise on key issues. An example of a country hounded by the West and punished in ways that resulted in massive suffering is Iran. No Western country has openly apologized or even acknowledged that tens of thousands of children—yes, children—have died in Iran due to sanctions. White privilege allows a Western government to get away with these large-scale horrors.

Thus the way we judge sanctions depends on whether or not they actually achieve their objectives. The international sanctions against Iran may have succeeded in bringing it to the negotiating table over its supposed nuclear arms program, but did so by inflicting a great deal of pain on ordinary Iranians, who did not have access to key goods. In addition, sanctions distort the economy, making access to even permitted goods more difficult.

Sanctions that *don't* work are crimes against humanity, because they inflict pain with no benefit. If inflicted against a White population, sanctions would be demonized and even unthinkable. One can't argue that the ends justify the means if the policy doesn't even achieve the ends. The US-led round of sanctions against Iran, begun in 2020, proves this point: the sanctions are clearly being enacted to punish a regime (by cruelly punishing innocent citizens) Washington does not like, with no real attempt to achieve any kind of mutually beneficial arrangement with Tehran. White privilege allows the West to remain collectively silent on these crimes against humanity and not to be held accountable to the global community.

Sanctions are now increasingly targeted against specific leaders and policymakers who are believed to be responsible for certain actions. But even if you accept the premise that wider economic pain will not result from these targeted sanctions, this approach reveals the limitations of sanctions as a policy instrument. There is no evidence or theory that explains how sanctions on already isolated leaders will lead to changes in policy—meaning that they are being implemented as punishment, as a warning to others, and in a desire to showboat a fake morality.

Conclusion

When considering how a post-Western world may look like and be run, it is important to look at and learn from examples that are working and not part of the Western world's prescriptions on geopolitical issues. Here are two examples that provide a pointer to how other models work in the geopolitical front.

Looking for Geopolitical Lessons: ASEAN

In discussions of international politics, experts and commentators largely ignore non-Western institutions when looking for lessons about peace, cooperation, and international security. Only experts attached to Western think tanks are invited to comment on and analyze events and developments in the international system.

One glaring example is the longtime ignorance of the Association of Southeast Asian Nations, or ASEAN. As Kishore Mahbubani notes in his book *The ASEAN Miracle*, ASEAN has an amazing track record of fostering international cooperation and peace in one of the most multicultural and multiethnic regions in the world.[10] Southeast Asia includes many of the world's largest countries, whose populations follow very different religions and have very different histories. Also, as a region nestled between China and the United States, it is at risk of having its divisions exploited by nearby great powers.

Despite this, the region has been not only peaceful but largely unified in its foreign policy. ASEAN has not fallen apart, nor are there pressing disagreements or disputes between its member countries. The prospect of armed conflict between the members of ASEAN is nigh unthinkable.

Mahbubani notes how the West has dismissed the value of institutions outside the West. He observes that the European Union has long been held up as the model for regional integration, whereas other models such as ASEAN and the African Union have been dismissed as not going far enough.

Even now, with the European Union beset by internal differences and divisions, ASEAN's success in keeping a multicultural, multiethnic, and multilingual region at peace has gone overlooked. The reason commonly cited for ASEAN's limitations is its culture of consensus building, nonintervention, and respect for internal sovereignty. Yet ASEAN appears to have truly bolstered the power of Southeast Asia as a collective body, maintaining an independent position on key issues between the United States and China. By contrast, the European Union continues to struggle to define an independent role for itself within the Western bloc.

Looking for Geopolitical Lessons: AIIB

Countries are made to jump through hoops in order to join the important international bodies. China needed to make significant changes to its internal policies in order to join the World Trade Organization, yet today countries claim that China did not do enough and must do more.

The furor over the Asian Infrastructure Investment Bank (AIIB) is an example of how an institution created to challenge White economic dictates and power will be treated as somehow illegitimate.[11]

AIIB was proposed by Beijing in 2012 as an alternative to Western-led organizations like the World Bank and the Asian Development Bank. It was never presented as a competitor to these organizations, but instead as an organization to complement existing development institutions.

Many countries throughout Asia were willing to support such an initiative. Even Western countries in Europe were open to supporting a new addition to the development finance landscape.

However, one country was strongly opposed: the United States, which saw AIIB as a threat to the existing Western- and US-led development finance institutions. Washington engaged in an international behind-the-scenes campaign to lobby governments to reject AIIB. Some countries agreed, Japan prime among them. Many other countries ignored the United States, much to the chagrin of Washington.

The irony is that Beijing developed AIIB in response to long-standing calls for it to become a responsible stakeholder. Throughout the 2000s, China was continually lectured by Washington to start playing a greater role in world affairs and to support an international order that fostered international peace and stability.[12]

AIIB was intended to be an effort in that regard: a new development institution that would show that China was willing to use its newfound economic power to improve global well-being. Yet when Beijing actually did offer to act as a responsible stakeholder, Washington strongly disagreed. The overarching objective of maintaining Western economic power is simply unable to tolerate such a proposition.

It turns out that by *responsible stakeholder*, the United States and its allies in fact meant that Beijing should accept the US-led order and contribute to its operation without fundamentally challenging the existing power structure. To join their world order, China must play by their rules and be subservient.

The narrative has, of course, shifted in recent years. Now, China's presence in international organizations—even ones set up by the West— is seen as a fundamental institutional challenge. China, as a major economic power, contributes a great deal to such organizations as the United Nations and the World Health Organization. Yet now an increasing number of Western commentators see these organizations as "tainted" by Chinese influence, to the point where they think that the West should not even take part in them anymore.

It is undoubtedly true that China's investment in these institutions is not wholly selfless: Beijing has probably made the calculus that its interests are suited by playing a large role in these international institutions.

Yet all major powers feel this way. The United States feels that its interests are served by being a major contributor to these organizations, and in fact feels that its contributions should give it a much *larger* say in how these organizations are run. China's attitude toward these organizations is not unique, nor is it indicative of behavior much different from that of other major powers.

Fighting Global White Privilege in Geopolitics

How can we fight structural White privilege in the area of global geopolitics?

One major avenue would be to recognize the successes of other regions in preserving peace and prosperity. The West is not the only region to have had decades of peace between its members: East Asia, Southeast Asia, Latin America, and Africa have also seen decades of interstate peace. They have lessons worth taking seriously as we try to chart a new path for global geopolitics. These successes also challenge the need for a single, powerful "global policeman": a title often claimed by White Western major powers and led by the US.

International institutions should also be humbler in their prescriptions. The track record of these global bodies is decidedly mixed, whether in terms of peacekeeping, global economic management, or fostering development. Rather than assume that Western-based framings are the best way to understand global issues, these international bodies need to elevate non-Western voices and examine whether their suggestions would work in non-Western contexts.

CHAPTER 2

THE RETELLING OF HISTORY
This Version Ain't Mine

I was wondering about our yesterdays and started digging
through the rubble/And to say, at least somebody went to a hell
of a lot trouble/To make sure that when we looked things up,
we wouldn't fair too well/And we would come up with totally
unreliable portraits of ourselves.

—Gil Scott-Heron, "Black History/The World"

Since I was a teenager, I have often wondered what it would have been
like to have read books about the colonization of Asia and Africa, written by Asians and Africans. Most of what I read were textbooks written
by Westerners—a bit like reading the account of a fire written by an
arsonist.

I could not find in the literature the robust explanations that I was
searching for to come to terms with what I saw and understood from my
lived experience. I was someone who was already fairly well versed in the
discussions about racism, the injustices of colonialism and the fight for
liberation across the world against Western domination, the Black power
movement, and the fight against apartheid. The failure to find these issues addressed concisely in nonacademic literature made me think that I
needed to write about it.

I clearly remember getting my first copy of *How Europe Underdeveloped Africa* thirty-five years ago and wondering if there was an error in
the title. I had to read it a couple of times to get my colonized mind
switched on to this bold new narrative by the Guyanese author Walter

Rodney. The same year, I read *Wretched of the Earth* by Ibrahim Frantz Fanon from Martinique. Both these books brutally exposed my "mind capture" by Western versions of history and elegantly opened new ways of understanding colonial history and its continuation to this day. My history education seemed to be filled with lies. I began to understand that his-story is not our-story, your-story, or my-story.

It was obvious to me that Western supremacy and White privilege manifest themselves in how history is told. The history of Europe and the West sits at the core of most discussions of global history; the history of other regions is taught in the context of the Westernization of the world or is studied as an elective. These curriculums often do not explain how historical Western dominance via colonization enabled the West to continue its economic and cultural influence in the present day. Imperialism, colonialism, and racism are painted as things of the past, ended by the decolonization and civil rights movements of the twentieth century.

Colonizing Minds through His-story

The justification for the West's authority over the global system is aided by a specific reading of history that favors the actions and ideas of White Westerners, legitimizing a belief that the West has acted as a benevolent force toward other cultures and that it continues to have a positive influence on the world through its economic models, governance systems, cultures, and more.

There is surprisingly little mention in popular Western history of the scale of the atrocities committed against colonized populations. Most of these are hardly ever mentioned today. Downplaying these deeds actually helps perpetuate the belief that the dark nature of colonization does not outweigh its supposed benefits—the spread of "civilization," infrastructure, education, and trade (despite its being plunder in reality). The societal, cultural, political, and institutional transformations of colonized countries have been described as the introduction of modern development to the underdeveloped world, and inculcating this belief is important for the reproduction of White, Western power, because it helps "colonize the minds" of non-Westerners.

What does *colonization of the mind* mean? In the context of the retelling of history, it refers to how key historical viewpoints are used to construct opposing identities in the minds of Westerners and non-Westerners, to the benefit of Westerners. These opposite mindsets that frame identities are superiority (as a Westerner, believing you and your culture are better than others) and subservience (as a non-Westerner, believing Western people and cultures are better and wanting to emulate them for this reason).

For example, by attributing modern global civilization to European colonization of the world, people are led to believe that Western forms of civilization sit at a pinnacle, and that global progress is owed to the West and its people. The common description of the Renaissance as the apex of human achievement in art and science is one example, as if the rest of the world lived in darkness and ignorance before and during this period. Yet this is patently not true. Take the Taj Mahal, one of the wonders of the world, which was constructed around 1650.[1] This wasn't achieved by Leonardo da Vinci or Machiavelli, but by Ustad Ahmad Lahouri, an architect of the Mughal Empire. Nonetheless, the conventional wisdom of Renaissance fundamentalism explains why many of the elite in former colonies such as Hong Kong, Singapore, and Malaysia are more interested in emulating British and Western culture than their own or that of any others.

Many history curriculums are marked by the West's conflicts, where Western countries are characterized as fighting against "evil" across the world. Glorified war heroes stand as exemplars for unassailable Western virtues, such as freedom, bravery, and honor, as if others do not hold these dear. But little mention is made of the non-Western soldiers and civilians who suffered and died in the West's pursuit of its own values during World Wars I and II, or of the nature of the fight for freedom from Western imperialism, as in Vietnam, Mozambique, Haiti, Algeria, the Dominican Republic, and so on.

Finally, Western narratives trace a path for global values from the Ancient Greek philosophers through the Enlightenment to the present day, placing the West at the center of human progress. Yet many discoveries vital to human progress were actually rediscoveries or transportation of works from one civilization to the other, including discoveries from Asian, African, and other non-Western scholars. That is in essence the story of human progress.

These three areas are examples of how history has been Whitewashed, where non-Western and non-White people are written out of history, and where events are framed to favor the achievements of White people. This narrative must be corrected to include the achievements and efforts of non-Western people if the cycle of repeated Western dominance is to be broken.

To dismantle global White privilege, the non-Western world needs to delegitimize the inaccuracies of the past as represented in Western historical narratives and relegitimize the truth through their engagement in telling their-story.

Colonialism Then: Imperial Glory Now

"Colonialism may have caused suffering of colonized populations; it also laid the foundations of the world we know today." This is the common Western historical narrative, and it demonstrates how people forget and exclude the more atrocious aspects of colonialism while emphasizing the positive changes that resulted from colonization (i.e., "civilization").

The British Empire invaded all but twenty-two countries on the planet and committed atrocities in many of them. In India, up to thirty-five million Indians died of starvation under British rule—three million as a result of Churchill's policies in Bengal—yet this is not common knowledge globally.[2] However, everyone seems to know of the failures of the Great Leap Forward in China and Mao's involvement. Both are of course appalling. As one of my English colleagues pointed out, British students are taught about famines caused by Mao, but not those caused by Churchill.

These kinds of discrepancies can be attributed to the selective version of history that is taught in schools around the world with a view of promoting the myth of the benevolent West. While it is true that a student in Japan will learn favorable histories of Japan, they will also learn Western history, often in a way that mirrors Western interpretations of history. But Western nations will not teach the history of Japan in core syllabuses. By exporting a version of history that glosses over certain negative past events, Western education ensures that the positive perception of Western countries is not overly impacted. Essentially, it is very effective propaganda, and it has become instituted in the West.

The impacts of maintaining this positive perception are apparent: a 2014 poll revealed that 59 percent of British people viewed the British Empire as "something to be proud of." Similarly, 49 percent of British people believe that colonialism benefited Britain's former colonies.[3]

Views like this are tied to a nostalgia for former imperial glory. I find this attitude common among expatriates in Hong Kong who are never tired of deriding China or India, but are quick to jump to the defense of the atrocities committed by the British. They will not entertain a discussion about a war crime having been committed in Iraq, such is their en-trenched view of the moral superiority of the West.

After all, how do you hold on to your White privilege with that on your record, and how do you teach your children that they belong to a superior culture if they are lumped together with all those other awful nations with blood on their hands? It is easier to maintain national pride if you are told that your own country has not committed heinous acts, unlike others around the world, or that your country is responsible for creating modern civilized world order. Beliefs like this actually inform the West's domestic and foreign policies, directly affecting non-White people around the world. The UK's decision to leave the EU is an example of this, wherein certain segments of the British populace see the nation as distinct and better than the rest of Europe because of its powerful imperial past—it is why Prime Minister Boris Johnson was a user of the "Make Britain Great Again" tagline.[4]

Whitewashing Colonial Histories

No major former colonial power or the United States has actively faced the sins of its past; at most, the government offers some sort of qualified "official" apology. None of these countries have addressed the deep harm that centuries of colonial rule and military intervention have had on the world. Instead, the recurrent imperial nostalgia felt in countries such as the UK is a direct result of historical amnesia on the part of government, education, and the media, which actively downplay the impact of European colonization on the world. The result of this institutionalized selective memory is a misinformed pride in Western history. In America, it is almost a national psychosis, and most people subscribe to alternative facts.[5]

This Whitewashing of colonial histories also has impacts in the non-Western world. By deliberately ignoring non-White histories of colonialism, non-Westerners are adversely affected by the delegitimization of their pasts. People in former colonies are told that their country's development and ability to modernize were a result of colonialism. For example, India's extensive railway network, built by the East India Trading Company, is still often referred to as a beneficial legacy left by the British. In actuality, it was built to benefit the outposts of the company, which were extracting vast quantities of wealth from India. It was paid for with Indian taxes, not British investments, and was for the most part built with what was essentially slave labor.[6] Retelling history through a Western lens in this way is essential for the West to continue its contemporary economic and cultural influence over non-Western territories, because it highlights the presumed benefits of colonial influence, ultimately leading to the belief that contemporary Western influence can only be a beneficial thing as well, and should not be resisted. In fact, Shashi Tharoor, a former UN undersecretary general, has made a career of identifying the positive myths of British rule in India, ranging from the railways to tea to cricket.

This Whitewashing of history strongly plays into the colonization of the mind of non-Westerners and contributes to why they seek to emulate Western views on politics, business ideas, and lifestyles. For example, Asians who have relocated to a country such as Australia often do not seek to learn of the crimes committed against the First Nation peoples, and without this education, may even discriminate against these communities, in spite of their own national history of subjugation by the West.[7] This rejection is rooted in the historical racism toward these people by the White population in Australia. Rather than sympathizing with the First Nation peoples, non-White immigrants seek to mirror White attitudes toward these people as a form of integration. Their racism toward the First Nation peoples is a price they are willing to pay for integration and proximity to White Western capital and cultural influence. Acceptance is critical, and this phenomenon is to be found among US-based Asians of Indian and Chinese origin, many of whom even supported a White supremacist, Donald Trump.

The Impacts of Silenced Colonial Histories

The link between colonialism and contemporary events is not commonly made because during key stages of education, colonialism is often taught as a thing of the past, and the lessons from these teachings imply that the modern world is no longer marked by empires and is thus somehow free from colonial legacies. Such teaching thus avoids explanations about the preservation of past privileges and how they contribute to Western dominance and injustice to this day.

African societies, for example, did not invite the West to define their borders, impose Western definitions of identity, or enslave its populations. They did not decide to place Egypt and Tunisia in the Arab Middle East. Yet because the Western telling of history brushes over the negative aspects of Western rule, the catastrophes that followed decolonization were blamed on postcolonial governments, not on the chaotic and wounded state in which colonialism left those countries, their social structures, and people.

A powerful example is the 1994 genocide in Rwanda. The mainstream view is that the genocide was sparked by internal sociopolitical rifts between the elite and the masses, defined along ethnic lines. Yet this was a narrative cultivated by the Western media, and one that missed how successive colonial powers laid the foundations for the divisive ethnicity-based policies that led to genocide.

German colonizers were the first to exploit the division between what they saw as Rwanda's two most populous ethnic groups, the Hutus and the Tutsi. Prior to colonization, the identity of all Rwandans was associated with eighteen different clans, including the Hutu and Tutsi. The Germans placed the Tutsi in administrative positions because they believed them to be racially superior (taller and with higher, more Germanic-looking foreheads). Later, during Belgian colonial rule, Rwandans were even issued identity cards that had their ethnicity on them. This immediately created different race-based social classes in Rwandan society, which collapsed into racial hate over time, leading to one of the most brutal civil wars and genocides in history: six hundred thousand to one million Rwandans died in just one hundred days. There were even reports after the genocide concluded that the French government had been actively supporting the Rwandan government with arms, which were used to perpetuate the killings.[8] But very little of this—neither the history nor the French involvement—is taught in the West. Instead, a prejudiced reading of the genocide focuses on the immediate events and hides decades of history, which helps to absolve the European colonial powers. The same is true of other countries, such as Myanmar, which has experienced the most civil wars of any country in recent history, due to the manner in which the British exited and destabilized the country.

Rwanda shows that the historical amnesia and Whitewashing of history by the West are extremely dangerous. They support the superiority complex in the West and an internalized sense of ethnic or cultural inferiority in the Rest, even resulting in colonization of the mind, which has been well documented around the world, such as by the author Frantz Fanon as mentioned previously and others such as the Brazilian thinker Paulo Freire.

I saw a form of this widespread sense of inferiority and fear on my first trip to South Africa with members of the band I was in, when we were invited to play in Johannesburg. I traveled with a fake passport—Malaysia did not recognize apartheid South Africa—and should have been the most afraid. But my South African band members seemed to change when we crossed the border, and became subservient and fearful in the land where the White man was king. I was brutally reminded of this master-slave construct when I saw a poor Black man shot in the leg for apparently stealing a pair of socks, and this being seen as an accepted way to maintain order and administer justice.

History plays a role in the development of identity—of individuals, of groups, of nations and generations. Celebrating the achievements of colonialism enforces White privilege. Furthermore, many of the most powerful international organizations/institutions of the modern world, such as the IMF, the United Nations, and the World Bank, have their roots in the colonial period and are therefore designed to reinforce the steep imbalance in power between the West and the Rest. Recognizing the impacts of selective interpretations of colonial history is thus very relevant to understanding contemporary identity formation and even geopolitics.

Glorification of War and Liberal Interventionism

The core events in our telling of history tend to be wars. Western wars have been repeatedly glorified over the past few centuries, which has led to the acceptance of historical and contemporary Western military interventions throughout the twentieth and twenty-first centuries. In an article in the *Guardian*, Geoffrey Wheatcroft explains how "the glorification of the second world war has had practical and baleful consequences. It has led us to an easier acceptance of 'liberal interventionism,' founded on the assumption that we in the West are alone virtuous and qualified to distinguish political right from wrong—and the conviction that our self-evidently virtuous ends must justify whatever means we employ."[9]

This narrative of liberal interventionism was employed in all Western-waged wars: South Korea and Vietnam were meant to prevent the global spread of Communism, while wars in Iraq and Afghanistan were supposedly meant to counter extremist Islam, spread "freedom," and even liberate oppressed Muslim women. The West has taken it upon itself to invade or sanction other countries on the pretext of furthering the goal of global peace. The Western fight for "the greater good," while perceived by many as a necessary fight, has had incredibly damaging impacts on non-Western countries—including destabilizing entire regimes—and has persisted as the commonly taught historical narrative.

One of the most pertinent examples is the nuclear bombing of Hiroshima and Nagasaki. Estimated casualties lie somewhere between 129,000 and 226,000, most of whom were civilians. The United States remains the only country in the world that has used nuclear weapons in armed conflict.[10]

The monumental decision to bomb Japan is often referred to as a necessary act despite debates in the historical community that there were other options available or that the Japanese were on the verge of surrender.[11] However, these debates are not part of the common understanding of the event, and even though the "nuking" of Japan is taught in classrooms across the world, the lay sentiment is that the bombing was not a crime against humanity and that the Japanese deserved it for their cruelties during the war. Instead, the atomic bombing is seen as a military tactic to bring a swift end to a war that the United States and its allies were dragged into, and a tactic ultimately less deadly for both the United States and Japan than other possible options. This perception is the ultimate perk of White privilege: committing a crime against humanity no matter the military justification and being granted a free pass. This would never have occurred with a non-White country committing an equivalent act of war.

This belief in a swift and decisive end to the war is perpetuated by Western historical narratives, which focus on the future without reflecting on the past, helping justify certain atrocities with myths. The repeated justification of certain war decisions taken by the West has had modern-day impacts—continual defensible interventions by the United States over the last century have seen the country emerge as "the world police," the only one capable of invading another with or without international consent.

The implications of this foreign policy are serious. So-called international support for the Vietnam War led to decades of atrocities. More than two million tons of bombs were dropped on Laos from 1964 to 1973—about a planeload of bombs every eight minutes for nine years.[12] Operation Ranch Hand, which sprayed seventy-three million liters of herbicides over Vietnam, Cambodia, and Laos between 1961 to 1971, included the use of Agent Orange, a deadly chemical mixture, even though chemical warfare like this was banned under international humanitarian law. Almost four hundred thousand Vietnamese were harmed as a result of exposure to herbicides, and reports show that Vietnamese mothers still have traces of it in their breast milk, while as many as two million people are suffering from cancer or other illness caused by Agent Orange.[13]

Thus the biggest legacy of the Vietnam War should not really be seen as a containment of Communism; rather it should be taught as the half-century of disaster that Agent Orange has imposed on the Vietnamese people and their environment. This legacy continues to the current day and is certainly not forgotten by the victims: in 2004, Vietnamese citizens filed a class-action lawsuit against more than thirty US chemical companies, but US federal judges dismissed the suit.[14] There has been no call by Western countries for an international inquiry to put this to bed—another example of Western privilege at work on the geopolitical front.

In War, White Lives Matter

The narrative of war taught in Western classrooms—particularly in the US—and spread through Western media imparts messages and values that glorify the Western role in war. This glorification serves as a veneer that obscures the sheer scale of the atrocities committed, atrocities that are not commonly explored as completely as victories. Are American children taught about the atrocities committed by their country, and *can* they be taught, given that blind patriotism does not seem to allow an honest discussion of war crimes? This failure can be attributed to the belief that the value of a non-Western life lost in war in a far-flung inferior society is not considered as important as the life of a White Westerner.[15]

During the first Gulf War in Iraq, which was the first globally televised war after the war in Vietnam, the deaths of tens of thousands of Iraqis went unreported in Western media, while the unfortunate casualties of every Western soldier or reporter were mentioned in detail. The same is true of the war in Afghanistan. The Western military was portrayed as the savior, with non-Western casualties as secondary, again perpetuating the belief that the interventions or even invasions by the West are premised on moral objectives, with sacrifices from soldiers fighting for the greater good, granting the West the right to decide which military conflicts are initiated and conducted "justly." Hence why the former US secretary of state Madeleine Albright is famously quoted as saying, "We think the price is worth it," when publicly answering the question of whether "sanctioning Iraq was worth the half a million children who died as a result."[16] It is White privilege that allows this to pass. If a spokesperson from a non-Western country had said this, even about their own people, the Western media would be in an uproar over the lack of care for human rights.

Consider World War II and the number of military and civilian casualties: combined, the US (420,000 deaths), the UK (451,000 deaths), and France (600,000 deaths) lost just 7.5 percent to 10 percent of the number of Chinese who died (15–20 million). The Chinese decision not to surrender to the Japanese Empire is one that impacted the fate of the entire world.[17] Yet this is not often taught in the Western telling of history, which describes China as incompetently defending against the Japanese and relying on American intervention to save it.

When interpretations of history that glorify Western wars, military, and heroes are perpetuated, Western violence is also glorified. A similar process occurs in all countries—it has become a part of national myth making—but in the case of the West, these myths are exported to the rest of the world. These lies are in fact taught to people who bore the brunt of these atrocities. This reinforces the view of Western armies as protectors of freedom and liberty, and defenders of the weak. Ultimately, these distorted versions of events enable the West to pursue further military interventions, guided by its own dubious moral compass—which it has decided is the only one worth following.

Human Progress: Non-Western Contributions to Science and Philosophy

Another major area where the narratives of history have been told in favor of the West is that of human progress: innovation, science, and philosophy. Although it is important to recognize just how severely non-Western populations were impacted by colonization, it is also necessary to include the history of non-Western people as part of and contributors to the modern world as we know it, rather than simply as beneficiaries (or victims) of Western thought.

Thus, when considering the milestones of human progress, we should acknowledge the achievements of non-Westerners. At the moment, it is a global norm to see human progress as a product of the West, itself portrayed as the progenitor of modern civilization. The West uses this historical legitimacy to claim ownership of leading the world into the future, through Western governance, institutions, ideas, products, and services, ultimately maintaining the West's economic and cultural dominance.

The history of science and philosophy was fashioned by Western educators and institutions that forget major figures from non-Western countries. For example, Westerners often attribute the origin of many scientific concepts and theories to the Ancient Greeks or to Renaissance thinkers: Plato, Aristotle, Leonardo da Vinci, Michelangelo, and others. Yet many people would struggle to identify non-Western thinkers portrayed as having equal stature.

Mainstream (Western) society has become oblivious to the essential role played by cultural plurality and knowledge exchange across history in shaping intellectual development. In Ancient Greece, the cross-fertilization of ideas with African and Asian civilizations contributed to many discoveries, through the Greeks' links with learning and commercial centers throughout the Mediterranean. It was Arab Muslims who preserved and translated Greek works into Arabic, sustaining this tradition of cultural and intellectual exchange after the fall of the Greeks and Romans, correcting errors and advancing these ideas. The Renaissance was fueled by these Arab works.[18]

There are countless examples of contributions from non-Western thinkers. The Indian mathematician Baudhayana Sutra wrote a theorem on right triangles one hundred years before Pythagoras. The Bengali Jagadish Bose was the first to discover ways to receive and emit radio waves, before Marconi, and he also anticipated the existence of semiconductors. The Persian mathematician Muḥammad ibn Mūsā al-Khwārizmī was the first scholar to use Hindu numerals in his work, introducing the concept of zero to the West. Arab writer al-Jahiz proposed the concept of natural selection far before Jean-Baptiste Lamarck and Charles Darwin did.

By excluding the innovations and discoveries of non-Western thinkers from the historical narrative taught in schools around the world, Western countries pave the way for their societies to be held in high regard as the founders of the modern world. By contrast, certain non-Western peoples are more likely to be unaware of their historical lineage, which may have been eroded by the combined forces of colonialism and globalization.

For instance, colonialism replaced the rich and fluid cultural identities of Southeast Asia, where I am from, with rigid identities based on allegiance to enforced ethnicities and nation states (the nation itself being a concept established in Southeast Asia through colonialism). This has resulted in frequent "culture clashes" in which neighboring countries claim many symbols and cultural elements: Indonesians, Malaysians, and Singaporeans, for example, have made repeated attempts to claim ownership of the common heritage of the *batik* design, shadow-puppet theater called *wayang kulit*, and traditional musical instruments such as the *gamelan* and *angklung.* Furthermore, colonial influence also affected the Malay language, commonly spoken among the Southeast Asian islands, dividing it into Malaysian and Indonesian variants. Now, many Malaysian Malays do not recognize the shared heritage they have with Indonesian Malays, and vice versa.[19]

The Science of Controlling Narratives

Clearly, non-Western contributions to human progress have been incredibly significant. Yet by excluding their innovations and discoveries from the historical narrative taught in schools around the world, Western nations pave the way for contemporary Western societies to be held in higher regard, as the founders of the modern world we live in now. Equally, non-Western societies that are unaware of their historical lineage (which was at times deliberately destroyed by colonial empires) will carry little national pride in the achievements and contributions of their nation. Ultimately, this manifests in a belief that Western modes of governance, economics, and social organization, together with Western goods and services, must all be of a higher caliber than non-Western equivalents.

A contemporary example is the vaccine for COVID-19. On November 9, 2020, Pfizer announced a COVID-19 vaccine trial that had a supposed 90 percent effectiveness rate. The *Financial Times* and many other Western publications quoted the CEO of Pfizer as saying, "Today is a great day for science and humanity," reinforcing the view that the West would come to the rescue of the world.[20] However, on July 16—almost four months before Pfizer's announcement—Sinopharm, a Chinese pharmaceutical company, announced a vaccine trial conducted in Dubai that yielded a supposed 100 percent production of antibodies in its subjects.[21] In fact, Sheikh Mohammed bin Rashid Al Maktoum, the vice president and prime minister of the United Arab Emirates and one of the richest people in world, was so confident in this vaccine that he took it himself on October 16, 2020. Yet both China's and Russia's vaccine attempts were not covered with the same ubiquity as Pfizer's vaccine announcement.

It is true that at the time neither the Chinese nor the Russian vaccine had been tested according to Western standards, but during a time of global crisis, one would expect that the collective desire to beat the virus would encourage Western leaders and commentators to cover international efforts with positivity, not overt criticism. Instead, China's and Russia's vaccines were repeatedly scorned, with French president Emmanuel

Macron and other commentators declaring how the West must oppose China's "vaccine diplomacy" (the supposed bolstering of Chinese soft power) when Sinopharm began offering its product to developing countries around the world. But surely diplomacy is much preferable to *no vaccine at all*—especially given that richer Western countries have rapidly bought up the first stocks of vaccines: Canada, for example, bought six times the number of vaccines it needed.[22]

On December 8, 2020, a UK grandmother became the first person in the West to receive the Pfizer vaccine. The Western media wasted no time in calling it the world's first "authorized" vaccine, thereby claiming leadership and immediately delegitimizing the scientific credibility, governance systems, and sovereignty of non-Western nations. This is how the history of human progress is manufactured. The role of the Western media in this process is addressed in Chapter Four.

Stock markets across the world rebounded on hearing Pfizer's headlines. And herein lies the mechanism of White privilege: a White Western company produces an innovation of significance that takes precedence over the *same* innovation produced by China and tested in Dubai. The result is economic capital channeled into the markets and pockets of the West. The White retelling of history produces moments like these, repeatedly.

By recognizing that discourse on human progress is heavily biased toward Western innovations and ideologies, we have the opportunity to change how these narratives affect our modern world. Doing so will require a reexamining of the sources from which we draw our central ideas of economics, politics, ethics, philosophy, technology, and the organization of society, and imagining how non-Western countries will make decisions when no longer beholden to constant Western pressure to accept their innovations and ideologies.

Conclusion

History is not simply what *has* happened. It is interpreted, retold, ignored, and silenced to achieve specific ideological ends. How history education is being delivered and received around the world is yet another way in which White privilege and Western dominance of global economic and cultural systems are perpetuated.

Colonial history has been repeatedly retold from the White perspective to minimize the damage caused by colonialism. Even as atrocities are exposed, colonialism is nonetheless painted as a "civilizing force."

The stories of the millions who suffered at the hands of White colonizers are hardly told. And the West is rarely blamed for the underdevelopment of countries postindependence and for the global inequality we see today.

White history also paints the White Western side of World War II and the Cold War as martyrs, fighting the good fight. Of course, there is an element of truth in this, but global war narratives are far more complex than right versus wrong. This is why certain readings of history even justify the use of horrific weaponry, from incendiary bombs to napalm and even nuclear weapons. The commemoration of wars in this way, which reinforces much needed moral justification, can spark nationalistic fervor and thus lead to increased support for unjust practices.

It was precisely this narrative of military-based "justice" that enabled the invasion of Iraq just seventeen years ago, which has led to the death of hundreds of thousands of civilians.[23] White privilege ensures that the US, the UK, and their allies are not held accountable for the true extent of what they have done.

The ability to initiate conflict across the world with little condemnation or intervention from the non-Western international community is a visceral manifestation of both economic and military superiority often in pursuit of maintaining economic interests. But the Western influence over historical discourse also enables the attribution of human progress and moral imperatives, and Western nations deepen the narrative of "West is best," the end result of which is an incredibly lucrative marketing play that legitimizes Western products and services over non-Western equivalents.

$$\bullet \ \bullet \ \bullet$$

So what needs to change?

We need a vision of society that does not depend on historical narratives that place White Western societies above the rest. This entails changing how history is recounted the world over, in both the Western and the non-Western worlds. Educational institutions and governments must heed this message and take active steps—such as including non-White perspectives in their curriculums and recognizing the importance of non-Western nations—to dismantle the systems and institutions that uphold the pro-Western world order in which we live. Only then can the decolonization of the mind begin.

It is important to note that this is not a solution that must come only from the West. Non-Western countries should take the steps to reconfigure the curriculums in their schools. To meet this challenge, and to inform as well as educate older generations outside of schools, a wide range of literature needs to be made available. This will require the development of high-caliber publishing houses outside the West that work in unison to achieve this goal. How about publishing one thousand history books over the next ten years from publishing houses in Africa, the Middle East, and Asia? While some accounts exist, they are often retained in the world of academia; a more mainstream discourse is badly needed to achieve greater impact. Such practical actions would help document a plethora of non-Western viewpoints on historical events and help capture voices that otherwise might have been ignored, silenced, and ultimately lost.

CHAPTER 3

THE WORLD OF BUSINESS
Uneven Playing Fields

We sacrificed [the interests of] individuals and families for the sake of an ideal, to stand at the top of the world. For this ideal, there will be conflict with the United States sooner or later.
—Ren Zhengfei, founder of Huawei Technologies, "Huawei CEO Says Clash with US Was 'Inevitable'"

Reacting to the Asian Financial Crisis

It was during the height of what was called the Asian financial crisis between 1997 and 1999 that I experienced my first awakening about the global power of Western financial institutions.[1]

I was then chairman of Asia's largest environmental consulting firm, with twenty-two offices in twelve countries, and the business was being impacted by the crisis. I was invited to a briefing by the global rating agency Moody's on the risks facing the different countries in the region and their currencies.

As an Asian, I was struck by the fact that for the second time in about two weeks I was listening to Western experts—not an Asian in sight on the podium—who were rating and ranking various Asian countries not simply as an academic exercise but with the power to downgrade them, influence investor decisions, and even affect the price of food for the poor. These countries seemed like vectors in an analytical framework of the global economy that these Western institutions used to do their business of rating sovereign states. It is a business in which they have an unchallenged monopoly. Yet they are meant to be trusted, as they are part of the architecture of the global financial system.

I remember asking the speaker one question: What gave his company the right to rate an entire nation and thereby affect the lives of millions of people using risk assessment tools that are prone to so much subjective analysis and thus manipulation? His response was the usual: his company is fair, the data and analysis are robust, and they have a reputation to protect. Knowing a bit about risk assessment methodologies, I am very aware of the limitations of these models and could not help but come to the conclusion that these institutions simply reinforced Western economic power over the world. The playing field seemed very clearly to be extremely uneven.

Who Gets to Be a Business Success?

This chapter will describe how these uneven playing fields work across the world of business, and it will provide examples of this power, some of which are so commonplace that they are now just viewed as the norm, such that we do not even recognize them as damaging and plain unfair.

Global business is, unsurprisingly, a significant sphere of human activity. A large portion of our lives is governed by the decisions of major and, increasingly, global corporations. In May 2020, seven out of ten of PricewaterhouseCoopers' top global companies were from the United States.[2] We buy from large global companies with global supply chains, we engage with the financial system through major global banks, and we earn our income by working for, or working with, big global companies.

Yet successful companies—or, more accurately, the companies we generally consider to be successful—are all based in the West. No matter the sector, corporate leaders and entrepreneurs who are featured on panels, on the business news, and on magazine covers are all Western, with the odd exception. If they are Chinese, they are viewed with suspicion. The pronouncements of these Western corporations are seen to represent the firm judgment of what it means to be a business or an innovator.

For example, in 2019, the Business Roundtable, an organization of American CEOs, declared that the era of shareholder value was over, to be replaced with a new concept of "stakeholder value," a term first developed in Western discourse by R. Edward Freeman in his 1984 book *Strategic Management: A Stakeholder Approach.*[3] The Roundtable's statement was hailed in the Western press as a new vision for global business, marking a new era in corporate responsibility and how we understand the role that business plays in society.

Except the more honest appreciation and conversation about the role of business, especially outside the West, never got the same headlines. Businesses in Asia have been constituted in different ways for decades, from the family business to the *keiretsu/chaebol* and the state-owned enterprise. All of these violate certain rules for how businesses should be owned, managed, and run, and certainly have different conceptions of their role and responsibility toward customers, the government, and their employees. Yet these models and merits are rarely part of the conversation because they are seen as failing to meet the Western gold standard.

In this chapter, we won't focus on business as a whole, but rather the array of professional and business-related services that supposedly help global businesses operate. These are the investment banks and legal firms that facilitate the deals, mergers, and acquisitions that create ever-bigger multinational companies. These are the accounting firms that judge whether or not a firm is behaving properly, and the rating agencies that determine whether a business or bond is a safe investment. These are the management consultants who try to improve the operations of existing businesses built around Western ideas about productivity and the obsession with shareholder value.

All these different businesses come together to determine the "right" way of doing business. Follow their prescriptions and, supposedly, a business will succeed and be accepted in the West. Follow the prescriptions of a management consultant and hire from the big Western business schools, and the business will be seen as a safe investment. With records evaluated by a Western accounting firm and with bonds graded by a Western rating agency, suddenly the valves of global capital are opened.

Reject these prescriptions, and the business is seen as being run incorrectly and is punished by Western investors not used to other ways of doing things. Accusations of lack of transparency will swirl. Worse, if a business achieves success despite ignoring the prescriptions of management consultants, accountants, and investment banks, then unease turns into suspicion: the business must have cheated somewhere, and so cannot be trusted, such as when Japanese, and then Chinese, companies were suspected by Western politicians.

Such suspicion and even punishment creates a strong material incentive to follow the rules as set down by Western gatekeepers and reinforces Western superiority as well as White privilege. There is little room to chart some new, non-Western way of doing business. Thus the globally successful companies—the ones that can operate in any country or market around the world—all end up looking the same and strengthening the stranglehold of the gatekeepers.

There are three particular areas where we see the manifestation of this global White privilege:

- The "proper" way of doing business is set by Western institutions and organizations and is reinforced by business media, consultants, and business schools. These suppress non-Western ways of thinking about business.
- The major accounting firms, investment banks, and auditors act as gatekeepers controlling entry into the major Western financial centers and preventing access to the largest capital markets. Connections to the "Big Four" in either auditing or accounting connote trust, whereas operating outside that system isolates non-Western businesses.
- Firms that succeed despite Western gatekeeping are seen to have cheated and thus are distrusted, and may even be punished by governments and regulators.

These gatekeeping and enforcement attempts are very effective because they are backed by the power of the world's most developed financial markets: the United States and the United Kingdom. If a firm wants to draw on these markets, it needs to follow those countries' rules and norms—which are stronger than whether the policy in question is led by a White or non-White leader.

Why the Rules Matter

Why do the rules of global business, and how it operates, matter in our discussions of global White privilege?

Business governs much of our lives, and so long as we live in today's system of global capitalism, business ends up governing much of the upward paths for economic development and social mobility in the non-Western world. Much of value is created through the efforts of the private sector. Constraining the ability of non-Western businesses and even governments to operate to their fullest extent thus constrains the potential benefit of a truly equal global economy.

The global private sector also creates many harms. Large global companies have been complicit in significant environmental damage, labor exploitation, sociopolitical disruption, and other major externalities. The current global economic structure, as developed by the West, ignores these costs and perhaps even celebrates them as the price of doing business. Much of this damage is now outsourced to the poorer countries via complex supply chains, despite pious statements about social responsibility.

More often than not, these harms fall upon non-Western communities. Poor communities throughout Asia and Africa grow the food that keeps us fed, manufacture the cheap products that line our store shelves, and extract the raw materials that go into our high-tech products. But this damage is rarely rectified, beyond token efforts related to codes of conduct and corporate social responsibility.

Global White privilege ensures that there is no accountability for these external impacts. They occur far from the minds of corporate leaders, Western consumers, and government regulators. How many really are aware of or are willing to look into the business models of electronic devices, for example, and the huge impact on natural resources such as rare metals in Africa, among others? An investigation can be released revealing forced labor among suppliers for the world's major companies, yet no heads will roll at the board level, nor will stock prices take a deep dive. The most one might expect is a press statement expressing concern, and perhaps some new codes of conduct. Look at the 1MDB scandal, which involved Goldman Sachs as a party to nationwide fraud. Even as the Malaysian government levied fines, major rating agency Fitch said that it saw no need for a rating downgrade. Cozy relationships make sure of this.[4]

This interdependent and crony relationship involving key Western entities in the global financial system is merely one reason why we need to confront the persistence of global White privilege in global business: it ensures that the benefits flow primarily to Western organizations and populations, while the costs flow primarily to non-Western—and non-White—communities around the world.

Of course, fostering a culture that lacks accountability around the world also means fostering a culture that lacks accountability at home. I am sure there are many in the West who see how the corporate disconnect affects their own society, from the rampant push for deregulation to increasing financialization of all aspects of the banking and money system that risks the loss of trust of investors and stakeholders.

Setting the Standards: When Best Practices
Are Western Practices

The proper ways of doing and conducting business are set by Western institutions and organizations. Western companies are highlighted as role models that companies around the world need to follow, from how they approach operational and organizational questions to how they understand the world around them and business opportunities within it. Business schools in the West have spent decades legitimizing Western practices through the case study method, and the business media reinforces those practices and methods with the stamp of approval.[5] To understand how pervasive this desire to introduce Western practices across the world is, it is important to understand the following.

First, Western business schools train the world's population of corporate leaders. Harvard, Wharton, Stanford, and other prominent major US business schools ensure that all business talent is steeped in the same concepts. There, they learn the doctrines of Western business: maximize shareholder value, maximize profits, minimize (or externalize) costs, run a slim organization, and do not overinvest in caring for labor as it will be a drag on business. But do not ever openly admit to the latter.

The major business schools rely on international students, who make up a sizable share of their student body. In the UK, 22 percent of the total postsecondary student population is international, while almost 48 percent of Harvard's MBA cohort in 2019 were international students, thus demonstrating the appeal Harvard's brand has around the world, how it reinforces Western ideas, and the connection of Whiteness and capitalism. This appeal—despite the outdated ideas being taught—speaks to the mind capture I referred to earlier in the book.

The popularity of these business schools is in disregard of the limited evidence that they provide any real educational benefit. The common observation made about MBA programs is that the actual value comes from networking and signaling, not from the classes themselves.[6]

Second, Western management consultants are contracted to improve business operations. A handful of US companies—McKinsey, BCG, and Bain—perpetuate the Western ideas developed in Western business schools. They hire their storm troopers for a region such as Asia from the pool of young Asians who obtain their MBAs in the West, where the indoctrination starts.

When a consultant is called in, they apply the same Western framework to suit any problem. The checklist is the same:

- Slim down operations and cut costs by reducing overhead.
- Offload parts of the company that don't contribute to shareholder value, and offshore what can be offshored.
- Hire agile management talent trained in general business skills applicable across many different sectors, and diminish the importance of technical competency.
- Employ technology, especially technology created by Western companies.
- Use sophisticated financial arrangements to reduce tax obligations and increase valuation.

These end up forcing one particular way of doing things. For example: the Western (or, specifically, American) idea of shareholder value has dominated discussions of the purpose of business and of whom it is meant to serve. For decades, business schools have followed the mantra of thinkers such as Milton Friedman and Jack Welch, who saw the purpose of business as narrowly focused on increasing profits and delivering value to shareholders.

But are there different, non-Western ways of thinking about business, such as the Japanese or Chinese ways of doing business, that never got their footing because of the dominance of the West? How would ideas about the purpose of business, or the ways that businesses could contribute to society, have changed if the world's first major companies had been non-Western?

The Gatekeepers: Guarding Access to Global Capital

The West offers a lucrative opportunity for global business—if you can get in. It has the wealthiest consumer markets, the deepest financial markets, and the largest buyers, including Western governments themselves.

Yet access to these markets is heavily controlled.

This may be a surprising insight. After all, the common refrain about Western economies—especially the United States and the United Kingdom—is that they are extremely open, pushing for free trade and open financial markets. This is true to some extent. However, to take full advantage of the West's economy, a company needs to work with established gatekeepers. These companies and services govern access to the West's lucrative markets. They may not necessarily have the force of law, but the Western business community accepts that these Western gatekeepers are the only ones with the authority to provide the necessary assurances.

Take global accounting. The accounting firms PricewaterhouseCoopers (PwC), Ernst and Young (EY), KPMG, and Deloitte—commonly known as the Big Four—are all Western and led by White people. All are headquartered in Europe; three are headquartered in London. All have Western CEOs.

These firms dominate global business as gatekeepers. They guard the rules of international business, determining which firms are compliant with international standards. Yet all of them have failed the test of integrity and breached the rule book numerous times as they serve their clients to secure exorbitant fees. The phrase "Too Big to Fail" from the book of the same name, used to describe the phenomena of governments bailing out the big banks during the financial crisis, will soon be accompanied by "Too Few to Fail" because of the supposed lack of alternatives from other nations.[7]

Every major company relies on these firms to audit their records and prove to investors and regulators that they are financially sound and legally compliant. Without a stamp of approval from one of these firms, the company in question is not considered trustworthy, and potential investors are warned away.

This has real consequences: non-Western companies in which one of the Big Four does not have a large presence are seen to be more untrustworthy than their Western counterparts. This means fewer opportunities to engage with the global capital markets, access major global investors, and conduct business with major suppliers or customers. And the cozy relationships that exist among all these Western players are only known to those who are insiders; it is the ultimate "White man's club."

Excusing Western Wrongdoing

Of course, the status quo remains unchanged, with the Big Four retaining their positions as trusted gatekeepers, despite a number of high-profile scandals where the accounting firms missed significant financial misconduct on the part of major companies—or worse, deliberately ignored such misconduct to preserve their relationship with the client.

Take the Wirecard scandal in 2019. An investigation by the *Financial Times* uncovered that the Asia-Pacific operations of Wirecard had artificially inflated the company's profits to a significant degree.[8] Wirecard's Singapore office had even been raided by the Singaporean government, yet no measures were taken against any of the key individuals.[9]

Even more embarrassingly, it was revealed that Wirecard's auditor, EY, did not do any of its due diligence regarding Wirecard's fraudulent statements, not even verifying whether Wirecard's supposed cash reserves were real. This was all uncovered in a "special audit" conducted by KPMG, another member of the Big Four.

These aren't even the only scandals EY faced in 2020. First, it was revealed that NMC Health, based in the UAE, had been understating its debt on its balance sheets.[10] Second, the Chinese company Luckin Coffee had falsified its financial and operating figures.[11]

The Luckin Coffee scandal has supposedly prompted the United States to propose legislation preventing Chinese firms from listing on American stock exchanges without providing clearly audited statements. Except, of course, Luckin was audited by one of the Big Four, which suffered no consequences.

There is nothing wrong, of course, with requiring a firm to have its statements independently checked by a trusted authority. But one might assume that investors would not accept an audited statement from a Chinese, Indian, or African auditor. There is no place for a Krishna, Ali, and Wong global accounting firm.

A similar gatekeeping role is played by the rating agencies, which determine the credibility of any bond. The Big Three rating agencies— Standard and Poor's, Moody's, and Fitch—are all Western. All are headquartered in New York (though Fitch operates a second headquarters in London).

Unlike the Big Four, the Big Three are backed by the force of law. Until 2003, they were the only agencies that could provide financial firms the information needed for regulatory compliance, a determination by the US Securities and Exchange Commission. Things are not quite so limited now, but the list of "nationally recognized statistical rating organizations" is still dominated by US companies: Japan Credit Rating Agency and HR Ratings de México are the only non-US companies on the list.

These agencies' ratings carry a great deal of weight. Downgrading a country's bonds is seen to be a serious negative judgment of its fiscal responsibility, especially if the rating crosses the "junk" threshold. By contrast, rating agencies will reward attempts to play by the rules with positive changes to ratings.

Negative media coverage can become self-reinforcing. Investors' concerns end up motivating the rating agencies to downgrade a company or country. That becomes a media story in itself, discouraging investors even further, leaving countries and companies with even less room to recover.

Much like the Big Four, the Big Three have not had a very successful track record. In 2007, the securitized mortgages held by major Western banks all had safe ratings from the rating agencies, meaning that they were supposed to be safe investments. When the American housing market collapsed, these banks suddenly learned that the safety of these assets was entirely fictional.[12]

Non-Western Parties, Western Facilitators

Major investment deals need to be facilitated by both Western banks and Western legal firms. If a non-Western firm wants to launch an initial public offering (IPO) in a Western stock market, the offering needs to be shepherded by one of the big US investment banks: Goldman Sachs, Morgan Stanley, and the like. Without their cooperation, no company can offer its shares on the NYSE, the Nasdaq, or the London Stock Exchange. Even major Asian financial markets involve the big Western financial companies: three of the four banks working with Ant Group for its ultimately aborted IPO in Hong Kong were Western. That might explain the outrage of the Western media, which once again reverted to type and accused Chinese regulators of a host of wrongdoings.

In addition, any major deal must be led by a trusted Western legal firm, either from the United States or the United Kingdom. No non-Western legal firms, even highly qualified ones with experience in common law systems such as those of Singapore or Hong Kong, are ever granted the opportunity to write up one of these deals.

• • •

The harm caused by these gatekeepers is not necessarily in any active oppression of non-Western options. Companies could choose to work with non-Western auditors, legal firms, investment banks, or rating agencies. But in doing so, they would likely be laughed out of any Western financial market.

The selection of Western gatekeepers means that ideas of "Westernness" are innately connected with authority and credibility, and the ability to grant credibility to others. Investors do not question the judgments of a Western auditor or rating agency; by contrast, any judgment from a non-Western organization is at least open to second-guessing on the part of investors.

This is not to say that non-Western firms should be as free of scrutiny as their Western counterparts. Instead, we should note how global White privilege turns off our critical thinking: we take shortcuts, assuming that statements from a Western firm must be accurate. We need to treat these firms with just as much scrutiny as we treat their non-Western counterparts, and accept that each is equally capable of making rational judgments and grievous errors.

Enforcing Authority: Suppressing Competition

When a non-Western disruptor of the status quo emerges, there is a strong reaction among the Western corporate and government world in order to suppress the business. This reaction is especially fervent when the upstart company performs well in a sector that is closely tied to the West's sense of self-worth, such as manufacturing, aviation, or technology.

When a non-Western company begins to make inroads into one of these strategic sectors, Western politicians immediately call for controls. None can accept the premise that these non-Western firms are just as good as—if perhaps not better than—their Western counterparts. This non-Western success is chalked up to something nefarious: either some nebulous non-Western cultural values, unfair support from non-Western governments, or outright theft or cheating on the part of the non-Western company.

In other words, the non-Western company must not be behaving properly. Only companies that follow the West's rules can be successful, and if a non-Western company succeeds, then it must not be following the rules.

The world saw this phenomenon with the first major challenge to the West's corporate supremacy, the rise of Japanese companies in the 1980s. When Japanese car companies began to outcompete their Western counterparts, Western media responded with a great deal of fearmongering. Japan's working culture was threatening to overtake the West, forcing Westerners to submit to Japanese norms and companies. Even popular culture got in on this: *Back to the Future II* features a hypothetical future where an older version of the main character is harried by his Japanese boss; *Blade Runner* features a dystopian future where Los Angeles's polluted skyline features prominent advertisements with Japanese characters.

In the end, the supposed Japanese takeover never took place. This was in part due to the economic slowdown in Japan, but it was also due to restraint on the part of Japan and Japanese companies.

Under pressure from the Reagan administration, Japan agreed to voluntarily limit its export of cars to the United States—"voluntarily" to get around WTO rules governing barriers to trade. Even now, Japanese car companies need to ensure that there is some amount of local US manufacturing in order to satisfy US politicians. Japan also signed the Plaza Accord, which appreciated the yen vis-à-vis the US dollar, making Japanese exports less competitive.[13]

Japanese companies also hired locally, ensuring that the face of their Western operations would be Western, or at least those who could speak English with no accent. Any hint of foreignness would need to be hidden away to avoid any perception of the Japanese company being foreign. But in Asia and Africa, Western companies still have White CEOs acting as if it were 1950 or, in some cases, 1850.

Japanese companies have long been accused of being insular, unable to integrate non-Japanese corporate leadership into their working culture. Of course, one wonders why Western companies are not judged according to the same standards.

Western Business versus Chinese Business

The need to remove potential non-Western competitors has perhaps been most clear in the approach the West has taken to Chinese technology firms. Although Chinese tech firms do present challenges to both China and the West—as do Western tech firms—these firms are uniquely and unfairly targeted, not because of these challenges, but rather due to the threat they pose to the West's technological superiority.

Take Huawei, China's first real global technology company. Through investment in 5G, Huawei was able to secure contracts to develop the communications infrastructure of countries throughout Asia, Africa, and, increasingly, Europe. Its biggest prize? A contract to upgrade the communications infrastructure of the United Kingdom.

This was met with a furious reaction from the United States, which normally retained its technological superiority. Huawei's rise triggered a long diplomatic effort to encourage countries to tear up their contracts with Huawei and remove the company from their communications infrastructure. Under the Trump administration, these actions were bolstered with sanctions, banning Huawei from the United States and denying it access to key components. One of the company's corporate executives was arrested in Canada for supposedly violating US sanctions against Iran.

Despite the brave face put forward by China and Huawei, these actions may have succeeded, at least in part: Huawei now admits that without access to high-end chips produced outside China, it will not be able to produce the latest versions of its high-end smartphones.

TikTok is another major Chinese tech company that came under pressure from the US. If Huawei was the first Chinese tech company to go global, TikTok is perhaps the first Chinese software company. TikTok is the first, and so far only, social network to compete against the titans Facebook and Google in the United States.

In 2020, concerns grew around TikTok's treatment of user data—concerns that many outside observers felt were inflated. In fact, TikTok offered to reform its practices to assuage these concerns, first offering to open up its algorithms to outside inspection (something Facebook and other tech companies have refused to do), then agreeing to a deal where American user data would be hosted in the United States by a trusted local partner. None of this appeared to be enough, as pressure against TikTok continued, even to the point of its being branded as a national threat.

Ultimately, the US is not going to accept a competing business from a non-Western country, especially in sectors around which the US has wrapped much of its self-image, such as the digital technology sector. More broadly, companies work together to keep out competitors. Aviation is a clear example: Boeing and Airbus may engage in harsh competition with each other, yet work to keep everyone else out of the sector. No other company—not Brazil's Embraer, Canada's Bombardier, or Russia's Sukhoi—are able to break the duopoly. We will have to see whether China's aviation company will be able to break through.

Conclusion: Legitimacy and Privilege

There's a structural reason why the major institutions of global finance—the investment banks, ratings agencies, auditors, legal firms, and so on—are Western. Namely, the world's deepest financial markets are Western, the United States and the United Kingdom prime among them.

When you have to raise money from Western financial markets, you end up needing to follow their rules and expectations: be audited by a Western accounting firm, get rated by a Western rating agency, partner with an established Western investment bank, and have the deal constructed by a Western legal firm. The heads of all these organizations are typically White, thus reinforcing the power of White people over the rest of the world.

It's a matter of not just the rules and regulations but the expectations of the investing community. One of the reasons why the Western gatekeepers keep their role is that the investing community still sees them as major sources of authority. Western and White equal authority and legitimacy.

One can see how these expectations persist. These gatekeepers are presented as the pinnacle of the financial system, attracting the best global talent. Their brand name is leveraged in non-Western markets to attract big local clients, outcompeting any local firms; in fact, big local clients need the stamp of approval from Western firms if global investing communities are to trust them.

At some point, the only way a company can be seen as serious is if it contracts with a "serious" firm—that is, one from the West. The privilege of being seen as serious is only ever attributed to Western firms and their White leaders. If you are African, Arab, or Chinese, you cannot be serious unless you work for one of the big Western corporations or are a self-made success story.

Thus the companies at the top of the heap preserve their position. And the West remains the sole arbiter of what is and what is not considered good business.

$$\bullet\ \bullet\ \bullet$$

How can we fight White privilege in the arena of global business?

A starting point may be recognition of the issue on the part of economic blocs such as the G8 or G20 and their setting into motion studies of what policies would be needed to change the institutionalization of White privilege within their structures and the time frames involved. Regional blocs such as the European Union and ASEAN could also in parallel begin a dialogue in this regard. A start can be made on one of the key issues: the monopolistic positions enjoyed by the Western rating agencies and the Big Four accounting firms. Other specific issues should be prioritized and global discussion initiated. Needless to say, there will be resistance from some Western nations, but that is only to be expected and worked through.

The best avenue may also be to confront and demand change within the professional bodies that set the rules and standards for global business. These bodies often elevate business leaders and companies, who quickly become the standard for multinational companies looking for assistance. A conscious effort to elevate non-Western leaders and companies within these bodies will help create a more balanced and more global approach to the professional services that guide the global economy. Non-Western leaders will have a more nuanced idea of the expertise and competence of non-Western professional services, and thus develop a more balanced set of standards that does not rely wholly on a Western experience.

The global Western business media, such as Bloomberg, CNN, the *Financial Times*, CNBC, and *Fortune*, can also shed light on these issues and draw attention to both the unfairness and the unsustainability of such business practices. The key question, though, is whether these Western media outlets are willing to do this, as it would have implications for their business models and operations.

CHAPTER | 4

MEDIA AND PUBLISHING
Captive Minds

> The media's the most powerful entity on earth. They have the power to make the innocent guilty and make the guilty innocent. Because they control the minds of the masses.
>
> —Malcolm X, *Malcolm X Speaks*

The Role of the Media

According to most histories of the press, the first Western newspapers published outside the West were in Mauritius, Kolkata, and Indonesia in the 1770s and 1780s, published by European merchants, traders, and colonists.

The press has often been portrayed as born from a Western historical context. The modern newspaper is a European creation, and its origins go back to Italy in the middle of the sixteenth century. In China, government news was handwritten and read out to the public. It was in 1582 that the first privately published news sheets appeared in Beijing, during the late Ming dynasty. Japan produced its first newspapers in the seventeenth century.

In Europe, a combination of international commerce, widespread literacy, and the "coffeehouse culture" spurred the creation of publications to cover shipping news, then political debates during the Enlightenment and the "Age of Revolutions." The press's central role in the American and French Revolutions solidified the idea of freedom of the press as a core part of the Western set of political freedoms. The end of World War II and the creation of the International Declaration of Human Rights then promulgated the idea of the free press to the rest of the world.

However, the idea of the free press, as normally conceived, comes out of a Western experience. As the idea of a free press is applied globally, to different places with different languages, histories, cultures, and experiences, it will inevitably be transformed.

Yet Western governments, societies, and publications still see the press as operating according to a Western model, and judge other versions of the press that do not align with that image. Non-Western reporters and publications are viewed as operating in a global yet Western-defined space in which Western publications, reporters, editors, and commentators are seen to be more qualified and naturally suited to premier positions in the industry.

In the Western liberal tradition, the media is deemed to have a critical role in speaking truth to power, exposing injustices and scandals, and even seeking notoriety to attract eyeballs. The journalist is viewed as beyond reproach as a member of the "free press." This is not in fact the basis for how media works in practice, with economic and business considerations driving many of the decisions of the mainstream media, especially in more commercial fields such as television. But rather than focus on how media operates in the West, this chapter will instead focus on media's power outside the West and its motivations for leveraging its White privilege.[1]

The impact of Western media became increasingly visible throughout 2020 and early 2021, as mainstream media outlets have attracted blame for how they have covered tensions between the United States and China. Asians in the West were increasingly targeted for harassment and violence throughout the COVID-19 pandemic, yet observers have pointed to increasingly dangerous media rhetoric around China that presents the whole country as a threat.[2] Mainstream Western media cannot run away from the view many non-Whites hold that the media has fueled racism against Chinese citizens, especially in the US.[3] Western media outlets will have to come to terms with the realization and the growing awareness in the non-Western world that their coordinated attack on China is rooted in racism and White superiority to preserve global White privilege.

Understanding the Western media is thus core to our understanding of global White privilege. It is where the status symbols of global Whiteness are spread around the world, and a sphere where the West is seen as the paragon of a Western-defined set of values. Scores of Western journalists have made global reputations reporting on Asia, Africa, the Middle East, and other regions as if they were residents, and customizing stories for "folks back home." In that process, they carry that ultimate free pass—that of the "independent" White Western journalist, the servant of the almighty free and fair Western press and therefore the guardian of the truth.

The Importance of the Global Media

In this chapter, we are primarily discussing the so-called global media: large media institutions with a truly global presence. These are the international news agencies, such as the Associated Press, Reuters, and Agence France-Presse. These are the major global newspapers: the *Financial Times*, the *New York Times*, and the *Wall Street Journal*, among others. These are the global news networks, primarily the BBC and CNN. These are the media institutions with enough influence to set the tone of global discourse about a particular issue or news story. And in discussing the global media, we are talking about a very small number of companies and organizations: media consolidation and the decimation of smaller and local media outlets mean that more and more of the press is dominated by a few giant outlets.

The reach of these outlets cannot be understated. News Corporation owns Fox News, Dow Jones, the *Wall Street Journal*, the *Sunday Times*, HarperCollins, and more than a hundred Australian papers. CNN is owned by AT&T, the ninth-largest corporation by revenue in the United States. The BBC reaches 468.2 million people—a population greater than that of the United States—every week.

It is critical that we have a truly global media and press landscape. In our more globalized world, it is now the norm that events happening on the other side of the world can have repercussions on how we live our lives. Decisions in Beijing, Mumbai, and Lagos will soon, if they are not already, be just as critical to understanding world events as decisions in Washington and Brussels.

A more representative media that sheds the shackles of global White privilege is long overdue and will help both Westerners and non-Westerners. Westerners will be able to truly understand what is happening around the world, with a clear view of how those outside the West think, act, and make decisions. And non-Westerners will have a clearer idea of what is happening in the West, with stories and analysis tailored to their needs rather than to the needs of a purely Western audience. They do not need relentless attempts at mind capture, or news, narratives, commentaries, or images that reinforce the stereotype of the White world as right and superior.

Global Media: Does It Even Exist?

The core issue regarding global media is that there really isn't any truly global media to speak of. All the outlets we consider to be "global"—whether news agencies, newspapers, or news networks—are all based in the West and run by White people. No non-Western outlet has the reach that outlets in the West do. The reach of these global publications is itself a function of an imperial past, and thus their outlook and ideology are fully drenched in all the prejudice, biases, and bigotry of that era.

It is worth exploring these briefly. First, these global outlets operate primarily in English—the world's lingua franca due primarily to British and then US dominance of the international media space throughout the twentieth century given their historical advantages. The dominance of English crowds out insights that may never be published in English: no one spends the time to research, translate, and disseminate stories that may never escape a country's borders.

Second, all these former colonies developed a governing and economic elite that was closely tied to the imperial center: attending its schools, working in its businesses and, important for this discussion, reading its papers. These elites seek legitimacy through association with the institutions of the West, and the global media is one route to them. These status symbols continue to persist today.

Members of the global elite, but especially those in the business and corporate fields, read the *Financial Times,* the *New York Times,* the *Wall Street Journal,* and the *Economist.* They watch CNN, the BBC, Bloomberg, and CNBC. They follow the thoughts and commentary of prominent Western politicians, business leaders, and commentators. And they want their arguments to be published in these outlets, which they see as the greatest validation of their ideas or the only way to be heard where it matters globally or even back home. Even then they have to pander to editorial dictates that are geared toward ensuring that their views will sit comfortably with a predominantly conservative Western audience.

This is how the dominance of Western outlets in the global media space constrains the way we think about global issues and reinforces the existing structure of privilege we see in international culture today. It reinforces the idea that Western publications are superior and that the White view of a given situation is the one that lies closest to "the truth," that its ideas and positions on issues are the right ones, that its sense of style is the very essence of modernity, and that its values are the ones that matter. It muzzles the very diversity it claims to seek and represent. This spectrum of influence ranges from ideological positions on geopolitics— for example, treating China as a threat—to economic solutions, climate change, the best books, and what is fashionable.

Why We Shouldn't Confuse Global Media with Western Media

Any objective reading of these Western global publications will come to the conclusion that they are primarily concerned with what happens in their own countries, catering to the needs of local readers even while purporting to be global publications. Any discussion of non-Western events is generally a pleasant distraction from local news, or an opportunity to reinforce ideological beliefs and Western notions of what is right and wrong, as seen and demanded by their predominantly White readership. In the US this is the same for both the *New York Times* and *Fox News*, but each with a different local and political audience base.

Yet there is a problem when it comes to when Western outlets report outside their own countries. As explained earlier, Western publications are primarily responsible to their own Western societies. Their societies, and more specifically their readership, ensure this relationship of accountability.

Yet Western publications are not accountable to non-Western societies in the same way. Members of British society, including minorities in Britain, have avenues to seek redress if something is misreported or misrepresented. Yet an Indonesian person whose story has been misrepresented by a Western outlet does not have the same power. An Asian business or government has no way to correct harm done by poorly analyzed commentaries and viewpoints that are prejudicial to their interests. Any attempt to do so is seen as an attack on the free press and becomes an international scandal.

The justification often is that Western publications are giving "voice to the voiceless"—to those who do not have outlets to present their views domestically, especially in countries that lack an open, free, and fair media themselves (as judged by Western eyes and often influenced by ideological agendas). The irony, though, is that many of the issues in these countries arise from Western colonization and current-day geopolitical intervention by the West. Yet these facts are rarely mentioned to provide the context, as they do not suit the narrative.

The Western journalist is transformed into a freedom fighter for the cause of the oppressed and in turn seeks notoriety, which further burnishes their credentials. Yet this is a somewhat patronizing view: that people in non-Western countries need saving by a White reporter whose modern-day privileges arise from the subjugation of others in the past and continuing to this day—or, perhaps, that a story published in the United States or Europe will be the thing that leads to change elsewhere in the world.

There is an uncomfortable question at the heart of these Western publications. If they are primarily Western publications serving a Western audience, then many of these concerns about being too focused on Western framings go away. However, that means they cannot portray themselves as global or international publications, and will be (correctly) perceived as particular vehicles for a Western mindset. If Western publications truly want to be global, however, then they need to split themselves from their Western focus and truly become more international. Yet that would mean losing much of the cachet that makes them so respected and would deny them access to a great deal of privilege that they receive from being Western and typically staffed by White males.

And these Western outlets do rely on Western power to ease their ability to report on the world. Western publications may conduct harsh investigative reporting at home, but overseas, they rely on their country's diplomatic corps—not to mention military power—to help them operate in these countries.

Locally, Western governments and Western publications may have an antagonistic relationship, but overseas, they work together. Western governments clearly see the operation of foreign correspondents as working in their national interest, and so push for increased access, more open immigration rules, and lack of government interference in non-Western countries. A classic example of this was when the liberal US media, which missed no chance to criticize Donald Trump, went into hyperdrive for a few days as they applauded his decision to drop bombs on Syria and the mother of all bombs in Afghanistan.[4] When it comes to war and displaying US military might across the world even when it is destructive and illegal, the media—both right and left—gets in line, as doing so is simply being patriotic and all values go out of the window. After all, do "Foreign Lives Matter"?

One could perhaps understand why non-Western governments may then look skeptically on a Western media outlet's claims that they are not a vehicle for Western power. In the end, Western media outlets seek to leverage Western power in the way they conduct business.

Diversity: Writing and Reporting, Not Practicing

There has been a conversation in Western news outlets about the importance of diversity in their newsrooms. "Diversity," in those cases, is defined according to a domestic frame of reference—whether or not these outlets reflect the true diversity of Western society, be it in terms of race, educational background, income level, or even where people live. The past four years have intensified these conversations, as national publications wonder how they missed major trends such as the rise of White "populism" or the strong undercurrent of discontent among minority communities.

But if national publications need to reflect the diversity of their national populations if they are to accurately report on national affairs, it stands to reason that global publications need to reflect the diversity of global populations if they are to accurately report on global affairs.

Most of these Western outlets are hesitant to hire locally when it comes to staffing their bureaus, instead choosing to fly someone in from overseas. Or, worse, they won't base anyone permanent in other than a few important countries, instead flying a correspondent back and forth.

These correspondents, without deep knowledge of the place where they are reporting, are thus forced to rely on a network of "fixers," local writers and analysts who often go uncredited in the stories that are eventually released. This is sometimes justified on the basis of personal safety—protecting local staff from retaliation—but is often just a function of neglect.

Fixers and local writers have themselves discussed feelings of being ignored and exploited by Western publications looking to report on happenings in their own country.

Priyanka Borpuhjari, writing in the *Columbia Journalism Review,* noted the stark dichotomy between correspondents and fixers:

> The difference between a correspondent and a "fixer" is not one of experience or qualification, but of geography. Local journalists hired

as fixers by foreign journalists are often established reporters and
can offer in-country expertise in the form of helpful contacts and
language skills—and, again, may well have already covered the story
in question. What they lack, in comparison with the correspondents
and outlets paying for their services, is the big-name cachet that in
the end only money can afford.[5]

Her article accurately describes how experienced journalists with
deep experience of their country and its local political and economic
issues—and even sometimes with long experience *working* for Western
publications—are tapped by parachuting journalists looking for a short-
cut for local experience and a way to jump last-minute hurdles.

She notes the mental barriers that non-Western and non-White journalists need to jump when conducting international reporting.

The expectation that the most authoritative journalists are from the
West is stubbornly pervasive. Last year I reported from Sarajevo.
When my American and European colleagues introduced them-
selves as reporters working for major papers, the locals didn't blink.
But I was asked: "Are Indians interested in Bosnian elections?"[6]

She ends her piece with a stark assertion: "But there's a word for the
act of flying in to claim ownership of the stories of others: imperialism."
And there is no better symbol of this imperialism than the Foreign Correspondents' Clubs dotted across Asia and Africa, remnants of the empire seeking to tell folks at home how the natives are coping.

When we think about diversity in media, we need to have a broader
frame of reference. Media outlets do not need just to reflect the diversity
within Western society but also to reflect the diversity within global society.
This entails, where possible, hiring locally, working with local media partners, and crediting local reporters with the story. It entails promoting from
non-Western sources: sending their non-Western reporters to cover the
"prestigious" beats in North America, Europe, and other international institutions, and filling their editorial ranks with non-Western editors.

For example, Western media outlets could hire non-Westerners to
report on American elections, to demonstrate that they can analyze US
politics just as well as a Westerner can. This would be a paradigm shift:
even non-Western news outlets feel the need to hire Americans to conduct their US reporting, a behavior that is not emulated by Western news
agencies in the non-Western world.

One response may be that America's opaque immigration system makes it difficult to send foreign correspondents to the United States. This would be an understandable complaint if the United States itself did not criticize other countries for not allowing American reporters into their country. White privilege emboldens Western journalists to believe they have a right to an immediate visa to any country where they want to cover a story and embarrass a government. Any hesitation or refusal by a country to issue one without delay and embracing arms elicits a concerted attack by all Western media about cover-ups, human rights violations, and dirty tricks. But you would not even know if an Indian, Chinese, or African journalist was not allowed into the US, UK, or Germany—it is simply not news.

Dictating the Tone: The Front Page Agenda

Everyone likes to be praised and especially to be flattered by organizations and outlets seen to be prestigious. Governments that choose to follow a pro-market and pro-Western policy are likely to be praised in the op-ed pages of major Western publications, building a strong international reputation. By contrast, those who pursue more radical and disruptive policies are more likely to be shunned by the international media, leaving them as pariahs.

Many technocrats following classic Western prescriptions have passed policies that are celebrated on the editorial pages of major Western publications, only to be revealed much later that these economic policies were flawed and masked massive discontent and unrest on the ground.[7]

Praise is not connected to democracy or actual popular support: many leaders are credited with implementing pro-market policies without any real reference to what is happening on the ground or what people are actually thinking. Thus Western journalists can often be surprised when something changes: they miss the actual undercurrents of popular support.

One can look at the initial reporting of the coup against Bolivian Evo Morales. In October 2019, President Morales won reelection to the presidency, defeating his closest opponent by over 10 points. However, accusations of election fraud from organizations such as the Organization of American States (OAS) led to protests, and eventually the police and military asked Morales to step down. He complied, and the opposition speaker of the Bolivian Senate took control.

Many Western publications accepted the narrative that Morales deserved to be ousted from office. It took over a year for the truth to emerge: the OAS made a basic math error when analyzing the vote. When the error was accounted for, the evidence of election fraud disappeared entirely. The error was basic; other researchers and think tanks were astounded that it was never detected.

Yet Western publications accepted the story that Bolivia's "coup" was good. Morales was seen as a radical, especially considering his pressure on the hydrocarbons sector and his close ties to Venezuela and Cuba. Undoubtedly many were happy to see him go, so did not think too closely about a story that presented Morales as a man trying to steal an election.

Non-Western Media: Al Jazeera and the *South China Morning Post*

Non-Western media outlets often struggle to be taken seriously and may be roundly criticized by their Western peers for their choice of story.

Al Jazeera is perhaps the only non-Western news network with any international reach. The network plays an important role in the Middle East, often acting as an independent source of Arabic-language news with the power to resist government interference. The network reaches millions of viewers across the region, and its stories have helped spur political change.

However, Westerners continue to criticize the network. One criticism is that Al Jazeera's reporting line stems from an "Islamist" perspective. This is a bit like saying the *New York Times* covers stories from a Judeo-Christian perspective. This criticism, of course, ignores the fact that Al Jazeera's reporters and its audience are primarily Muslim—though the network employs many Westerners—so stories are likely to be tailored for that audience. Al Jazeera's tone, in this case, is a function of the environment it operates in, much as CNN's tone is a function of its American environment.

Another complaint is that Al Jazeera sometimes avoids criticism of Qatar, its funder and patron. Yet this says nothing about the content of the stories Al Jazeera *does* cover elsewhere in the region. To dismiss Al Jazeera's coverage based on this argument is to reject a non-Western media outlet for not achieving some Western-defined standard, not agreeing with Western media group think or to fail to understand the network's constraints.

The *South China Morning Post (SCMP)*, Hong Kong's major English-language newspaper, is another example. The newspaper thoroughly reported the protests that rocked Hong Kong in 2019. But as a Hong Kong–based paper, it was able to report on the various ways the protests affected people's lives—on both sides of the political divide. It took the same approach in its publication of opinion and commentary, publishing pieces from both those who supported the protesters and those who supported the government.

Like every other publication, *SCMP* has made mistakes in its coverage. Also like every publication, it has divisions between reporting and editorial staff. There are many Hong Kong people who disagree with its editorial stance, and so exercise their right to read other publications. But unlike the *New York Times* or the *Financial Times*, it has reports that are positive about China and others that are critical, much of the latter written by contributors who have a track record of being anti-China. One cannot say that of many leading Western publications these days.

Yet the problems faced by *SCMP* and the mistakes it has made are portrayed not as problems faced by every newspaper but as unique problems stemming from its nature as a Chinese paper. Opinion pieces that support Beijing's view on a matter are seen not as an attempt to present both sides of an issue but rather as nefarious acts of propaganda. Observers ignore the investigative reporting done by *SCMP* and its criticism of both the Hong Kong and Chinese governments, characterizing the paper as de facto Chinese propaganda. Thus a potential English-language competitor to Western papers in the region is dismissed.

The end result of these criticisms of Al Jazeera and *SCMP* is that these non-Western outlets are not considered "serious" in the same way that the *Wall Street Journal* or the BBC is considered serious. These outlets are held to a Western-defined ideal—one that Western outlets often fail to achieve themselves—and then dismissed when they fail that standard. When a non-Western outlet gets close, the goal posts are moved, and the outlet remains relegated to the second tier.

Publishing: An Adjacent Instance of White Privilege

We've focused primarily on the global media in this chapter, but some time should be spent discussing the global publishing market, which has its own significant problems with global White privilege.

Every airport bookstore—perhaps the closest thing we have that reflects the book consumption tastes of the "international" audience—features the same books, primarily from Western authors. These may be memoirs of Western politicians or business tycoons, stories of business or technological success from Western companies, or Western history books written by Western historians. Non-Western topics, if they are covered at all, are usually written by non-Western authors.

Anyone looking for a non-Western perspective would likely be unfulfilled by what they find. The same could be said for someone poring through the standard best-seller list or the most prominent book reviews. The Nobel Prize in Literature has been awarded to only five Asian authors in its entire history.

The reason for this odd situation has nothing to do with English fluency: there are likely to be countless writers with excellent command of English even in nonnative-English-speaking countries. And then you have a wealth of stories *not* written in English, waiting to find a new audience through translation.

Instead, the reason is structural: the channels for getting published—going to the right creative writing programs, having the right agent, getting the right meeting with a publisher—are all easier to navigate for Westerners, and specifically White Westerners, than for anyone else. Someone from small-town America is probably more likely to be published by the major Western publishers than a writer in Ho Chi Minh City or Jakarta.

Coverage of books is also oriented toward Western and White authors. Like it or not, "buzz" around books is partly created by connections, and Western authors and agents are always going to have more connections with the major Western publications than are non-Western ones. This is true even when talking about non-Western topics: publications will release lists of "the best books on China" featuring not a single book written by a native Chinese person (regardless of their political leanings).

Conclusion: Confronting White Privilege in the Media

Thinking of ways to resolve these structural problems is admittedly harder than it is for some of the other areas we've discussed. Media and publishing are tough businesses: unless you are part of a few key outlets, publications, or publishers, your efforts are unlikely to succeed. Concentration of power and influence is an unhappy by-product of an industry where an increasing number of consumers are interested in or are being channeled toward fewer and fewer sources of information.

There are primarily two paths that can be followed in dismantling global White privilege in the media sphere.

The first is to encourage Western media outlets to become truly global in their operations. That means hiring and promoting more non-Western reporters, and elevating more people outside the usual media tracks to editorial and management positions. It means staffing locally where possible and properly crediting local reporters who write for these outlets. It means that outlets should treat non-Western stories with the nuance and care that they would treat stories in their own countries. And it means giving non-Western reporters the privilege of reporting on their own countries, trusting that a non-Westerner can report a Western story in its entirety.

The second is to encourage the growth of entirely non-Western media outlets, which would report on global news from a non-Western perspective. These outlets will be different from their Western counterparts. They may make, or may have to make, different decisions about what to cover, how to report on issues and events, and which ideas should be provided a platform. This will lead to a more vibrant debate on global issues and broader and deeper reporting of non-Western topics and perspectives.

It is true that non-Western media outlets are operating in a different political context, so will make different choices than will their Western counterparts. But one should not dismiss a non-Western outlet's true reporting or its commentary on a subject because of these different choices. Doing that would be just as bad as dismissing the reporting of a Western outlet because of its political choices.

The end result of either of these two paths is to build a non-Western media sphere that is treated seriously by the global elite. When a news network based in India or a newspaper based in Nigeria or Hong Kong can be held in the same high regard as the *New York Times* or the *Financial Times,* we will know that we have succeeded in eradicating global White privilege in the media.

CHAPTER 5

EDUCATION
Schooling and Grooming

Colonial education annihilates a people's belief in their names, in their languages, in their environment, in their heritage of struggle, in their unity, in their capacities and ultimately in themselves. It makes them want to identify with that which is furthest removed from themselves.

—Ngũgĩ wa Thiong'o, *Decolonising the Mind*

Why Shakespeare?

I have a confession to make. I never understood why as a child in a developing country I was required to study and understand the works of Shakespeare. I never quite appreciated the Bard, and to this day his works have not touched a chord with me. The language frankly does not speak to me, and the context quite simply remains alien.

So why was I meant to study Shakespeare at the expense of all other forms of literature, and what was I to get from it? Millions of students in former British colonies had to continue to study Shakespeare and were led to believe that his works are the pinnacle of literature and the use of language. Meanwhile, these students are completely uninformed about the Upanishads, al-Jahiz from Iraq (*The Life and Works of Jahiz*), Omar Khayyam, the writings of Confucius and Laozi, or the wide range of profound literature to be found in the Buddhist world, from Tibet and Mongolia to Myanmar.

Even in social circles and as a working professional, the study of Shakespeare and your ability to make references to *Macbeth* or *Hamlet* immediately grants you a certain acceptance in the Western-dominated world within which real success is to be found. It does not matter if you have no interest or zero insights in the literature from the non-Western world, but if you can cite *King Lear*, you are immediately considered well read, sophisticated, and welcome. You have been indoctrinated, and now you are ready for the privileges that might accrue from your proximity to and appreciation of White culture. Throw in a bit of Tolstoy, Twain, Joyce, Woolf, and Nabokov and you are all set.

Capturing the Mind

My little anecdote should make clear that Western education and thought have been exported across the world and are universally hailed as the pinnacle of schooling and the most desirable way to achieve success in later life—if you can afford it. The curriculum design, access to educational experiences, ideologies, styles of teaching, systems of schooling, and institutions of Western education have been emulated or disseminated into education systems the world over. The active introduction of Western education into the colonies and its perceived effectiveness in spreading Westernization make it an incredibly potent tool for maintaining global White privilege. This is because education shapes the minds of generations—Whites and non-Whites alike—during their most impressionable years, creating entire populations and societies that are sympathetic to Western worldviews, ideologies, historical readings, and cultures.

At a personal level, this means that Western populations are advantaged by an education that is perfectly designed for the world they created, and they thus have a privilege in the global marketplace—for example, lawyers practicing "international" law, which is a pseudonym for Western law. Western education is thus perceived as superior to that in the rest of the world, giving those who attended elite Western colleges access to the best employment opportunities in their own nations and across the world, including in the largest multinational companies of our time, most of which are run by White leaders—assumed to be better educated and qualified. A Western education can even give them privileged access to lucrative employment in the non-Western world, where they are placed above educated locals. This is a common lament of many in former colonies where "expats" still receive perks that are shaped by attitudes that belong to the nineteenth century. Simultaneously, the minds of non-

Westerners are colonized through selective content and ideological promotion, which convince non-Westerners that West Is Best and White Is Right while ignoring, belittling, or silencing non-Western knowledge and ideals. Thus these non-Westerners will inevitably want to pursue Western lifestyles and beliefs, resulting in the maintenance of White privilege.

At a macro level, pursuance of Western education also results in the promotion of Western ideas at the expense of others, including economic models, governance systems, foreign policy, and cultural ideals that the West has created or aligns with. This occurs at all levels of the education system and is particularly effective at the higher education level. The consequences of this are serious, as these ideas ultimately influence the economic and political trends shaping nations, geopolitics, and the world order. And this is where White privilege literally gets systematized and hardwired at a global scale.

These are tangible, instrumental outcomes of the Western education system that the world has been nurtured to desire. More intrinsically, the Western education system is also a major contributor to non-Western acculturation or Westernization, the process by which non-Western cultures are eroded and eventually replaced by Western variants. We are losing knowledge, beliefs, traditions, writings, languages, art, and ultimately lifestyles in favor of Western preferences taught in schools around the world.[1]

An interesting example of this is the teaching of history in schools in an independent British colony such as Hong Kong. As the curriculum has not been updated since the colony was returned to China in 1997 and is still very much reliant on a colonial and imperial prehandover worldview, Hong Kong's role as a part of the new China has not been properly taught. What has transpired is that a whole generation of young people have been educated in ways that have not allowed them to understand the history of colonization, the nature of British rule, the history of China, or what is happening in today's China, which has been modernizing and at the same time changing the world in many ways. Instead, they are taught history, economics, and politics that are Western in outlook, rooted in early twentieth-century ideology and that depict China in outdated ways and even as a "backward" country because it is not a democracy as defined by the West. Students and even their teachers had thus easily bought into the views being pushed by an insecure West that China is a threat to the West and the world and that Hong Kong needs to be independent. This narrative about the past and the depiction of a bleak future has resulted in dividing the society and in the crisis the city faced across 2020.[2]

It is also incredibly profitable to be in the business of educating the world. Fees for attending prestigious Western-born education institutions (in Western and non-Western nations) are astronomical, and non-Western elites will happily pay to educate their children according to Western standards of excellence. In Hong Kong, there is a Harrow private school based on the system of the elite British school from which it gets its name. The land for the school's construction—worth millions—was granted for free by the Hong Kong government. Here we have White privilege at work again. No Chinese, Indian, or Islamic school, no matter its pedigree, would have been granted such terms.

Beyond being a lucrative business for education institutions, a Western education system will obviously create consumers interested in Western goods and services, to the detriment of local goods and services. Pair this with how Western education helps promote economic models and modes of doing business that the West prefers, and the result is a global system of markets that advantages Western institutions and populations. In a survey of former students of private English-language schools in Hong Kong, a Hong Kong–Chinese woman reflected on her experience and described how it caused Asian students to be "enthralled" by all things Western. Therein lies the grooming and capture of minds.

This chapter will therefore look at how Western education systems have selective curriculums that promote White Western worldviews while also diminishing local knowledge. It will also discuss why Western education institutions are viewed as the most prestigious, and how this view, in tandem with selective curriculums, aids the economic dominance of the West and the presumption that White Is Right.

I must point out that what I discuss in this chapter is not in any way suggesting that Western education is inferior or that non-Western nations should not be learning from the best that the West has to offer. What I seek to do is expose the harm that the unfettered global spread of Western education with the objective of spreading Western ideas at the expense of all others can do in specific areas. These are primarily in culture (literature and the arts), political history, business education, public policy, and economics.

Western Prestige

Western education, particularly higher education, is perceived as the best and most desirable in the world. Just think about the prestige accorded to the Ivy League colleges, the amount it costs to attend one of these institutions (the average undergraduate fee for an Ivy is US$56,425), and even the lavish donations that are paid out to them (e.g., Michael Bloomberg paid US$1.8 billion to Johns Hopkins University in 2018).[3] This prestige even attracts Asian donors, thereby further strengthening the stranglehold these schools have and deepening the primacy of their business models.[4]

Similarly, Oxford and Cambridge have a continued global preeminence, particularly in former British colonies. Beyond this, they are also officially ranked as the best in the world by various ranking agencies. (In the top fifty *Times Higher Education* World University rankings, only six are non-Western.) But have you asked yourself why? Is it simply because the standard of teaching and students is of a higher caliber? I would argue otherwise.

There is of course an element of historical prestige that comes with Western education institutions. The University of Bologna in Italy is the oldest university in Europe, having operated for over one thousand years; Harvard has produced more than 161 Nobel laureates; and Oxford has hosted people who have impacted the world, including Adam Smith, J.R.R. Tolkien, and Indira Gandhi. This prestige is well known, but it is also very selective. China, for example, has a history of higher education that spans two thousand years, when Confucius established a private academy in 4 BCE.[5] Equally, Middle Eastern universities are responsible for some incredible innovations, including surgery and algebra. In fact, the oldest operating university in the world is in Fez, Morocco, the al-Qarawiyyin University, set up in 859 CE. Yet the historical importance of these institutions is not valued by the international community to remotely the same degree as that of Western schools.[6]

These education institutions are not only sidelined but actively rejected in many cases. Take, for example, the Confucius Institutes in the United States, which are set up to foster cultural and academic exchanges between higher learning institutions in the US and China. You might expect that, much as how the historic British school Harrow was very readily accepted in Hong Kong, a university of Confucian learning would also be welcomed in the US on the grounds of its deep academic history. Instead, these institutes have been branded as "communist mouthpieces" and have even been investigated by the US Government Accountability Office (which turned up no evidence for the claims after a yearlong investigation in 2019). Yet we see Christian universities and pro-free-market business schools the world over. Clearly there are specific ideologies that enable universities to have "prestige" while others do not—and these ideologies are selected by the West.

The need to conform in order to achieve success in a Western-ordered world leads us to the next issue: the belief that the quality of education and the caliber of students that Western institutions create are somehow superior. Droves of non-Western students attend Western universities every year because of this exact belief and will pay extortionate amounts to do so. They often do so in pursuit of "cultural capital": the knowledge, traits, or associations with what is perceived as desirable, successful, or powerful, for the purpose of improving socioeconomic status. And when ambitious non-Westerners talk about higher education on a global scale they invariably refer to the popular Western institutions and hardly ever to first-class institutions in other non-Western countries.

But again, what defines "quality" differs among cultures, and I would argue that the prestige of the Western university—the brand, if you will—outweighs the actual niceties of the differences in university education among nations.

These biases about perceived prestige, achievement, and education quality are all then codified through the process of ranking universities, a process that is dominated by Western establishments and perpetuated by Western publications. For example, of the three major international ranking establishments for higher education, two are Western; the other is Chinese, the Academic Ranking for World Universities, and was the first of its kind. These ranking systems use the number of publications per faculty member and peer reviews from other universities. Needless to say, this criterion poses serious challenges for non-Western universities: most major journals are in the English language, and the Western higher learning network is very deeply connected and a closed shop to outsiders. For example, just 1 percent of scientists capture more than one-fifth of all citations globally, and the inequality is growing.[7] The issue here is that this only serves to legitimize Western science and innovations as the best in the world, and mainstream media plays a big part in this too. How many have heard of Dr. Zhong Nanshan, a leading pandemic expert in China? He is as qualified as Dr. Anthony Fauci, the director of the US National Institute of Allergy and Infectious Diseases (NIAID) and chief medical advisor to the US president, who has become a household name globally. Scientists from China, Japan, Korea, and other parts of the non-English-speaking world have found it very difficult to be published and taken seriously.

Further, university ranking results are published through Western mediums that reach across the world, but there is no osmosis the other way: India's university ranking never makes it into the *Financial Times* or German media, for example. It is no surprise, then, that very few Westerners take the leap of faith to attend non-Western education institutions—they are told repeatedly that they are better off staying and learning at their own universities. Going to a university in Asia or Africa is simply an adventure for immersing oneself in a foreign land and burnishing one's resume.

Combined, these codified biases and deeply held "truths" about the effectiveness of Western higher education endow Western students who attend these universities with cultural capital that enables them better access to more lucrative employment opportunities across the world, ultimately ending up in stronger economic positions than non-Westerners who do not attend these same institutions. This is the very definition of privilege.

In pursuit of this same privilege, many non-Western students are encouraged to leave their home countries to pursue a supposedly better education at Western universities, at immense personal cost. In the process, they open themselves up to further Westernization, including absorbing ideas about economics and business that are totally unsuited to their own countries, and from this point onward will try to emulate Western culture and lifestyles, even to the point of leaving their home countries to apply their aptitudes in the West, draining their home nations of talent, wealth, and leadership. Places such as Silicon Valley, finance centers in New York and London, and biotech parks across the US and Europe are all beneficiaries of this colonization of the mind, because White privilege works to link education *attained in* the West with well-paid careers *in* the West, leading to a global brain drain from non-Western countries to the West. We will further cover just how this colonization of the mind takes place in the following section.

Selective Curriculums: Colonization of Minds

Education systems all over the world have curriculums that favor the teachings of Western thinkers and leaders across all fields, which results in the selective silencing of non-Western teachings and value systems, ultimately degrading non-Western culture while promoting Western culture as the global aspiration for all nations. This outcome is a direct result of colonization, during which Western countries set up entire education structures and modes of classroom-based pedagogy in their colonies. English-language systems were implemented throughout the Commonwealth, French-language systems were taught in Francophone African colonies, and Spanish and Portuguese systems made it to Latin America.

Take literature, for example. Writings and learnings from White Western authors have a special place in the literary canon taught in schools around the world. Plato, Shakespeare, Tolkien, Homer, Adam Smith, Kant, and so on are venerated as literary greats. They are core components of curriculums at all stages of education, with entire courses dedicated to exploring their works. Of course, there is nothing intrinsically wrong with this—these individuals all produced incredible works worthy of study and appreciation. However, they are not the *only* individuals to contribute to the literary canon—consider Confucius, whose writings have deeply shaped the culture of the most populous country on the planet; or Imru' al-Qays, the great Arabian poet whose pioneering use of form and linguistic technique eventually led to the creation of the ode and the sonnet, which Shakespeare is world renowned for using; or Rabindranath Tagore, Bengal's most renowned philosopher and poet, whose compositions were chosen for both India's and Bangladesh's national anthems ("Jana Gana Mana" and "Amar Shonar Bangla" respectively).[8]

So why is it that White Western writers take primacy of place in schools outside the West, but Western schools do not regularly teach works of literature from non-Western nations? The answer is a selective curriculum, one that values White Western literary work above that of non-Western literature, giving the false impression that the West was—and still is—responsible for the works of literature that shaped our world. This encourages all students—Western and non-Western—to think that non-Western countries are incapable of producing thinkers and writers who match up to the Western authors they are taught at school.

This is a particularly powerful and active way of instilling notions of White superiority into young people, because literature is one of the key ways in which we all learn, form ideas of ourselves, and try to understand the world around us. Thus students' being primed to see White Western writers as superior to their non-Western equivalents has a potent effect: Western students are reared with the assurance that their culture is the literary leader; non-Western students are influenced in terms of the books they choose to read and the learnings they choose to follow, as well as in terms of their mindset and values, which may ultimately shift away from the values of the country of which they are a part. This is then reinforced in adulthood by the annual list of book recommendations by supposedly global publications such as the *Financial Times*, the *New York Times*, and the *Economist*, which are dominated by Western authors. The end result is a non-Western population that is more aligned with Western ideologies, ideas, and values, and even fantasies about being White.

The other impact of this process is of course the erosion of non-Western literature, which is a global tragedy. The immense diversity in writings and learnings from work across the world is becoming increasingly Whitewashed. For example, children around the world are exposed to stories from other cultures only when they have first been sanitized and co-opted by Disney. You know Mulan, but what about *Hei An Zuhan*? You know Aladdin, but have you heard of *Taghribat Bani Hilal*? You know Mowgli, but what of the *Ramayana*? Yet these same children all know of Hansel and Gretel and Harry Potter. I have even been told by Tibetan friends that the story of the *Lord of the Rings* is drawn from their folklore. Ultimately, this Westernization reduces the diversity in schools of literary thought, and vital aspects of non-Western culture are no longer being celebrated as they should.

And this process doesn't apply only to literature. The selective nature of curriculums extends to science, too. Scientists and scientific discoveries by Western nations are taught as the greatest in the world. Leonardo da Vinci, Isaac Newton, Albert Einstein, Stephen Hawking; the steam engine, the plane, the refrigerator, the internet. Being selectively exposed to these thought leaders and innovations again paints the picture of Western historical supremacy in these fields. By teaching these historical successes, Western people and nations gain credibility and legitimacy to be the leaders and authorities for developing the science and technology that will shape human progress in the modern day.

Delegitimizing the Rest

This narrative contributes to the Western practice of delegitimizing non-Western science and technology. Inventions developed outside the West are questioned for how successful they will be in application, how rigorous they have been in production, and how ethical the process of innovation has been. Upon reading this you might think, "For good reason: products and services from non-Western countries do not meet exacting Western standards sometimes, right?" Rarely do we consider, however, that this is just a continuation of the narrative we have all been educated with. After all, some of the biggest, most trusted Western brands are guilty of bad production (planned obsolescence in all iPhones), unethical practices (Nike, Adidas, and Reebok have all been accused of using child labor to produce shoes cheaply), and even the use of slave labor (cocoa picking in West Africa for Western chocolate brands). Despite knowledge of Western wrongdoing, the focus is always on the failings of non-Western business practices and innovation. This active cultivation of narratives to reinforce that the West is on the right side of contemporary issues is perpetuated by the selectiveness of the Western education system and media reporting. This results in the maintenance of White privilege in this sphere by enabling the continued dominance of Western people and organizations.[9]

For anyone who is not in denial, it should be crystal clear that the Western education system has captured people's ways of thinking, their value creation, their ways of innovating, and their perceptions of the meaning of legitimacy. This control is then converted into economic dominance via the pushing of Western economic models, namely free markets, with minimal state intervention. The free-market, neoliberal capitalist economic doctrine taught in Western education systems is built on a laissez-faire philosophy (i.e., favoring less regulatory intervention).

Adam Smith's *The Wealth of Nations* in particular is often cited as the ideas that frame the ideology of the foundation of modern-day capitalism and the genesis of much of current-day neoliberal economic thinking. The core tenet: individual selfish actions in the marketplace ultimately help achieve social good via the "invisible hand of the market." Yet Smith published his theories in 1776, and despite the world's having completely changed since then (e.g., an increase in global population from less than a billion to about eight billion), such archaic ideologies still prevail. In fact, the model has been constantly critiqued throughout history for achieving inequality, not social good, yet it is *still* taught in schools around the world. Paul Samuelson—the first American to win the Nobel Memorial Prize in Economic Sciences—made precisely this same critique in 1948: "This unguarded conclusion has done almost as much harm as good in the past century and a half, especially since too often it is all that some of our leading citizens remember, 30 years later, of their college course in economics."[10]

So why has this economic theory not left Western classrooms across the world for three hundred years? Because it is rooted in the history of colonization—it was in effect the economic model of colonization—when free markets literally meant what it says on the tin. Thus these ideas, so wholly unsuited to a crowded and resource-constrained twenty-first century, were institutionalized, and these Western-born curriculums have persisted through the decolonization process and into the modern day. Despite their weak intellectual basis and even self-serving roots, they have been retained to this day because these education systems are still perceived as superior to other forms of trying to make sense of the world and markets. In addition, many non-Western educated individuals making decisions about what economic theory to teach were educated in or by the West, and have thus reproduced their learnings in their home nations. This is the capture of the minds of elites.

Ultimately, this process of indoctrination, which has produced several generations of these ambassadors of Western thought at the expense of cultivating other schools of thought, works in favor of the West. The light touch of regulation, a key feature of the laissez-faire system, benefits the West because it permits Western business interests backed by their governments to leverage their historical advantages (economic and otherwise) to retain control and expand in new markets by trampling on weaker local entities. This behavior has been enabled in the modern day through education and the power of the Western media, which helps control narratives of Western excellence in economics, science, and other fields. This grants legitimacy to the goods and services the West produces, and the result is a global export of goods and services from the West to the Rest as the crème de la crème. As you can imagine, this business model is incredibly lucrative—after all, if you capture markets outside your own nation, your consumer base dramatically expands. In this sense, you can think of the selectiveness of the Western education system as the ultimate form of subliminal marketing to generation after generation. This contributes to and exacerbates the continued inequalities between wealthy Western nations and poorer non-Western nations.

In sum, this selective programming of White Western literary and scientific brilliance perpetuates White privilege by explicitly valuing these achievements above the contributions of non-Western writers and scientists. This legitimizes Western people and nations as contemporary leaders in these spheres. When coupled with the dominance of Western theories of economics, this de facto leadership becomes a very powerful means for the West to maintain economic supremacy, because both Western and non-Western recipients of a Western education will work to maintain the global economic system they were taught from when they were young, despite the host of inequalities it has created.

Business Schools: Spearheading the Ideology

As with universities, Western business schools are held in the highest regard and have a global stranglehold. One can see why this is the case: top executives, government leaders, and business owners have invariably attended these business schools because these institutions are perceived as a ticket to high-paying employment opportunities and the networks it is possible to build just by attending. Everyone wants a slice of this particular pie.

These schools have immense potential to influence the trends in popular business thinking in favor of Western norms because they so neatly represent the marriage between Western prestige in higher education and the use of selective curriculums. They are so powerful that they are a strong feature of one of the world's leading newspapers, the *Financial Times.* Martin Parker, a British business school educator with nearly ten thousand citations to his name, once remarked on this, saying that "the virtues of capitalist market managerialism are told and sold as if there were no other ways of seeing the world."[11]

This dominance results in the same harm that we have covered in the discussion of Western universities—graduates of these institutions become inculcated with economic and business doctrines of the West, which ultimately enable the active maintenance of White privilege through the perpetuation of economic models that inherently create and rely on inequality, drive unsuitable practices, deepen the subordinate role of non-Western countries, and favor Western businesses.

Business schools differ from universities in that not only academic students attend them but also employees of multinational corporations (MNCs) and governments, and future leaders of all sectors, from across the world. These schools create what I like to call the "economic storm troopers" of our time—students enter the business school at one end and exit the other as firm believers in the potential of the free-market model to create wealth (more often than not, just personal wealth) and even in the shameless pursuit of the "greed is good" mantra. These ideas are then spread across the world as non-Western students return to their respective countries, usually to then become successful individuals themselves, in positions of power where they are capable of implementing these ideas across entire organizations. In some cases, they need not even journey to the West to receive this education—India, for example, has over three thousand business schools, all teaching the same Western curriculums. But you will be hard pressed to see any Indian-sourced curriculums in France, or a Chinese curriculum in the United States. Hong Kong and Singapore are modern-day colonial outposts of these business schools, with governments supporting their establishment of campuses with the usual White-privilege perks.

Business schools are seen as an apex when it comes to practical education for individual and organizational success. But now it is time to remove this venerated veneer to instead consider the role that their educational service plays in perpetuating inequality, and in particular how these schools help to reproduce economic models that favor the West and associated White privilege without actually furthering economic ideas to meet the existential challenges of our time or the real needs of developing countries.

Conclusion: Fixing a Powerful Mechanism for White Privilege

Education is an incredibly powerful means by which White privilege is enabled and reinforced in our contemporary world. The historical prestige of Western education institutions, particularly those of higher learning, has been maintained into the current day. This is often well justified given the impressive list of achievements these institutions have racked up, drawing on their historical advantages. However, this prestige is actively marketed to feed the big business of education, attracting copious numbers of non-Western students to the West, where they seek the increased access to gainful employment that Western-brand universities provide. This not only diminishes the significance and contribution of non-Western education institutions but also exposes non-Western students to curriculums that selectively favor Western knowledge, history, cultural ideals, economic models, and lifestyles. Ultimately this is a vital tool in preserving the dominance of the West in the minds of generations of people across the world who are educated according to Western belief systems and standards. This chapter has shed light on only a few key areas.

In addition to this colonization of the mind by Western cultural be-liefs, Western economic and business education also synchronizes with the global inequalities of the free-market trade system, which although supposedly based on fairness is in fact rigged in favor of the West. It is easy to sell a Western product or service in an unregulated market when the world is already taught that Western products and services are the best in the world and that Western companies play by the rules where others do not. The business schools are the holy sites where this conversion takes place.

Although this process is deeply embedded in the way we are brought up and how we see the world, it is not unassailable. Initially, the selective-ness of curriculums must be changed to include diverse cultural view-points across all subjects. Imagine a history lesson taught from the perspective of the Indian soldiers in Malaya during World War II. This would teach Western students that White Western perspectives are not the only views that have shaped the world. It would also teach non-Western students the value of their own cultures and the contributions they have made to the world, beyond Western examples.

But, more important, non-Western countries should break the trend of relying on the West to provide leadership in education. They must in-vest in and review their education systems to critically analyze where their systems are designed to encourage the West Is Best mindset, or where they focus on Western ideas at the expense of their own. There will need to be major efforts across the world to develop educational institutions of ex-cellence that are distinct from Western norms—and to seek academic success through this diversity of thought, rather than ignoring it or even actively shunning it.

CHAPTER 6

CULTURE AND ENTERTAINMENT
Gone with the Wind

The colonized is elevated to above his jungle status in proportion to his adoption of the mother country's cultural standards.
—Frantz Fanon, *Black Skin, White Masks*

The Seduction of Western Culture

This chapter is an important one because it addresses what is perhaps the most seductive and powerful tool of Western design, which instills subservience and dominance in societies across the world. Although the influence of Western culture and entertainment on the rest of the world has been termed "soft power," it is clearly anything but soft. It has been called "cultural imperialism" by its critics, which is most certainly true as it still reigns supreme across the world, and its harm is conveniently ignored by its perpetrators. This chapter seeks to shed some light on why the Western cultural promotion and entertainment industry seeks to infiltrate other cultures to promote and preserve Western power, what harm it does, and what actions might be taken.

The impacts of music, film, and television are certainly not immaterial—they have serious real-world implications that capture and shape the zeitgeist of the times in which they are produced. These mediums are a substantial part of how we connect with people in our immediate communities and even with others around the world. They are also an essential component of how we form our own identities. Over the last two to three centuries, Western culture and entertainment have been leveraged to create an overwhelming impact on the rest of the world, subjugating and controlling societies for economic gain. And by no accident, this extends to rock and pop music.

It was pop and rock music that had a particular effect on my identity as a teenager—but not in the way you might expect. As a teenager, I found myself listening to and being force-fed the music of the Beatles, the Rolling Stones, and every other pop/rock band that the global Anglo-Saxon music industry could infect you with. You caught the music as though it were a virus, such was its economic power in a world full of unsuspecting and gullible non-Western youth who had been groomed in the emerging postcolonial era to worship everything exported from the West. We were enthralled by all things Western because although the armies and administrators had left, the use of soft power was now in full swing, working to ensure that we did not forget that White Is Right and the source of all things superior. Pop music was undergoing some sort of revolution in the West and heavily appropriating from African American musical forms. English as the language of pop made the music a product that could be easily imposed on others too weak at that stage to resist this cultural tsunami. The irony was that these White stars were singing about White experiences that hardly anyone in the non-Western world could identify with, yet they had global followings. Their popularity told us perhaps less about any inherent appeal or power of the music and the lyrics but more about the desire of previously colonized people to identify with White culture and its idioms.

Yet after a few years of being swept up by this thrill, I wondered at the absence of any non-Western and Indian music—my cultural heritage—in my life, and even at the way I actively rejected the traditional Indian music my mother would listen to daily on the radio. As for rock music, when I attended university in the UK, it was all my friends would discuss. They would question me to make sure I wasn't from some disconnected village in Asia: "What is your favorite band? Do you like David Bowie? What do you think about Hall and Oates?" If I answered correctly, then I was that guy from Asia who was "with it" and invited to their gatherings. I played that game to an extent because I knew the rules. These rules included knowing the top British and American bands of the day; being familiar with UK and US sports, movie, and TV stars; being "Western fashionable"; joining in jokes about other non-Whites who are not as "cool as you"; and of course learning to speak like them, with the right accent. Get enough of these wrong and you are out.

In retrospect it dawned on me that these student friends of mine—who could never even pronounce my simple name—had never experienced the cultural indoctrination that I and millions of others around the world were faced with daily, via the export of Western entertainment culture. They were comfortable in the knowledge that the popular music produced by their Western culture and exported to the rest of the world was a "global good" and the pinnacle of modern music, a symbol of modernity and global youth culture. Thus they had no need to learn of music from other parts of the world. In many ways, they were as impoverished as I was.

Globalization of Western Culture

It was and remains an unwelcome daily assault—radio, TV, cinema. This soft power truly did not feel so soft. Western norms, lifestyles, and ideas were—and still are—constantly advertised through these mediums as the greatest and best in the world. The messaging we receive every day directly links Western culture and entertainment with the notion of superiority and the economic dominance of the West, because for every song or movie, there is a product or service to buy associated with it. This is relentlessly messaged by the clothes that are worn and depicted as fashionable, the cars one must have, the houses that depict modernity, the food that is associated with being cultured, the slang used to underline a certain progressiveness—the list is endless. Herein lies the ultimate good: the marketing opportunity to reach the billions of consumers outside the West, one that was actively cultivated during the early years of radio and television to help set up a deeply rooted belief in the superiority of Western goods and services.

In this regard, one could view the Western pop and rock bands of the 1960s and 1970s—despite their songs of protests and rebellion—as playing a key part in the continuation of neocolonialism and the perpetuation of imperialism. I began to see these musical icons, such as Elton John, Mick Jagger, and Axel Rose, as symbols of the empire, but just in psychedelic clothes. I often wondered if they ever thought of what they were exporting to other unsuspecting cultures not quite ready for their assault: a heady mix of sex, drugs, and narcissism. This journey of decolonizing my mind, in addition to a strong curiosity for other cultures, was what also drove me to discover Black music—blues, jazz, reggae, calypso, salsa, Afro-beat, high-life, juju, Mbaqanga—and then later the glorious and raw music from around the world.

Beyond this economic dominance, the exportation of culture and entertainment to the non-Western world has resulted in many of the current concerns surrounding globalization—among them Westernization and acculturation. But it is not simply the corrosion of non-Western culture that occurs. It is also the colonization of the minds of non-Westerners, who, after years of listening, watching, and embracing Western culture, want to pursue Western lifestyles as a means to legitimize their arrival in the modern world. And not just by replacing the goods and services they traditionally use—a *sarong* for a Burberry suit, a futon for a Western bed, or *nasi goreng* for a Happy Meal and a cupcake—but also by transforming their cultural values: what is humorous, how to express affection, how to share a meal, how to greet elders, what defines career success, or even what rights we have as individuals in a society.

This colonization of the mind through the soft power of music and entertainment has led to entire societies finding themselves engaged in a struggle where there is active rejection of various aspects of their native cultures as the next generation views them as inferior to Western equivalents. In 1979, the prolific Black American writer James Baldwin identified this phenomenon in African Americans, describing it as a form of self-hate—rejecting parts of their cultural identity in favor of a culture that is perceived as superior, but into which they will never truly be accepted. This internal struggle of self-regulation is true for non-Westerners too, and this self-hate and loss of cultural identity have serious implications for national stability in any country in which these are occurring en masse, as it is in many non-Western nations. In my experience, these internal struggles within non-Western societies have accelerated in the last twenty years, particularly with the advent of the internet and the omnipotence of US social media and entertainment business empires such as Facebook, Netflix, and YouTube, just to name a few. The assault of modernity through Westernization is now ongoing 24/7, and a click away on your mobile device and a threat in more ways than one.

Thus it is essential that we analyze how global music, film, television, and the performing arts are primarily shaped by a White Western narrative and have very harmful impacts on societies in the non-Western world.

Music: Popularity and Prestige

As a Westerner—or someone with Western music taste—if you walk into a mainstream music shop, you will likely find records organized by genre: pop, rock, jazz, electronic, classical, world music. Catch that last one? Callously labeled under one category, the entire musical repertoire of the non-American and non-Anglo-Saxon world is simply termed "world music." Sadly, you can find this nomenclature in music shops across Africa and Asia too. This is the case because Western music is associated with being both popular and prestigious, so its various forms take precedence over all other musical types. This has not come about by accident.

Let us begin with the popularity of Western music. Following World War II, the US and the UK fully embraced their roles as global cultural leaders, given their status as victors and their higher level of socioeconomic development. During this time, American and British music was broadcast around the world through mediums pioneered and controlled by the West, first the radio and then the television. This immediately gave Western music a huge competitive advantage—not only was it available for people in India and Togo and Japan to listen to, but it also was associated with the cultural and economic superiority attributed to the West at the time, meaning that people from around the world were *told* that this music was what they *should* be listening to. This was a key element of being modern in the non-Western world.

This dynamic has not changed today. The global reach and pervasive influence of Western music are not something anyone in the West thinks about or questions, nor would like to see changed, because like other key exports, Western music represents an enormous market opportunity and confers a sense of cultural superiority. In 2020, only one in the twenty-five of the highest-earning musicians were from outside the West—BTS, a Korean band, whose members are themselves inspired by the Western pop music tradition, to the extent that they even dye their hair blonde.[1] Control of the music that people are listening to around the world enables entire Western industries to thrive—radio stations, TV channels, award shows, producers, artists, designers, stadiums, paraphernalia, streaming services, advertisers, even the international success of the iPod when it was first released. The list goes on.

And it is not just the popularity of Western music that matters, but the prestige it affords. This prestige is cultivated around the perception that the historical weight and technical skill behind certain forms of

Western music are superior to other non-Western equivalents. Take classical music, a genre that is associated and synonymous with *Western* classical music. There is an association between high-brow status and playing classical piano, violin, French horn, and so on, while there is no global awareness of ancient and complex Chinese instruments, such as the range of stringed instruments called *dihu*. In fact, this association is the very reason why musicians such as Bach, Mozart, and Rachmaninoff have a global following, while you are unlikely to have heard of the legendary Indian *shehnai* player Ustad Bismillah Khan or know that there is a difference between North Indian and South Indian musical traditions (Hindustani and Carnatic). If you have heard of some "ethnic" musicians, it is because they have been integrated and accepted into Western societies (e.g., Ravi Shankar, a very successful sitar player) and/or play Western instruments—for example, the wonderfully talented American cellist Yo-Yo Ma, who was born to Chinese parents.[2]

Echoing Impacts

The global belief in Western music's popularity and prestige has serious ramifications. As mentioned, it is of huge economic benefit to be associated with Western industries. But beyond this, Western music also helps reinforce deeper Western cultural norms: music disseminates vernacular, guides our emotions, paints powerful examples of relationships, and describes lifestyles. As the global popular music industry stems primarily from the West and is dominated by its performers, the potential to influence non-Western populations into thinking and behaving like Westerners is very real.

Of course, it is not intrinsically bad to think and behave like a Westerner when it comes to music. But Western music tastes are overriding traditional music traditions at a rate that is silencing and causing the loss of entire non-Western schools of music. Imagine if the number of people playing the violin or piano dwindled, as is now the case with Japan's national instrument, the *koto*, and with West Africa's *kora* and Zimbabwe's *mbira*. It would be a musical tragedy, forever changing the way music is produced in the future. Now imagine that the reason for this is due to instruments from another country taking precedence, and in particular because they are associated with a "superior" culture that is at the same time being actively promoted. Practicing traditional music should not be threatened by colonial history or contemporary globalization, yet it is.

The loss of musical styles is one cultural impact. But it is part of a wider loss of cultural identity as a result of Westernization. Young people around the world are now consuming and relating to music that is largely disconnected from their own cultural settings. For example, the White American singer Lauv has a fan base of three hundred thousand in Quezon, Philippines, alone—the largest of his fan bases across the world. Again, there is nothing intrinsically wrong with this, but over time the messaging in Western music—concerning Western lifestyles, ideas, and "Whiteness"—has steadily promoted a dislocated Western cultural legitimacy in the minds of non-Western listeners. And as we have discussed, that is a powerful tool for the West, indeed.[3]

Music is potent. Although it may not be viewed as actively weaponized by the West, it is most certainly actively pushed for its clear impacts that contribute to the everyday promotion of Western superiority and power.

Film and Television: Tarzan and Friends

As with music, the popularity and prestige of the Western film and television industry reigns supreme. B-movies from the Hollywood archives have now been declared as works of art of the twentieth century and key features of global culture, from *White Zombie* to *Body Snatchers*. The industry has resulted from the same colonial history and the same globalized all-powerful Western media, which took pop music to every unsuspecting corner of the world. But unlike the music industry, the film and television industry has been successful in selling Western norms, distorted versions of history, ideas, and lifestyles at a scale that was not previously possible. In this regard it is even more toxic. For example, in 2019, *Avengers: Endgame* became the highest-grossing film of all time, making a staggering US$2.8 billion as people around the world queued up to watch an army of White superheroes save the world, including the aptly named Captain America. Just this one film made more money than the GDP of twenty-seven countries.

This movie is a good case study: virtually all the titular characters are White, while some supporting roles are filled by minority actors. Beyond the cast, entire non-Western cultures are presented as a distinct *other*—Middle Eastern culture is frequently used as a terrorist foil throughout the film franchise, while the only representation of African culture is a fictional nation (in the form of a hypermodern super city-state called

Wakanda), and the leader of a supposed Nepalese school of mystics is a White man called Dr. Strange.

Misrepresentation like this in Western film is nothing new. Entire books have been written about how Hollywood is selective and protective of its White leadership and White casts, with campaigns and watchdog groups having been set up to counter this trend—with good reason. Non-White, non-Western actors clearly struggle to achieve the same level of success or even access to employment in visual media.[4]

One example worth mentioning is *Tarzan*, a story that has White supremacist roots and overtones, even in the most recent depiction of the story in 2016.[5] The story line operates on the premise that the jungle is the ultimate arena for survival of the fittest, and thus, through brawn and brains, the White male will rise to the top. This assumption of White male superiority in non-White lands is made throughout Hollywood, from *The Last Samurai* to *Avatar* and *Lawrence of Arabia*. Hundreds of reality TV shows about surviving in harsh terrains and dealing with strange local people in far-flung corners of the world are the new versions of the Tarzan concept to reinforce notions of the fearless and pioneering Westerner, who has a penchant for adventure and risk taking, and ultimately to reinforce in locals the aura of superiority of Western people. They are dominated by White men—with White women at times playing a modern-day Jane—acting as superheroes while locals watch bemused and the rescue helicopter is of course hidden off screen.

But then again, it is important to remember that on many levels, Hollywood is a "local" industry that went global because of the economic power of the US in the postwar era and the American belief that White culture is exceptional, a global good, and a money spinner once the "natives" get hooked. This was perhaps best explained by Bong Joon Ho, the Korean director of the movie *Parasite*, which won the 2019 Academy Award for Best Picture. When interviewed by Korean media about the significance of the award, he described how one should not get too carried away, as the Academy Award is really just a "local" US award.

The same is true of dance and theater. Ballet, a French-derived dance, is considered the world's most prestigious dance form, yet literal "White ballets" such as *Swan Lake* and *Giselle* exist, which "require" White dancers to represent ghostly figures, naturally precluding people of color from capturing leading roles.[6] Meanwhile, other forms of dance and theater have never gained an international reputation; we all know Shakespeare's tragedies, but what of the various Chinese operas? What about the Japanese *Noh* theatre, the Turkish *Karagoz*, the Indian *Kathakali*? These art forms are for the most part restricted to their country of origin, so for a budding non-Western artist to achieve international standing or recognition, they must simply choose from Western theater and dance forms. One example is Carlos Acosta, the great Cuban dancer of ballet.[7]

White, Black, and Brown: Fiddling with Race

Because this issue is quite literally in the limelight, the manifestation of White privilege and structural discrimination in entertainment culture receives a lot of attention. It is why, when the 2016 Oscars were all handed to White people, the #OscarsSoWhite hashtag started trending on Twitter. People can see the Whitewash, can see the talent of non-White actors and want to address their challenges.

This is a legitimate concern, but it is also a peculiar obsession of White liberals and the press in the US. So, to pose a controversial view: giving Oscars to more non-White people is largely unimportant. Although it is important to give platforms to deserving non-White role models, frankly speaking the central part of our debate on discrimination should not be whether someone who is already successful is recognized for their success—and, more important, by a White establishment. Structural discrimination among the minority elite is far less important than structural discrimination among the everyday masses, yet we are happy to accept publicity stunts such as choosing more non-White Oscar winners over any real change to the structures that caused the problem in the first place. We are missing the point and directing energy toward putting out bush fires by superficial means instead of looking upwind for the source of the blaze.

So there is a need for a deeper analysis beyond the discriminatory structures of any one nation. The issue with the portrayal of White people (particularly men) in leading roles perpetuates the belief that only White people are important or worth focusing on; this becomes a powerful tool to reinforce White privilege in the minds of people across the world, given that billions of people now consume Western media in which White-washing is a common occurrence. Anyone from the non-Western world who was introduced to Western movies and TV shows during the 1960s and 1970s should be able to identify with this sentiment, if they are honest with themselves. Uncivilized Native Americans; lazy, drunken Mexicans; wicked Communist Chinese; bloodthirsty Vietcong; murderous Japanese—the stereotypes were force-fed, and most swallowed it hook, line, and sinker.

What we must do now is make this important link between mass visual representation and its damaging influencing power and apply it to on-screen Western culture as a whole, and not just skin visibility: clothes, houses, cars, beauty standards, romantic norms, political ideologies, and so on. Marilyn Monroe's "blonde bombshell" look inspired women around the world to dye their hair and aspire to become a White beauty. Equally, James Bond's presentation as a suave (yet misogynistic) sex icon with an Aston Martin helped spark an obsession with White males and luxury cars. At the same time, the on-screen presentation of sex or sexualized acts dramatically changed global film norms and the definition of what it means to be progressive. (And if other cultures did not want to ascribe to this Western model, it led to their being labeled "inhibited" or "restricted.") The power of film and television is undeniable, and people around the world are now being incredibly effectively programmed to pursue Western ideals through the shows and films they love, accelerating colonization of the mind. This global domination by the Western film industry and its associated elevation through economic means to being viewed as the most advanced and entertaining has also made Western societies less interested in movies from the non-Western world, and thus markets were never created. To this day, few Americans or Europeans are really interested in movies from China, Japan, or Nigeria. It is no wonder that one of the ultimate prizes of US trade talks with China is unrestricted access to the Chinese market for Hollywood.

Again, the belief that Western films are the state-of-the-art in entertainment helps with the process of acculturation, as non-Western people now aim to live their lives to mirror what they see in Western movies, instead of pursuing lifestyles unique to their own cultures and enhancing them. This has occurred in a big way in India, with the rise of Bollywood as one of the largest film industries in the world—by numbers of viewers, it *is* the biggest. Yet the moniker is certainly telling, and the embedded Westernization runs even deeper: the influence of Hollywood has meant that commercial Indian films have moved toward Western storylines, themes, sets, and even standards of sexualization (for both men and women). Actors aspire to Western lifestyles, many of them believing that global recognition can only be had through success in the West, despite having, outside of India, much larger fan bases in parts of Asia, the Middle East, and Africa. The message this imparts to millions is that being an Indian megastar is not good enough until you are accepted by the West.

This sort of mindset can also exacerbate other deep social issues that already exist. Take the generation gap we see in all societies. Now imagine that in addition to the usual social, cultural, and political differences between the generations, there is an overwhelming and unrelenting extranational influence in the form of film and television that younger people are actively consuming, which has tremendous potential to transform their identities, beliefs, and behaviors. Imagine if White youth in the US were constantly watching Chinese, Indian, or Arab films (with Islamic content) and television shows—the end result would be a deepening of rifts and even political instability. It would even be viewed as a form of subtle political subversion of the population and simply not tolerated.

Lastly, there is a propaganda element at play in Western film culture that has persisted since World Wars I and II. Films set in the American West of the past were incredibly popular after World War II, and they have been analyzed as depicting a White male Western hero who embodies a specific brand of American exceptionalism: he is masculine, ruggedly self-reliant, and freedom loving, while also using intelligence to outwit superior numbers of Native American or Mexican villains. Similarly, films depicting the Vietnam War often represent Vietnamese men as collaborating with the Vietcong, or Vietnamese women as prostitutes/bargirls; the Viet Cong are torturous and sly, not freedom fighters. The White Western hero versus the non-Western villain is a dipole that is set up in the modern day, too, with oppositions between heroic US Navy Seals and cowardly Middle Eastern jihadists, or the righteous British SAS and the murderous Taliban. These popularized depictions of war eventually feed into subconscious and conscious biases, helping preserve Western moral authority and bravery in wartime engagements.

Of course, film and television are not even remotely single-handedly responsible for these phenomena. But they are part of the wider Westernization process, and to dismantle White privilege entails addressing these deeply held norms that the world sees as acceptable or, even worse, hardly questions.[8]

Conclusion: The Great Potential for Cultural Change

While Western entertainment culture is enjoyed by many worldwide, we need to remember that it represents so much more than just entertainment—it carries cultural values, immense industry worth, and perceptions of skin visibility that, taken together, overtly advertise White Western culture to the detriment of others, leading to acculturation and Westernization across the world. This effectively exports Western goods and services as superior, enabling Western economic domination, while also reinforcing White privilege the world over. We must be aware of the role that culture and entertainment plays in promoting and preserving White privilege if we are to makes strides in dismantling it.

Fortunately, entertainment culture is not static. It is always shifting, and that allows room for entertainment mediums to effect positive change. There are certain obvious steps to take, such as having more accurate representations of non-Western cultures in Western entertainment and, in particular, ceasing sidelining, vilifying, or ignoring non-Western cultures through their portrayal in the media. This includes actually improving the access to opportunity for non-White, non-Western artists by hiring racially appropriate casts and promoting diverse musicians.

But we must not—and cannot—rely on the West to make these changes for us. It is time that non-Western industries make substantial changes to compete with Western dominance in entertainment. Unlike the realms of business, education, or geopolitics, where serious critiques of the status quo do not often gain traction, it is possible to effectively publicize avant-garde thinking about race and privilege through film and television. Within the West, there has been a rise in the number of films and television series that document the lived experience of non-Whites in Western countries, both historical and contemporary. So, in a similar vein, there is a need to now encourage the development of a film and television industry outside the West that captures these experiences and also popularizes narratives that do not portray the West as Best. It is essential that the spell of White Western superiority in culture and entertainment be broken if we are to dismantle White privilege, and it is not simply by being passive or pushing for more awards to non-White artists.

Entertainment culture is also a two-way bridge between the West and the Rest, meaning that changes sparked in the non-Western world have the real possibility of cascading into the Western world. It is this fluidity that non-Western nations must take advantage of. We are seeing certain elements of non-Western entertainment culture flourishing around the world, from K-pop bands to Bollywood films. This sort of exposure to non-Western culture is important, and now is the time to begin imparting messages of unique cultural identity through these mediums.

These changes are needed. The next time you watch a film or listen to a song, think about how it impacts your psyche—how you take messages from it that reinforce deep cultural stereotypes, including the superiority of the West.

CHAPTER 7

SPORTS
Match Fixing

> We hear racism being shouted on the terraces, but it also happens when a black official walks up to a boardroom [of a soccer club] and doesn't get recognized as an official . . . There's the culture of "black players play," and non-black players coach, manage, lead and are senior management in the company.
>
> —Iffy Onuora, equalities coach for the
> Professional Footballers' Association

Banana Skins, on and off the Field

My initiation into racism in sports occurred when for the first time in my life I got on a pitch to play a competitive game against an all-White team. I was, at the age of twenty, picked to represent the Malaysian field hockey youth team, and we played a friendly game against the Great Britain team, who were in Malaysia for the field hockey World Cup. I remember being called a "Black c**t" by one of the GB players, and in my innocence was left wondering why he resorted to such language simply because I had nutmegged him in a game of hockey. I did not take offense at all, as I was just thrilled to play my first "international game." And it is worth remembering that it was also the first time I had played a game with White men or even been in close proximity to anyone from the West, but something about it did stick with me.

A few months later, I left Malaysia to study in England and found myself playing in the leading league in the country. It was there that I came to terms with the inherent racism at that time at all levels of sports in the UK. I got used to being called all kinds of names when I got the better of a player. Fast-forward ten years and, after having not played for many years, I found myself playing in the premier league in Hong Kong for a local team made up mainly of ethnic minorities—Indians and Pakistanis—and some Chinese. We were the league leaders, and here too I saw racism directed by players from the leading expatriate clubs against these teammates of mine, many of whom could not respond to racist taunts, and I found myself fighting in their corner. I'm glad to say that things have improved since then.

Sports can also divide and be the basis for nationalism, racism, and even ethnic tensions. Yet, I firmly believe that sports have the power to unify rather than divide. Sports receive global attention and have a unique ability to connect people regardless of creed, class, or race. It is possible to share the common language of sports without any other connection, and the universality of sports enjoyment means that when sportspeople and sports arenas occasionally become the center of political issues— including race—they are particularly visible. As the manager and coach of the Hong Kong hockey team for seven years, I saw this intimately at various international tournaments.

The Changing Arena of Sports and Race

Many legendary African American athletes used sports to demonstrate that sports can unify, by using their global platform to take a stand against racism: Muhammad Ali, Tommy Smith, Jesse Owens, Wilma Rudolph, and Althea Gibson all helped further the cause of African American equality during the twentieth century through their sporting platform.

Outside of America, there is Jaipal Singh Munda, a leading figure on the 1928 gold medal–winning Olympics hockey team for India and a fierce activist for tribal rights. In Australia, the First Nation player Adam Goodes exposed the extent of racism in Australian rules football when he spoke out about the constant abuse he received from White people and even children. He was infamously called an ape by a thirteen-year-old girl during a game, and on calling her out was in fact further attacked.[1]

There are also other examples, such as American football players, rugby players, and others "taking the knee" during the national anthem to protest racial inequalities, or players wearing clothing in support. In 2020, Black soccer players in England refused to take the knee, which they said was because it had become a meaningless gesture and simply made good media and provided cover to a system that refuses to change. I have to say I agree.

All of these actions, although they are small and performative, have sparked considerable debate in Western countries around the issue of race. Not all of these examples are positive, however, as explicit racism in sports is exceedingly well documented—from fans, other players, commentators, and managers.

This chapter will move beyond a blinkered focus solely on explicit acts of racism in sports, because I believe that it is not well understood how White privilege impacts the very structures of global sports. It contributes to which sports are played, where they are played, the rules that control sports, which sports attract money, which have media/television rights, which institutions govern sports, and even who is allowed to participate in sports and achieve success through them. It goes much deeper than simply making monkey noises to non-White players on the pitch, and its solutions are much more complex than taking a knee or media-favored coverage about catchy slogans such as "boot out racism" in soccer.

The major popular sports—football, rugby, baseball, American football, golf, and tennis—have all for the most part been exported from the West to the rest of the world and are largely dominated by Western countries. Even if non-Western players are now capable of joining the elite ranks of sports, the rule-making bodies are Western, and key decisions are still being made in the West: FIFA is based in Zurich, World Rugby in Dublin, the International Tennis Federation in London, and so on. Even the World Anti-Doping Agency (WADA) is based in Canada and increasingly seen by some non-Western countries as becoming a tool for the geopolitical agendas of the leading Western nations.

Of course, there is nothing inherently wrong with these organizations being based in the West. After all, these sports are hugely successful in the West and are major parts of Western economies. But what has occurred is decision-making that favors the West in the approximately US\$500 billion sports industry.[2] It is this sort of favoritism that has been at the heart of the project to ensure that the West is viewed as the center of global sports, with all their positive contributions to the world, and that the West is therefore more justified than the rest of world to take a leadership role in the promotion of this global public good.

Excellent examples of this need to ensure that the center of global sports remains in the West occur with certain gated sports, such as tennis and golf. All four Grand Slam tennis tournaments and all four international golf tournaments are held in Western countries; although there are exceptions, these are distinctly middle- and upper-class sports, with high entry and maintenance costs. This means that while there have been successive waves of non-Western or non-White competitors, the dominant players in these sports still come from White, Western populations.

By exerting this level of influence over global sports, the West bolsters its soft power. Thus there is the belief that the West must have the best sense of fair play—which it relentlessly seeks to promote—are the best arbiters within sports of what is right and wrong, and have the best equipment, facilities, sports scientists, management systems, administrators, and athletes. All of this feeds into the wider belief in the cultural and moral superiority of the West.

This chapter will look at White privilege in the world of sports, including explicit racism, identification of sporting excellence, and sports management. It will then zoom out and take a bigger-picture view, analyzing White privilege in global sporting structures, particularly how White Western privilege enables all popular professional sports to be the preserve of Western nations and their institutions.

White Privilege within Sports: Race Leads the Race

The most obvious example of White privilege in sports exists in the differences between the explicit racism experienced by non-White players in Western sporting arenas such as soccer and the adoration Western teams and White players receive in non-Western societies. For example, in January 2013, Italian footballing giant AC Milan played against the smaller Pro Patria. The game was abandoned twenty-six minutes in, after Pro Patria fans consistently chanted monkey noises at Milan's Ghanaian midfielder, Kevin-Prince Boateng. It is important to note that the game did not end because there is a guideline that states that racist chanting results in a forfeit—it ended because Boateng took the initiative to lead his team off the pitch.

The Boateng incident is not an outlier or out-of-date—in this past year alone, Black British football players Moise Kean and Romelu Lukaku have reported hearing monkey chants from fans. The British newspaper the *Independent* even has a consistently updated page titled "Racism in Football."

It is true that explicit racism in sports has existed for as long as there has been a sport to play between different cultures. But what is of note is how acts of racism are managed in the modern day: Pro Patria's penalty was to have to play just one match with no fans allowed to attend. Astoundingly, Pro Patria had already been fined earlier in the season for a similar incident—only five thousand euros.

Ideally, actions would be taken to encourage and incentivize someone not to be racist in sports, but soccer in Europe is widely known to have notoriously resisted making the necessary changes. There are few regulations to deal with explicit acts of racism, and when the dots are connected between all the different occurrences in different sports, a pattern emerges that points to an inaction on the behalf of sporting institutions to truly effect any real change. One explanation for this is to see it almost as an admission on the part of sporting culture; it is woven into the culture that racist banter is not yet viewed as repugnant enough to prevent normalized use in sports arenas, or in conversations at home or in the workplace.

Further, racist rhetoric is not limited to negative comments, but also includes general observations on players. For example, in June 2020, Run-Repeat, a Danish sports data firm, collaborated with the Premier League's Professional Footballers' Association (PFA) to write a paper on racial bias in football commentary. Their findings were illuminating and affirmed the implicit racism that is prevalent in modern sports.[3] According to the research, when commentators talked about the intelligence of a certain player, almost 63 percent of praise was aimed at players with lighter skin tone, while 63 percent of criticism was aimed at players with a dark skin tone. Players with dark skin were also often celebrated for their "pace and power." They are almost seven times more likely than light-skinned players to be praised for their athleticism. This is not a recent development. In 1996, James Roda of Ithaca College researched racial biases by media networks in coverage of the National Football League (NFL). He also found that White players are likely to be praised for their intelligence and other positive character traits, whereas Black players are often commended for their physical abilities.

Non-Western Sporting Heroes

This selective recognition of sporting talent is not just restricted to race but to geography too—it is why non-Western players who have excelled in their sport are often not venerated to the same degree as their Western counterparts. Many in the world are aware of the achievements of athletes such as David Beckham, Michael Jordan, Roger Federer, and Serena Williams, among many others. But do you know who Nicol David, Jahangir Khan, Ali Daei, or Rudy Hartono are? Most people are probably not aware that of the top ten goal scorers in international soccer, five are Asian, and the leader, ahead of the two greats Cristiano Ronaldo and Lionel Messi, is an Iranian, Ali Daei.

Nicol David, from Malaysia, should be considered one of the greatest sportspeople in history. A squash player, she was ranked world number one for 108 months consecutively—*nine years* of being at the pinnacle of her sport. For comparison, the great Serena Williams was ranked number one for eighty months over the course of her entire career, and consecutively for only forty-seven months. My favorite tennis player, the sublime Roger Federer, was ranked world number one for four-and-a-half years, half the time of David.

In badminton, the great Indonesian Rudy Hartono reigned supreme during the late 1960s and 1970s and won the All-England Championship, the badminton equivalent of the Wimbledon Tennis Championship, seven years in a row, but is hardly recognized as one of the greatest sportsmen of the twentieth century. And then there is the legendary Pakistani squash player Jahangir Khan, who achieved the insane feat of being unbeaten in 555 consecutive matches over five years and eight months—the longest winning streak of any sportsperson in history. You will not find his name on any list of the greatest athletes compiled in the West.[4]

So the question now is: Why is it that Beckham, Williams, and Federer are household names, but David, Hartono, and Khan are not? Of course, tennis is a more popular sport than squash or badminton, but sports greatness is surely not only measured simply by media eyeballs and the economics. The answer is rather simple: there is not an opportunity for these non-Western superstars and the sports they excel in to gain the same international coverage because the West dominates the popularization and commercialization of what is deemed and instilled as a global sport.

There is little benefit to the West, either economically or culturally, in having various sports industries and related sports stars centered in non-Western countries. So returning to squash and badminton—these sports have proven harder to commercialize for various reasons, one of which is that players from the non-Western world have often taken the leading titles, and this in turn also affects economic decisions. After all, are Americans—despite their addiction to sports—really interested in seeing a petite Asian woman or a burly Pakistani dominate in a sport? No, because this would lay bare their worldview and naive assumptions that their local competitions are the best and make evident that their major sporting competitions do not necessarily represent the finest athletes in the world. Western audiences aren't interested in watching their players lose to those from the non-Western world.

In this, it is possible to glimpse how the West has a strong influence on the narrative of modern sports, the making of heroes and legends, leading to a self-perpetuating cycle in which only the achievements of White and/or Western athletes matter. Black athletes in the West are accepted as part of "us" given their sheer excellence in certain sports and for the economic contributions they make, despite being discriminated against daily. But there is no hiding that the White owners and coaches would love to see more White players in the National Basketball Association (NBA) and the NFL and even in the leading Premier League clubs in the UK, if not for any other reason than the reaffirmation of the masculinity of the White male in the sporting arena. Their media partners can shunt aside the achievements of the Asians and others, but how do you do that with Black athletes in your midst, who are also your breadwinners?

This, again, has soft-power consequences. If children in Europe knew more about the accomplishments of athletes such as David, Khan, or Hartono, they would gain respect and appreciation for the countries that these lesser-known athletes represent. They would even seek them out as role models. Similarly, global recognition of these athletes would help non-Western nations believe in and recognize the latest potential within their own society and develop these athletes accordingly. The resulting confidence might even reframe the stereotypical way in which they are portrayed in Western media as backwaters without sporting systems and with a lack of raw talent—the latter idea in particular playing into notions about White superiority.

White Managerial Control in the Global Sports Structure

The discussion of the soft-power implications of Western-dominated sports begins to touch on the deeper manifestation of White privilege in sports—namely that the wider sporting structures have been largely influenced by the West, from management of given sports in the Western world to the global operations of sports. This influence stretches from rule making to the antidoping system.

First, managerial control of sports in the West mainly rests in the hands of White people. In the US, the NBA comprises nearly 75 percent Black players, yet as of August 2020 the number of non-White club owners stands at three, with only one African American majority owner—Michael Jordan.

At one level, the Black athlete in the US is a modern-day gladiator serving a special need for a paying White audience looking for fantasy entertainment, working for a White business superstructure, helping the political elite espouse an imaginary multiculturalism and playing a role beyond which he must not stray; Muhammad Ali found that out, as did Colin Kaepernick.

Similarly, just 30 percent of NBA club general managers are Black. Why is it that Black people are trusted to take the game-winning shot at the buzzer, but not to oversee the direction of a sporting team or association?

The NBA is not the only professional sports league that has leaders who are not representative of its player base. In the NFL, 70 percent of players are Black, yet only two principal owners out of thirty-two are non-White: Shahid Khan of the Jacksonville Jaguars and Kim Pegula of the Buffalo Bills. Only three head coaches are Black. Two general managers are Black. The NFL's decision in 2018 that players kneeling for the anthem would be financially punished was made by a group of thirty White men, with two exceptions. In professional sports, minorities are valued for their athletic feats, but when it comes to entrusting someone with the fate of a franchise, most teams seem to follow the same mantra: White Is Right.

Beyond the management of sports in Western countries, the global structuring of sports is also largely controlled by the West. For example, there are five major sports played and televised around the world: soccer, basketball, cricket, tennis, and rugby union. All five originated in the West. In fact, almost every sport covered in the mainstream media and broadcast to a worldwide audience is Western-centric. Other sports from other parts of the world do not have the same global following at all, due to historical Western preference and spread; for example, cricket spread from the UK around the world during the colonial period.

Again, it is important to be reminded why the contemporary focus of Western sports is preserved: because it reproduces the economic structures that enable Western power and privilege. There is a lot of money to be made if a large Western audience is watching sports, and a large Western audience is guaranteed only if there are also Western clubs playing or owning the sport. This in turn will attract a large global audience raised on the superiority of Western sports competitions and their entertainment value.

In addition, the global network of popular professional sports is centered in the West, with the most prestigious leagues and clubs for most major sports based in Western regions—the English Premier League, Major League Baseball, tennis leagues, and so on. They exist in close proximity to the power centers of the global Western media, which has unrivaled channels and access to the rest of the world to promote sports and thus Western soft power—as seen through the lens of White privilege.

Even the Summer Olympics, which is the most popular and participated-in sports event in the world, falls under this banner, despite being the most international event in human history. There are thirty-four Olympic sports, and only one, *taekwondo,* was founded in and headquartered in a location outside Europe and the United States. Yet 206 nations competed in the last Olympics, the vast majority not from the West.

Not only do almost all Olympic sports originate in the West, but the governing body of the Olympics, the International Olympic Committee (IOC), is based in Switzerland. The president of the IOC is German. In fact, there has never been a non-White president of the IOC. Would there even be a Winter Olympics if not for the fact that it involves sports that are born out of outdoor activities in cool-temperate climates in the West and that are anything but cheap to take on as casual sports?

Impacts of Western Sporting Control

What does the global control of the major sports by the West mean? It results in a global flow of sport-related capital, coaching, and management expertise and talent into the Western world. Even if non-Western countries play and enjoy the major global sports and have thriving professional leagues domestically, these leagues will always play second fiddle to leagues in the US and Europe. This is the case with Nippon Professional Baseball, Senegal's and Ghana's football leagues, and so on. Culturally, this creates a power gradient in sport, whereby even the best sporting leagues a non-Western country can produce will never be enough to reach apex sporting status. It also results in a draining of the best sporting talent into the West, helping reinforce the belief that the West has the best leagues. And it is precisely this belief that leads people all across the world, even in the poor countries, to pay to support a team, watch the matches, buy the expensive merchandise, or fly to see a game.

Millions in Asia have been converted and become die-hard supporters of British soccer teams such as Liverpool and Manchester, places that have no cultural or historical connection to them. One would be hard pressed to find the same in reverse, such as Europeans and Americans supporting the world's largest cricket league in India.

Even with solo sports like tennis or golf, those who "make it" inevitably become members of Western sporting leagues and eventually residents in the West. Meanwhile, the chances of non-Western non-elites participating professionally are slim, given that these sports often require significant personal capital for someone to continue attending international competitions. The four tennis Grand Slams are perfectly designed to showcase Western excellence and lifestyles, and are scheduled around the holiday cycles in the West—Melbourne to Paris to London to New York. Thus, during every quarter throughout the year, the non-Western world is reminded via their TV screens of Western superiority through sports, thereby reinforcing global White privilege and all its significant economic benefits. Imagine a Grand Slam itinerary in which only two were held in the West in any one year, the other two in Asia and Africa.

Now look at the migration of sporting talent from the West to the rest of the world. It is commonly perceived as a demotion—that these athletes failed to make it in the West and must seek success elsewhere, or that they have reached their twilight years and can still use their privileges of having played in the West to find positions to play in other leagues. Asia has accepted many a washed-up professional soccer player from the West because, despite their inability to merit a place on the team, their Whiteness and past glories make them an attractive economic proposition for people craving White sporting heroes even if they are past their sell-by date.

These viewpoints are exacerbated by and inextricable from the fact that major media channels are focused on the sports that the West dominates, giving them coverage unattainable for other sports and ultimately helping deepen the global focus on Western-centric sports. The media contribution here should not be underestimated. The access to Western sports and the global fan base helps with the colonization of the mind, promoting the belief that West Is Best. A good example is the US media promotion across the world of the NFL, a sport hardly played anywhere else.

Cricket: Money in Indian Spin

There is a notable exception to the Western-centered focus of major sports and it is offered by India. It is one that proves the rule: cricket and India.

As a sport that is not fast-paced enough to be successfully commercialized and televised to the extent of football, rugby, or even tennis and golf, it straddles the boundary between control by the West and control by other non-Western countries. With less opportunity for commercialization in the West and other non-cricket-playing countries, there is less money involved in the cricket industry, meaning less incentive for Western business stakeholders to keep its center of organization in the West. This is why we have seen South Asian cricket become a global center for talent as much as in the West. In fact, the International Cricket Council is headquartered in Dubai, with an Indian CEO.

Further, although many excellent Indian and Pakistani cricket players have played in the UK in the past, these countries are now much more likely to retain their talent, and many are internationally recognized as some of the greatest of all time—for example, the great Indian cricketer Sachin Tendulkar.[5]

What the case of cricket demonstrates is that when there is less of an economic superstructure behind a sport, the various Western stakeholders are less incentivized to preserve its importance in the West. In the case of India and cricket, the economic power is exerted by the largest population in any country that is obsessed by a single sport. This quite literally balances out the playing field and gives space to non-Western nations to compete at these sports, even one with global reach such as cricket, which is now responsible for much of India's sporting soft power.

But even in cricket, White racism is not far away, nor is the presence of White privilege. In the 1990s, as Sri Lanka started to make waves, it produced one of the most successful bowlers of all time, the spin bowler Muttiah Muralitharan. As Sri Lanka became a cricketing power, the English and Australians—unused to this Asian upstart—tried everything they could, including calls for bans to discredit his unique bowling style, the result of a birth defect, but failed. Many other Asian cricketers will attest to this racism, which stalked cricket for many years as the English and Australians viewed themselves as guardians of the game.

There is another aspect of White privilege and the seemingly addictive need of the West to be the focus that needs mentioning: the demonizing of other nations by Western sports bodies, nations, and even athletes. I clearly remember the West's reaction toward China when it was granted the right to host the Summer Olympics in 2008 and the years of media smear campaigns against every aspect of the Chinese efforts to host a successful games. The same can be said of the soccer World Cup in Russia in

2018 and the upcoming World Cup in Qatar in 2022. In both cases, Western powers such as the US and the UK felt that they deserved to be the winners to host the events. And then there are the doping scandals, which are a scourge in sports. But here too the villains are typically always the others, and all it takes is for a leading Western athlete from the US, UK, or Australia to cast aspersions, and before you know it an athlete from China, Iran, or some African country is guilty until proven innocent. The Western media jumps on the bandwagon and becomes the judge and jury, pressing the various international bodies for action against the cheats.

All of this should leave few in doubt that the global sporting structure is currently set up to selectively favor the economically high-powered Western sports—for fans, players, managers, franchises, and associated industries.

Conclusion: Calling Time-Out on Uneven Playing Fields

Racism is well documented in sports. Players, fans, and managers have all been criticized for this, and White privilege works in ways that often shields White players from experiencing racist behavior in the same way, helps them deny its very existence, and in some cases even becomes a beneficiary. Similarly, as with other careers, the opportunity for career development is bolstered for White members of the sports industry, as they have access to better-paying roles and managerial positions.

But White privilege in sports goes beyond this. It is embedded in and influences the very structures of global sports norms, resulting in a perceived gradient of sporting excellence that starts and ends in the West. It starts there because the headquarters of all major sports are based in the West, which naturally make decisions to benefit the sports ecosystem in the West. It ends there because all non-Western players understand that to achieve sporting fame and greatness, they must compete in the West. Thus the Western sports leagues have the privilege of being offered the best talent, and with the unrivaled media focus, branding opportunities, tournaments, associated products and services, and institutions, the sports industry becomes unassailable in its Western economic entrenchment.

As discussed throughout this chapter, this entrenchment has significant economic implications for the world. Sports are universally enjoyed, with copious amounts of money flowing into Western sports industries from consumers worldwide. Also discussed are the significant cultural impacts. Sports are a competitive field dominated currently by Western powers, but there are signs of it being dismantled as we enter a post-Western world. Every time someone in, say, Cambodia turns on the television to watch a sport, they are reminded that they cannot compete in the same league as Westerners. There is no such thing as playing at "home," because every important sporting occasion is an "away game."

To begin to address this inequality in the global power structure of sports, conversations on race and sport should start to take a bigger-picture view, looking beyond explicit acts of racism in sports to analyze sports structures around the world. In the West, these conversations might result in the sharing of leadership for a given popular sport with a country in the non-Western world—for example, setting up a joint global football leadership center in Brazil or a squash institution shared between the UK and Pakistan or Egypt—the latter a leading squash power and, at the time of this writing, home to the top three female players in the world.

In the case of non-Western sports and sportspeople, more focus should be paid by non-Western governments and media to transform certain national sports into industries with their own soft power. After all, there are a plethora of sports that are well suited to becoming commercialized but have not yet received the attention or funding to do so, including Mongolian *bökh*, Indian *mallakhamb*, and Southeast Asia's highly entertaining *sepak takraw*.[6]

By deconstructing the socioeconomic and political superstructure that define sports in the modern era, and which in turn help further White privilege, by association we will also be working to deconstruct the economic power and cultural norms that continue to put White Western culture center stage.

CHAPTER 8

FASHION

Little Black Dress

The Brazilian models had their shiny moment and I remember girls from Rio and São Paulo being all the rage. Next, the African models were the "It girls" and when their turn was done, it was all about the Asian models, and then the Black American girls and so on and so on. Race is not a trend. My skin is not a trend.

—Tyra Banks

You Thought Fashion Labels Are Cool?

Tyra Banks's words may sound a bit rich coming from an African American model who made a living sexualizing the female form within the Western fashion industry and promoting its notions of style, beauty, and sexuality. Yet on the issue of race she is spot on, and this quotation exposes two issues. The first is how White culture uses race tokenism to dress down its real power. The second highlights the sad spectacle of non-Westerners wanting to be close to White culture due to having been mentally enslaved to believe in its modernity while embracing it (understandably) for its economic benefits.

One of the most insidious trends of the last few decades is the widely undetected and poorly recognized globalization of Westernization through one of the least obvious channels—fashion.

Modern fashion is perhaps one of the biggest culprits in reinforcing this phenomenon in mindsets and cultures across the world. It seems so innocuous on the face of it. After all, fashion is meant to make us all feel good about ourselves and be a way for us to express our individuality and culture. But nothing could be further from the truth. As many are aware, the global fashion industry is infamous for its widespread exploitative labor practices and poor wages, fully taking advantage of garment workers around the world—even children—to keep profits high. Nike, Adidas, Forever 21, Disney, Gap, H&M, Victoria's Secret, Zara, and even high-fashion brands such as Prada have all been exposed for their poor treatment of workers in non-Western countries.[1]

But the widely ignored problem goes beyond profits. Fashion is an industry, and like any industry it has an agenda of growing and seeking power and influence to ensure its success. And in this case, promoting Western culture is very much part of that agenda.

The total value of the fashion retail market (including footwear but excluding jewelry) is about US$1.7 trillion, and it is dominated by Western brands.[2] The fashion industry's products are based on the way White people think you ought to dress to look modern, civilized, and acceptable. Its power and influence are born out of its success in getting people around the world to believe that Western culture in all its manifestations is superior and modern, and to adopt it. People's adoption of this belief, especially in the non-Western world, reinforces the privileges that White people thrive off of economically in the globalized economy and that they take for granted or even believe is a right. Fashion in that sense is the perfect soft-power tool.

Thus, when we speak of the fashion industry, we are not talking about fashion as an expression of flair and identity in different parts of the world, which draw on the amazing variety of rich cultures to be found globally. Instead, we are talking about "White fashion" and its relentless spread across the world, which has been normalized through apparently innocent yet highly ignorant terms such as *global fashion trends*. There are no global fashion trends. There are only variations of Western fashion trends. Have you heard of Africans wearing Chinese clothes and fabrics or of Danes wearing African or Indian clothes and its being talked about as a global trend?

Fashion Stripping Identity

So how did the situation get to this point, and why? When the African American model Tyra Banks spoke about skin color trends, she was addressing one aspect of the tyranny of the global spread of White fashion. She was also a victim of the industry, and inadvertently helped promote it by modeling clothes that propagate White culture and its sense of fashion, ultimately serving its economic interests and cultural hegemony. Getting more Black models to promote White fashion is not going to change the fundamental White privilege that sits at the core of this issue; even though it may appear to help even the playing field in terms of job opportunities, it unfortunately does so only in a superficial way.

The truth is that race politics and economics are inseparable when we talk about the global fashion industry. Fashion today is so much about race—how to present yourself to be accepted by White Western standards—yet its damaging role is not deeply understood. So even though fashion is meant to be a visual manifestation of self-expression, the choice in this expression has become a myth, as Western fashion deliberately precludes representation of non-Whiteness except when appropriating a design or style to confer some form of "exotic" or "ethnic" look, which ultimately panders to a segment that wants to present itself as globally conscious—just for the occasion. It is an infuriating condescension that has sadly been normalized by high-end fashion in particular.

Try as a non-White person to wear a sari, sarong, or dashiki every day of the week as a fashion statement or because you are comfortable in it, in any of the leading Western institutions or even in an international business in the non-Western world.[3] The only place you might get away with it and not be seen as making a non-Western cultural statement and your career prospects not jeopardized is in the Muslim world, such as the UAE, India, and parts of Africa. This is particularly so for professional women. Fashion choices in these settings thus becomes more than an expression of individuality as conformity is demanded: it becomes a tool, whether we are aware of it or not, to trigger, reinforce, and perpetuate Western culture and thus White privilege, which is the ultimate objective. Race has become reduced to a fashion trend allowed within the structures of White privilege in fashion, rather than a celebration of one's identity and culture.

Naked Fashion and Body Modification

We can begin this much-needed examination by looking at the most fundamental, and the most personal, object of fashion we all possess: our bodies. In cultures across the world, people are modifying their bodies to reproduce White beauty standards. Some of these modifications are insidiously normalized in the everyday; others occur as extensive operations.

Let's start with complexion and skin color. In Hong Kong, cosmetic stores have entire sections dedicated to skin-whitening products. From lotions and creams to facial masks, these products come in a great variety. In 2010, the BBC reported that the market for skin-whitening cream was larger than the Coca-Cola market in South Asia.[4] By 2025, the global market is expected to reach US$13.7 billion.[5] In Nigeria, more than 77 percent of women reported using skin-whitening products on a daily basis; many of these women faced mental health–related consequences.[6] Myriad plastic surgery services are offered to those who feel that their features are not pronounced "White enough." In Thailand, such services are even extended to one's private body parts, with a surge of vagina-whitening or penis-whitening procedures.[7]

General makeup use across the world seeks to lighten skin too, and beyond that it can be artfully used to contour and hide features not aligned with White beauty standards. This has been taken further in many places across the world, and in Korea, it has become a common trend for both men and women to have their eyelids carved, nose bridges accentuated, cheekbones shaved, and chins slimmed to replicate White features. Korea has become the plastic surgery capital of the world just for this, and there are more than six hundred cosmetic surgery clinics in Seoul alone. The industry is entirely based on trying to erase Korean features. This time, money, and effort are dedicated not to trying to look like an Indonesian, Indian, or African but to try to look more Caucasian.

In fact, Julie Chen, an Asian American television host, admitted to undergoing surgery to change her eye shape because she was repeatedly told that her Asian eyes would hinder her further career advancement.[8] Imagine what has to go through someone's mind to alter their facial identity—the features of their parents and ancestors—to achieve the prize of Whiteness and its associated privilege, yet to know that their kids will not be born any different.

Body modification is also a daily occurrence for people with Afro-textured hair, who choose to emulate the straighter hair of lighter-skinned races. Commonly, girls with Afro hair have it braided until they are old enough to have it straightened, over and over again throughout the course of their lives, leading to premature hair loss. They are also told to refrain from swimming or even sweating, because straightened hair frizzes up on contact with water.[9] Malcolm X is quoted as saying, "My first big step towards self-degradation: when I endured all of that pain, literally burning my flesh to have it look like a White man's hair."[10]

Today it is hard to find female Black American celebrities or anyone of prominence who sports an Afro. From Beyoncé to Michelle Obama, it is now the norm to straighten one's hair. White media expects it and celebrates it, as was the case when Michelle Obama turned up to the Biden inauguration with "bouncing curls."[11]

Whitened skin and face and body modifications to attain Caucasian features are some of the hottest fashion trends today. But perhaps they go beyond typical temporary fashion trends; after all, having fair skin and sharp Caucasian features has been fashionable for centuries now. Hollywood even captured the imagination of millions across the world with these norms, and has successfully exported this version of beauty globally, literally weaponizing the "blonde bombshell" beauty ideal through celebrities such as Marilyn Monroe. The spread of these powerful Western notions of beauty and fashion were turning points in the postcolonial global project. Its aim was to normalize White privilege as Western movies and magazines were vigorously exported to all corners of the world to subvert the minds of hundreds of millions with Western notions about beauty, fashion, and even body shape.

But why exactly are fair complexions trendy, and why isn't my olive-brown skin, or my sun-kissed Asiatic skin, or my smooth Black skin fashionable? Why is beauty status unattainable in most parts of the world, unless we purchase beauty products to bleach our skin? Why does the majority follow the minority, and why are the minority the trendsetters? These are questions that people may not even think of asking, precisely because these trends have been so pervasive for so long. It is what "modern" has become associated with. You are not a modern and contemporary woman if you are not fair and do not have an overpriced handbag from one of the luxury brands. You are not manly enough if you do not have a pair of Levi's jeans and rugged White skin. Advertisements constantly bombard people around the world with the images of White fashion and beauty. Imagine being a non-White person and being inundated with these images since you were a kid.

It is thus imperative that we begin to question these trends if we are to effect change in a world of fashion that to date seeks to get the global majority to worship beauty as defined by White people and to thereby reinforce notions of White superiority.

Fashion Police: The Fascist-sta or Fashionista

Moving from bodies to clothes, it is clear that fashion trends incorporated by big brands help reinforce White forms of power. For example, White brands across the world use and appropriate designs from other cultures, from Polynesian tribal designs to Chinese characters and Hindu symbols. This goes beyond a simple appreciation of aesthetics; it is the ingrained belief that aspects of non-White cultures are free to be appropriated, while others are to be ignored, looked down upon, or destroyed. In the late 2010s, large Western retailers such as Nike and Gap began featuring advertisements of women in hijabs. Diesel, a German fashion brand, featured a topless, tattooed White woman wearing a niqab.[12] These ads drew the attention of a large number of young Muslims, who were further encouraged by *Marie Claire*'s Beauty without Borders campaign. This new trend, "Burqa Chic," turned the "veil" into a fashion icon. This is an obvious 180-degree shift in attitude toward women with veils: due to the War on Terror, Muslim women were painted to be dark, mysterious, dangerous, or even asexual and repressed beings. Now, however, even non-Muslim celebrities, such as Rihanna and Madonna, are seen wearing veils.

The veil is now a symbol of "edginess," with Muslim women even being transformed into a sexualized commodity. Young Muslims might see this as a celebration of their culture, in the hopes that one day wearing niqabs, burqas, and hijabs will be normalized and that they will no longer have to fear for their safety when out in the streets. But admission of certain clothing types into the halls of White privilege does not erase the history of Muslim repression, especially after 9/11. This peculiar trendiness points to how the desire for White acceptance and all the trimmings of White privilege have become the aspiration of non-White people around the world. This process of conditioning continues to this day, with massive marketing budgets set aside to convince people the world over to embrace the modern age by adopting the latest fashion statements of the White world. One could argue that this has had a more detrimental impact on non-White women than on non-White men.

These trends are problematic at best, but downright destructive at their worst. Young Muslims are coaxed into believing that finally their faith can become "modern," without their even questioning why their definition of *modernity* equates to wearing White Western clothing. Modernity in the non-White world is synonymous with a desire to be White or Western, with the terms and conditions set by the so-called fashionistas of the Western world. This directly leads to the erosion of traditional attire, which can be seen even among other Asian cultures, such as the Burmese longyi or Indian sari being "upgraded" with Chanel or Hugo Boss fabrics. The definitions of *trendiness, fashion,* and *beauty* are so limited to the Western narrative that non-White cultures are unable to see their own beauty until they are accepted by the White fashion world.

From Top(s) to Bottom(s): Apparel Domination

Simply increasing representation of people of color among corporate fashion brands, on fashion catwalks, and in advertisements misses the point. In reality, these are superficial attempts to build a façade rather than confront the insidious nature of the industry when it comes to race and culture. For those who are mindful of these issues, it is actually counterproductive to embrace or endorse these steps of tokenism. In reality, it is harmful to the agenda of dismantling White privilege in the fashion industry. Consider the example of Muslim representation:

1. Fashion brands begin to realize that the Middle Eastern demographic is a huge potential market for profit and expansion. They are also aware that there is a deep desire to be accepted by the West, and this can be exploited.
2. Fashion brands proceed to include Muslim clothing, such as hijabs and niqabs. For instance, MANGO now releases a Ramadan line every year, with Uniqlo, H&M, and Dolce & Gabbana following suit.
3. This visually appeals to Middle Eastern Muslims or Muslims living in Western countries, as they see themselves as finally being represented by dominant, often White fashion brands. They thus believe that they are empowered, and consume these products.
4. Profiting from the Muslim demographic in this way is a classic example of how White privilege works—for economic gain—through the promotion of Western culture, drawing on centuries of dominance and the subjugation of minds of non-Western cultures. The fashion market in the Middle East has no competing cultural influence other than that of the West and Whiteness. No other culture—Chinese, Indian, or African—has this privilege.

It is very clear that White fashion brands have now begun to incorporate elements of other cultures into their clothes, in the race to gain more market share and stand out with new designs and motifs. White brands are exported the world over, and selectively using and adapting non-White designs can advance market domination in the non-Western world. Equally, by branding themselves as "diverse" and "inclusive," they can successfully create a façade of a forward-moving fashion industry in Western markets—a lucrative ploy.

This is damaging for two reasons. First, the representation of Muslims by these White fashion brands is reductive, and it effectively collapses the diversities within Muslim communities into one. Even when these brands are choosing to represent Muslims, only a select few "good Muslims" that fit the brands' narratives are visually represented. Black Muslim women or South Asian Muslims are almost never featured in these ads. Marketing stereotypes like this adopt a message of "being Western is modern" that reinforces the generic image of a submissive Muslim woman hiding behind a veil, waiting to be conquered, while effectively weakening other cultures and races within the Muslim community, ultimately ranking different Muslim cultures against one other. It also creates, as mentioned in the chapter on culture, tensions within communities as this pressure to modernize and Westernize is driven by strong economic forces. No real change results, as Muslim representation is often only there to fulfill a certain quota or to uphold the diversity image.

Second, this fake embrace of liberal ideals driven by economic imperatives not only implies that the push for diversity and inclusion in fashion is merely performative but also reveals a bigger issue. Often in the discussion of racism in fashion, those at the bottom of the supply chain are excluded. Fast fashion brands such as H&M and Gap have been notorious for using sweatshops and child labor in countries such as Bangladesh and India. It was revealed that a line of feminist T-shirts with the words "Girl Power" and "This is what a feminist looks like"' were made by girls and women in Bangladesh and Mauritius, where they were earning less than US$1 per hour.[13] It goes without saying that this discussion was only held through media, as a bridge between the consumer and H&M—the voices of the very women being wronged were not even sought out.

The Trash Economics of Fast Fashion

But the true economic motive of many fashion brands can be revealed upon a closer look at the mechanisms of fast fashion, an industry that is worth US$36 billion.[14] People constantly fail to consider that the free-trade policies and agreements of the 1980s and 1990s enabled largely White fashion brands to move their production to Latin America, the Middle East, and Asia, where they can outsource cheaper labor and increase profit margins. The apparel manufacturing industry experienced a shift to the developing world, highlighting the willingness to exploit non-White communities with low wages and unsafe working conditions. As these largely White fashion brands outsource labor in poorer countries, they can step away from their responsibilities of maintaining workers' basic protections, which include minimum wages, a safe and hygienic working environment, suitable working hours, and so on. Coupled with the complexities of labor law in different countries, these requirements become hard to enforce, and fast fashion labels are able to ignore them altogether. This implies that a worker's job security is extremely low and that their legal protection is paper thin. In early 2019, more than seventy-five hundred employees at twenty-seven factories in Bangladesh lost their jobs after striking over wages. After rounds of negotiation, the new minimum wage reached only half of what they demanded—8,000 taka a month (~US$100).[15]

Even in 2020, Bangladeshi garment workers were forced to protest after not being paid their wages, because major retailers canceled billions of dollars worth of orders after the pandemic broke out. Nearly two million workers were affected,[16] and at least ten thousand were laid off.[17] But because these aspects of the fashion industry are not typically shown to the consumer base, they are almost invisible. By continuously exploiting non-White worker populations, fashion brands are perpetuating a racial hierarchy both within the industry and in socioeconomic terms. It is almost an extension of the colonial past, except that this time, workers are not enslaved as coolies in sugar plantations but exploited in fashion sweatshops.

Despite these issues, there is a whole subindustry involving some of the biggest names in fashion and their global media partners (e.g., the *New York Times* and the *Financial Times*) in promoting fashion's social responsibility and sustainability through features and conferences. Through these supposedly "socially conscious" platforms, the global White media lends respectability to these Western brands—the perfect cover to demonstrate caring, without having to consider changing the fundamentals of economic exploitation or addressing the issue of furthering cultural domination. No Chinese or Indian fashion company would be able to mount such marketing activities to cover up exploitative practices. In fact,

White privilege will ensure that these Indian and Chinese companies are attacked by Western media allies, with the intention of burnishing the liberal credentials of Western brands. This has led to most people believing that Western fashion brands are no longer involved in malpractice—meaning many may have great difficulty understanding or accepting the issues of White privilege outlined in this chapter. (On a different note, the culling of millions of minks in Denmark due to the pandemic revealed a brutal trade that many thought was no longer practiced in the civilized and sustainable West for the purpose of fashion.[18])

On April 24, 2013, the Rana Plaza factory in Dhaka, Bangladesh, collapsed, killing 1,134 garment workers.[19] This sparked outrage across the world as the issue of systemic exploitation in the fashion industry surfaced for the first time. Eight years later, many issues from that time still persist. To acknowledge systemic White privilege that is enabled by free-trade agreements, outsourced labor, and corporate structures in the fashion industry is paramount. Otherwise, those young Muslims who fall for the pretentious and ostensible diversity in White fashion brands become accomplices to the exploitation of their fellow Muslims in these poorer countries thousands of miles away from them. This is an example of how globalized supply chains are not only exploitative of labor but also tethered to maintaining Western economic power, despite pious declarations about the need to end these practices in the developing world.[20]

It is merely the tip of an iceberg.

Of the seventy-four million textile workers worldwide, 80 percent are women of color. At the same time, up to 93 percent of fashion brands do not pay a living wage to their suppliers.[21] As consumers continue to buy cheaper clothes while White brands enjoy larger profit margins, these non-White people bear the brunt of the knock-on injustices and exploitation that is hard-wired into the global supply chain. Yet they are never heard from, voiceless, and silenced by the superficial yet selective representation at the top of corporate chains.

More Than Meets the Eye: Racism in High-End Fashion

The world of high-end fashion has always belonged to White culture, yet its biggest markets are now in Asia. Take a glimpse of the four major fashion shows throughout the year: New York Fashion Week, Paris Fashion Week, Milan Fashion Week, and London Fashion Week. (There is a par-

allel in the tennis world, with the four Grand Slam tennis events—
Melbourne, Paris, London, and New York.)

Not only are all these flagship events held in Western countries, but
the star-studded catwalk shows feature mostly White fashion designers,
models, makeup artists, and hairstylists. For instance, until 2017 there
were fashion shows in the US that had an all-White cast. The model Beverly Johnson was once told this was the case because "Black women are
not as pretty."[22] More disturbingly, only around 10 percent of the fashion
designers were Black.[23] Even then, non-White designers pursue a framework of design that hinges around White acceptance of their designs—a
need that is cultivated during training.

Even fashion magazines such as *Vogue* and *Harper's Bazaar* seldom
feature people of color. *Vogue's* 2018 cover featuring Beyoncé was the first
cover photo shot by a Black photographer in its 125-year history, and it
was not even *Vogue's* own intention, but rather per Beyoncé's request.
Needless to say, this was a one-off feature, as the magazine failed to continue featuring Black photographers afterward. The desire to be featured
on this magazine by non-Whites perpetuates and reinforces traditional
ways of reproducing power: to Westernize people who seek the trimmings
of White privilege. Seeking recognition through White power structures
such as *Vogue* legitimizes these structures, enabling them to exert more
influence in dictating fashion norms and values. The question is, by engaging with this process, are non-White celebrities complicit, or simply
characters in the story of the weak?

Let's continue looking at the case of Black beauty in high-end fashion. Black models such as Beverly Johnson have reported that they have
needed to bring or even do their own makeup before shows because
makeup artists simply do not understand how to use the right colors on
Black skin.[24] Equally, many hair stylists don't know how to style Black hair:
the African model Anok Yai lost ten inches of hair within seven months
simply because hairstylists did not know how to style it and chose to cut
it off instead.[25]

There are also countless examples of cultural appropriation in fashion shows: Comme des Garçons' using blonde cornrow wigs and the use
of White models in an African fashion show are just two. And then this
pattern of appropriation and discrimination gets repeated. Black stylists
and designers find doors of opportunity slammed shut in their face, simply because the gatekeepers, mostly White publicists and managers, do

not care to recognize them for their talents. What's worse, White stylists are allowed to style whomever, but Black stylists are hired only to style Black models. Ultimately, their skin color becomes a hindrance to their self-expression. Unless Black models and artists fit a certain kind of skin color or change up their hairstyle, the structures of the fashion industry will never be able to accept them for who they are.

To make it big in the fashion world, you have to have more than talent. You have to have money and connections and to be willing to succumb to White male power too. But non-Whites are denied the first two because the industry is predominantly White. The White networks in the fashion industry all comprise White executives and managers, artists, and editors whom non-White people must struggle to pay to get themselves featured in fashion shows. The result: a lack of Black managers and publicists leads to Black models, designers, and stylists having trouble booking jobs and earning money; a lack of Black models whom the White audience see sends the message that it is OK to neglect Black talent. Thus, even when Black designers, makeup artists, and models get to the top of the ladder, they are then conditioned to be too grateful to even be included, and are too afraid to change things up. Thus, both White privilege and the structure that enables it continue to thrive and spread their wings globally.

The Dilemma of Non-Whites in Global Fashion

It is these entrenched protectionist practices that constitute the high entry barrier for non-White people. These institutionalized barriers and thus the opportunities for redefining the place of fashion in a world that should celebrate diversity is not just limited to the challenges faced by Black people.

When Alexander Wang, an American-born Taiwanese, was named creative director of Balenciaga in 2012, he was not honored with appraisals of his talents but beset by rumors: because he is Chinese Taiwanese, he must have ascended the corporate ladder by "playing the race card" and even exploiting cheap labor. Asians cannot rid themselves of these assumptions and accusations in the fashion world, which in turn harms their opportunities.

It is no secret that the world of fashion is exclusive; there is a high entry barrier for the high-end fashion world. Admittedly, the fashion industry has made some progress throughout these years. In the New York

Fashion Week Spring 2020 shows, close to 45 percent of the models were people of color.[26] Fashion shows now also feature designers of different races, such as Muslim Indonesian designer Anniesa Hasibuan, who made history by featuring hijabs in all of her forty-eight outfits.[27] Asian fashion designers have also risen to the top of many corporate ladders. For instance, we see Leon and Lim taking over Kenzo. Virgil Abloh became the first Black man as the artistic director for men at Louis Vuitton. British *Vogue* hired its first Black editor-in-chief, Edward Enninful.

But these achievements are mostly cosmetic. They do not address the deeper issues of how White fashion is used as a tool of cultural and economic domination and Westernization of the world, adding to the relentless assault on other cultures, traditions, and arts. Enninful is Black, but his fashion training and his job is to promote Western notions of style and fashion, even if he has the gumption to add a bit of Black flair and non-White models to his pages, which is, sadly, tokenism at its shameless best. But to those who are attuned to this assault, one sympathetic view is that these talented non-White designers have become captive to White privilege and perhaps even know it. After all, to enter the world of high fashion, non-White cultures have to be made digestible to the White audience. In this process, authority is given to the White creators and executives within the fashion industry to define which parts of dissected cultures can be appropriated to appeal to and satisfy the White appetite. Otherwise, non-White cultures become too threatening to White privilege.

Conclusion: Upcoming Trends?
Fighting White Privilege in Fashion

Achieving true diversity and eradicating White privilege in fast fashion require us to consider all aspects of the Western-dominated fashion industry; this is both a political and cultural project. It is more than filling the "diversity" quota while still refusing to pay a fair wage. It is more than celebrating the representation of a mixed-race Muslim American and calling it a day. It is to fully embrace different races, traditions, and cultures and level the playing field by exposing the nature of the subjugation of others to the superiority of Whiteness on which the fashion industry is reliant and thrives on for economic reasons. It is to destroy the hierarchical racial relationship embedded in garment manufacturing. From high-end, avant-garde fashion runways to everyday apparel and its manufacturing processes, systemic White privilege persists. This Whiteness is simultaneously glaringly visible yet unobvious, given that it is so ingrained in our fashion decisions.

The global acceptance of White fashion legitimizes White cultural control at an institutional and deeply personal level. This enables the vast economic success of the White Western fashion industry and convinces people around the world to change their very features to possess more Whiteness and even reject their rich heritage and cultures. Many of them are richer and older than those in the West and possess incredible sources of inspiration if one want wants to truly make fashion statements not curtailed by Whiteness.

Dismantling White privilege is not a fashion trend; it is a political and cultural struggle. Race is not a fashion trend. It is not OK to fetishize Asian culture and Hello Kitty cuteness for a few years, then turn to African cornrows and Middle Eastern hijabs the next. Each culture, race, and color is beautiful in its own way, and it is time that we recalibrate what it means to be beautiful, trendy, and fashionable. That change starts with non-White people across the world understanding the nature of the White fashion trends they follow, questioning why they follow them while rejecting their own culture, and understanding that doing so promotes and sustains global White economic privilege.

CHAPTER 9

ENVIRONMENT, SUSTAINABILITY, AND CLIMATE CHANGE

Zero Carbon and Other Myths

The White Savior Industrial Complex is not about justice. It is about having a big emotional experience that validates privilege.

—Teju Cole, "The White-Savior Industrial Complex"

The Whitewashed Environmental Movement

Ever wonder why the most prominent global thinkers, policymakers, commentators, activists, and authors on the pressing issues of climate change, sustainability, and environmental crisis are typically Westerners? From David Attenborough to Jeffrey Sachs and even Greta Thunberg, the people shaping narratives on most of these incredibly important topics—and lauded in the mainstream global media—are White Westerners.

There can be only three explanations for this:

1. Non-White people, their organizations, and governments do not care about environmental issues and thus are not engaged in addressing them.
2. Non-White people, their organizations, and governments *are* interested, but they do not have sufficient education, ingenuity, capital, institutions, or technologies to find solutions to environmental issues.
3. White people, their organizations, and governments seek to control how these issues are addressed because doing so grants them the

moral high ground, and they are thus able to deflect responsibility onto those who do not tackle these issues in the ways that White people have deemed appropriate—that is, non-White people.

I call this the unholy trinity of environomics. The first explanation is not true—environmental actions are clearly being taken by people all over the world, not just by Western governments and their populations. The second explanation may seem as though there is some truth to it (e.g., access to capital, institutions, and technology), but in reality, it speaks to Western superiority. It is a disdainful way of looking at how non-Western countries are dealing with environmental issues. Thus although the first two points are untrue they are the often unspoken assumptions that define attitudes in the West, born out of arrogance and a sense of superiority. Yet these issues are not black and white as non-Western countries too have to take responsibility where their inactions have furthered such viewpoints.

India, for example, clearly has an extensive pollution problem in the Ganges, and its inability to address it is an indictment of successive governments and India's politics. But its ecological footprint per person is 1.2 hectares, whereas Sweden's is 6.1 hectares, which is entirely unsustainable in the long term.[1] Yet Sweden is widely considered to be following a much more environmentally sustainable path. So, what defines success here? Pollution-free waterways? Or a per capita footprint that represents a sustainable economic pathway? Sweden possesses the former, India the latter. Both polluted water and an unsustainable footprint are serious environmental issues and addressing them is wholly dependent on local contexts, yet neither is excusable.

The West has decided what the worthwhile measures of success are, and regards Sweden as an exemplar. Why? Because Western lifestyles are not as *visibly* unsustainable, even if they cause more overall environmental damage. But shining a spotlight on these privileged and damaging lifestyles is, of course, very problematic in relation to the way Western populations live their lives. Hence, point 3 remains as a generalized explanation for the Western dominance of environmental narratives.

I am familiar with these arguments because I have worked in the environment and sustainability field for thirty years. A global movement is being created as awareness of environmental issues continues to rise, but the main actors and policymakers on the global stage remain Western—so let us be clear that even humanity's interface with the natural world is seen through a White Western lens, even though some of the largest green strides are being taken in non-Western countries such as China, which is the world leader in producing solar energy—at 205,000 megawatts in 2019, which is over three times as much as the US, in second place with 62,000.[2]

Climate change, the loss of biodiversity, global resource abuse, and pollution are the existential threats facing the planet and our species. Thus the people and organizations involved in addressing these environmental issues now wield tremendous power in shaping our world and how we think about managing our societies.

The vast majority of these people and organizations are Western—the Intergovernmental Panel on Climate Change (headquartered in Switzerland), Greenpeace (the Netherlands), and the Climate Action Network (Germany) are some examples. Their efforts have been branded as the world-saving work of our time, but in reality, they have not guided the world in the direction of solving environmental issues: only ten countries of the 1997 Kyoto Protocol met their targets (by buying carbon credits), and a landmark 2020 UN report found that the world has failed to meet *any* of its biodiversity targets.[3] France, for example, is home to 35 percent of Europe's biodiversity, yet one in four species remains endangered.[4] Similarly, Italy hosts 43 percent of European biodiversity, and 35 percent of the European species on the Red List of endangerment are in Italy, which is produced by the International Union for Conservation of Nature (the leading organization on tracking extinction levels).[5]

Concentration of Power, Dispersal of Responsibility

The cultivated moral authority and influencing power has allowed the West to assume leadership in addressing these global environmental challenges, which in turn has been utilized to serve Western needs—the ability to avoid any changes to current lifestyles (which are being exported worldwide for economic gain, as discussed) and privileges (which are reserved in the West) that are causing the environmental challenges we are facing. Instead, the solutions exported by the West focus on technological silver bullets, convoluted economic instruments, and democracy (which is meant to urge positive political behavior), rather than on an acceptance that our collective welfare is going to require drastic individual lifestyle changes, rethinking of the assumption that we need "constant growth," and stronger state intervention to keep economic activities from running amok at the expense of the natural world. Addressing these issues would be a shift away from business as usual and would require rewriting the narrative on sustainability as we know it. But this is a political impossibility for Western liberal democracies: they simply cannot make these changes, because it would require Western societies to sacrifice the standards of privilege they have become used to, which in turn are dependent on expanding their economic interests globally. Therefore, thinking is instead directed toward posturing and shifting the onus of major responsibility for environmental challenges onto the non-Western world, China in particular.

Although it is true that environmental concerns are global, that does not mean that they are caused equally by all different nations or peoples. Nor is responsibility for addressing and solving these challenges shared equally among every nation or every person. Yet this fact is conveniently ignored by Western nations, which are responsible for having leveraged incredibly environmentally degrading processes to fuel economic development (and still do), including excessive use of fossil fuels, overhunting, abuse of minerals, and extreme production of pollution. Western nations now critique these same processes in other countries in a way that is not sympathetic to the developmental challenges non-Western countries face, and that often overlooks the environmental destruction caused by their own lifestyles.

The White Western approach to environmental issues is created and maintained through three main channels:

1. Scientific legitimacy: the creation of "truths," approaches, and technology that empower Western policy frameworks to address environmental issues, even outside the Western world.
2. Moral authority: the self-belief of Western nations that they are working to fix the world's environmental challenges, even while their economic approaches, overconsumptive lifestyles, and modes of doing business externalize costs and perpetuate the destruction of the natural environment.
3. Economic dominance: the use of economic muscle to enforce solutions that perpetuate the success of Western business models (for example, the Biden administration's carbon tax that it wishes to place on products coming from high-CO_2-producing countries, including China).

Environmental issues affect everyone—most important, future generations. Western narratives have shaped received wisdom on these issues for the last fifty years at least. If globally cooperative solutions are to be found and followed, they should move beyond self-serving or poorly informed prescriptions from the West to include expert opinions from others who have legitimacy and whose knowledge is rooted in local realities.

Let us examine these power dynamics in three key areas: climate change, biodiversity loss, and pollution.

Climate Change: Western Staged Support

Climate change is possibly the most significant existential threat the human race faces. Yet it is unsurprising that the former president of the United States, Donald Trump, simply denied the existence of climate change. Looking back to when the Kyoto Protocol was first introduced as the seminal climate change movement, the president was Bill Clinton, and his vice president was Al Gore, two American leaders touted for caring about the environment. However, the United States did not even ratify the treaty, let alone abide by binding targets for CO_2 emissions. Fundamentally, the domination of Western countries in the climate-change arena perpetuates White privilege through legitimizing the Western approach to solutions, which ensures Western lifestyles are not affected, thereby maintaining Western economic dominance. Thus, although even President Biden may take climate change seriously, he has little power to change the minds of Americans—he could not even get them to wear masks during the pandemic—or take tough measures, as these would threaten the privileges of the original White American dream to which most Americans are beholden. This is why the top four banks still financing fossil fuels in 2020 were American—JP Morgan alone contributed US$51.3 billion to fossil-fuel financing in 2020.[6] That is more than the individual GDP of one hundred countries across the world.

One of the most visible ways of maintaining leadership over the global agenda is through the various international climate conferences, summits, and agreements. These events follow a pattern: the West initiates and mediates these conferences, which have positive motives for addressing climate change and purport moral direction, scientific rigor, and political commitment. These Western-led initiatives preach of the need to share the climate burden, only to refrain from acting on their historical debt to the planet from decades of overreliance on fossil fuels; and they are ultimately unable to lower their luxury CO_2 emissions to meet stated targets—unless using burden-shifting mechanisms. Here, good intentions take center stage, while the realities of enforcing serious climate action are masked.

This capture of the global narrative by framing it entirely through the Western lens enables Western countries that participate in these conferences to hold moral authority over countries in the non-Western world, which are seen simply as laggards, participants, or bystanders in these conferences, unable to lead change as can the Western world, whose leaders take the stage and make commitments on which they have typically failed to deliver. These forums act as symbolic reinforcements of the West's leadership position in the narrative of climate change, which shapes it as an issue that only the West cares about and that only the West can lead the world in solving, rather than one that requires global equality in cooperation and sacrifice on the part of Western economies.

Similarly, the developing world's "survival emissions" are critiqued as somehow worse and holding more responsibility for climate change than the Western developed world's "luxury emissions." These terms refer to the CO_2 emission per capita per year needed to maintain basic societal needs and stimulate economic growth, versus wasteful lifestyle maintenance. For example, while China does have the highest national CO_2 emissions, it is also the most populated country on the planet, and has low CO_2 emissions per capita, at 7.05 tons, which is significantly lower than that of the United States (16.56), Canada (15.32), or even Australia (16.92).[7] Hence the difference between survival and luxury.

Consequently, solutions proposed during climate conferences are skewed toward the West, whose governments and businesses seek to prevent changes to consumption habits and economic activity that fundamentally rely on producing CO_2 as part of growth. They especially refrain from intervention via political action. Being in control of these international forums in the first place allows Western countries to be irresponsible in the way they continue to produce CO_2, as non-White countries simply cannot restrain them.

Why Western Solutions Are Global Solutions

This is not to say that Western nations are not taking steps to reduce their per capita emissions. The EU, for example, is trending downward, according to the World Bank, from 8.46 tons of CO_2 per capita in 1990 to 6.47 in

2016, due to increased uptake of nuclear power and outsourcing of manufacturing to non-Western countries. However, as per the 2020 review by the United Nations Framework Convention on Climate Change (the originators of the Paris Agreement), the EU is only 70 percent on its way to meeting its emission targets.[8] This does not bode well for a 2050 CO_2-neutral scenario.

Despite being repeatedly unable to meet global climate commitments, the West is still looked to as the world leader. Take the *Stern Review*, for example: a seminal report released in 2006 by the British government that documents how climate change can be addressed with market-based solutions. It has been many years since its publication, and no such market-based instrument has come close to fighting climate change on the scale needed, yet Western countries are still unable to steer away from the outdated belief that the invisible hand of the market will dig us out of a mess that it caused in the first place.[9]

The alternative is to dramatically lower per capita emissions for Western populations, which would actually be a shift from business as usual and would require massive adjustments to Western lifestyles—imagine car ownership cut by 50 percent, food supplied seasonally only from local growers, direct intervention from governments to limit businesses that produce above-quota CO_2, and lowering ecological footprints to a global average to meet climate-change targets.

Instead, there is a great touting of silver-bullet technology that has not been applied properly or even invented yet. Or a deep belief in sophisticated economic instruments such as carbon-trading schemes, which have underachieved because they are almost impossible to administer and are often unsuited to the socioeconomic contexts of developing nations, or nations with larger, poorer populations.

The accusations against non-Western countries and the restrictions on them proposed by the West are thus missing some key points, namely White historical responsibility for a certain proportion of CO_2 emissions; White contemporary responsibility via high per capita CO_2 production; and that non-Western countries may be constrained in their development trajectories if they adopt Western approaches to the climate problem. Further, the active pursuit of leadership roles in international agreements allows the West to amass political and even scientific credibility, to offshore their responsibilities to those that are weaker in power, or simply to deny the existence of the problem. The ability to deny and shift responsibilities in this way is yet another form of White privilege.

White Savior Syndrome and Climate Change

White privilege and power also enable the cultivating of leaders and heroes, which dovetails with a strategy of denial. Western and White activists are often put forward as the face of global movements. Greta Thunberg is perhaps the most striking example, attending annual conferences and making magazine covers for her passion and commitment to climate activism.

But what about non-White climate activists who have been fighting this same cause for years or decades before Thunberg? Or those working in more difficult environments with far fewer resources? Renowned Nigerian author Chika Unigwe has commented on this very issue,[10] pointing to several non-White climate activists who have not received the media attention, outpouring of global support, or opportunities to grace magazine covers and win titles—activists such as Artemisa Xakriaba, a nineteen-year-old indigenous Amazonian youth leader and member of an alliance that protects six hundred million hectares of forest, or Yero Sarr, the eighteen-year-old from Senegal who founded a youth climate action movement in his country.[11] Frustratingly, these non-Western climate activists are now seen as "following in Greta's footsteps" despite having been committed to activism years before Thunberg arrived on the scene.

White heroes are deliberately built up as champions in the fight against climate change, which is a misleading way of entrenching existing racial hierarchies and power imbalances—that is, that White people care while others do not. Non-Western climate activists rarely make it to the front page because they do not fit the ideology of the White savior (that White activists will be the heroes to save the day, just like in the movies). No matter how much these non-White climate activists embody the values of environmental protection and sustainability or live on the front line of the struggle, they are no match for the moral authority that White activists possess, passed down from centuries of carefully carved out privilege.

This moral high ground is embodied not only by climate activists but also by conservation activists, business leaders, and political spokespersons. These people have the great privilege of being in close proximity to White centers of power: Western media, political and business leaders, philanthropists, multilaterals, and influential organizations. Thus they can exercise their moral authority to perpetuate White supremacy over sustainability-related matters across the world. Because these stakeholders are acting in ways that appear to combat the effects of climate change, they are often not criticized. It is how Greta is now the youngest *Time* Person of the Year, with two consecutive nominations for the Nobel Peace Prize; or how Elon Musk is held as a globally acclaimed innovator committed to changing the planet, yet his inventions seem aimed more at leaving planet Earth than saving it. It is how Al Gore has rebranded himself as a climate change activist after starring in an environmental documentary, with the tag "Nobel Prize laureate, author and founder of Climate Reality" behind his name.

Symbolically, therefore, this elevation of Western personalities to heroes creates the belief that Western approaches are the only right way to report, solve, and discuss climate change altogether. Not only is this unhelpful overall in the fight against climate change, as it limits the possibilities for solutions, but it renders all non-White voices irrelevant while forcing White and Western-tailored solutions onto these same people. Ultimately, the fight against climate change becomes yet another extension of White power, which is actively maintained through discussions, climate change forums, business models, and media reports. At a time when change is crucial for us to fight what is coming, nothing, in fact, has changed.

Biodiversity Loss: Extinction Narratives

Climate change is not the only environmental narrative that is controlled by a Western framing. Biodiversity loss is another major example, and the people who shape and influence that narrative have the ability to transform policy and economies: after all, animals and plants are the source of a vast number of products and services we use every day, from food to clothing to fuel.

Species are disappearing at over one hundred times their natural rate, and no country has been able to meet its biodiversity targets. This is clearly a major global challenge, yet if you follow mainstream Western media, you may be led to believe that only the West cares about the issue or that the Chinese and Indonesians are hell-bent on environmental destruction or even that simple solutions exist if one follows Western prescriptions for these poor countries. Western conservation leaders also dominate the narrative about which species are valuable and need to be protected, where they should be protected, and how.

This process of forming misleading narratives is both a historical and contemporary process. Starting with the former, let us look at the North American bison as an example. They were critically endangered as a result of overconsumption on the part of American settlers. In the nineteenth and twentieth centuries, bison were hunted close to extinction for their fur, skin, and meat, and to deprive Native Americans of bison as a resource.[12] A population of less than one thousand persisted by 1890. Just a century previously, there had been sixty *million* bison in North America, the largest herds of terrestrial megafauna ever. (For reference, the number of wildebeest we see famously migrating across the African plains is only around 1.5 million.) It is almost impossible to imagine the scale of slaughter.

But few even within the US are aware of how the bison was horrendously overconsumed and slaughtered for profit or how hunting them was weaponized against the Native Americans. This is because the narratives of biodiversity conservation are controlled by the West—and this is not only a historical occurrence. Just as the fate of the North American bison has been rendered invisible, narratives surrounding contemporary conservation have been selectively used to promote a Western conservation agenda, which is not always aligned with the needs of non-Western countries.

In fact, when it comes to biodiversity, most of the purported villains today are Asian and African: the poachers who kill megafauna such as tigers, elephants, and whales. It is why the Japanese are internationally critiqued for whale hunting, yet the Norwegians exported the practice to Japan in the first place, and to this day are responsible for killing the most whales of any country in the world.[13] Yet the need for biodiversity relates to more than the megafauna found in the tropics. It is also the bees, beetles, worms, frogs, and birds that are responsible for keeping our ecosystems in balance, which are dying out across all continents; their decline is not due to countries in Africa and Asia alone. The abject failure of Asian and African governments is an indictment of their incompetence and much has been said about it, but they are not the only culprits.

The Implications of Western-Style Conservation

Like climate change solutions, conservation in the modern day has been largely dictated to non-Western countries by the West. Let's consider the example of fortress conservation, the most widely practiced method of conservation, first proposed by environmentalists in the United States. Essentially, it is a system for the creation and management of large protected areas—such as the large US national parks—so that ecosystems can function in isolation from human disturbance. This sounds good in theory, but it is heavily ideologically laden: at its core lies the concept that the environment and people should be separated—but which people? Who decides who these people are? What about communities where people and the environment coexist? Here is where White privilege takes the driver's seat, as Western control of the conservation narrative means they often get to decide on these answers.

In the United States, for example, it was decided that Native Americans must be separated from their environments to allow White populations to enjoy the same spaces. Yosemite National Park, one of the most famous parks in the world, gets its namesake from a people: the Yosemite band of the Miwok tribe, who had been resident in the park for four thousand years before the US government evicted them between 1851 and 1969. Now, four million tourists visit every year. In this case, White Americans decided that Native Americans were not allowed on the land for the sake of conservation, but other members of American society were deemed permissible.

Fortress conservation like this thrives today because for several decades Western governments, NGOs, experts, and philanthropists have been able to export this model to other parts of the world. In Africa, studies have been conducted which reveal that countries with high levels of economic inequality and weak political institutions have the largest conserved areas—Namibia, Tanzania, and Zambia, for example, each have over 30 percent of their land set aside for conservation. In the process, many indigenous communities have been removed from their lands, often violently. In their place, commercial tourism operators and corrupt government officials can benefit from monetization of these spaces, such as by promoting and even permitting with licenses safaris or trophy hunting expeditions. The ability of Western environmental activists to separate non-White people from their environments on the grounds that they do not live according to Western "civilized" standards exemplifies the epitome of White privilege—that Western conservation ideologies can be placed above the traditions and well-being of non-Westerners. This would never happen in Western countries.

What is insidious about this approach to conservation is the assumption that local people use natural resources in irrational and destructive ways or are not capable of helping their surrounding environment as Western people can. The unmissable irony is, of course, that Western lifestyles are notoriously unsustainable.

This imperial mindset is part of the wider belief that to deal effectively with threats to conservation select elements of the environment are more important than the non-White indigenous communities that live in them and use them. In other words, certain plants and animals are ranked as having more value than certain people. As a result, many of these people are labeled "criminals," "poachers," and "squatters."

This ranking by Western organizations has serious implications. Consider the case of the World Wide Fund for Nature (WWF), one of the largest conservation organizations in the world. It has achieved incredible things during its campaign to "save the planet," but has fallen into the trap of expressing White savior syndrome: WWF made headlines in 2018 for the exposé that they had funded *militia groups* to protect conservation parks from poachers—poachers who used to be residents of these parks, as in the case of the Baka people in Cameroon.[14] These groups have since been accused of maiming or even killing scores of people across Africa and Asia.[15] In this case, non-White people trying to continue traditional ways of living or make a living in new economic situations have literally been deemed less valuable than animals.

The West can certainly extend considerable influence and use its power to command attention toward select species it deems worthy or in need of protection. For example, WWF's logo is a panda, an animal native to China, not the West. By using charismatic megafauna, such as the panda, traditionally found in non-Western countries as "flagship" species, Western environmentalists evoke empathy and support for animals outside the West, turning conservation into a non-Western issue and a political one. The truth is that the panda success story was led by Chinese conservationists, not WWF or some other Western entity.

The focus on Western conservation achievements deepens the White savior narrative. There is a lack of attention paid to the work of local animal rights activists and environmentalists, which creates an image that local activists are barely doing anything to conserve important animals or habitats and that their governments are incompetent or uncaring. In particular, this is a pattern proselytized by Western NGOs in non-Western countries. Invariably, these NGOs will have an antagonistic relationship with non-Western governments, arguing that corruption and lack of interest result in anticonservation efforts on the part of the government.

Conversely, they will happily collaborate with Western governments that are just as guilty (if not more so) of hampering biodiversity. The conclusion they reach, therefore, is that Western intervention is required as the ultimate savior to protect the animals and habitats in question. However, although biodiversity targets are not being met in non-Western countries, Western nations are also incapable of protecting their own species. For example, the UK has failed to reach seventeen of the twenty Aichi biodiversity targets, and this gulf between rhetoric and reality has been critiqued as resulting in a "lost decade for nature."[16]

To summarize, the case of biodiversity conservation demonstrates that White privilege enables the selection of which environmental narratives the world focuses on. This has caused non-Western nations to conserve huge swathes of their land following Western conservation modes, which may sound like a good thing, but is often at odds with local needs, especially those of the people residing in these lands. In fact, this process has manifested in historical and even contemporary value ranking, where non-Whites and their livelihoods are placed below their surrounding environments. Lastly, White privilege manifests in White savior syndrome, whereby non-Western environmentalists are given neither the respect nor the platforms they deserve, in place of White saviors.

Pollution and Waste: The Plastic Problem

The final environmental issue that warrants discussion is pollution. The narratives surrounding it have been dramatically influenced by the West, placing the West in a position of moral authority, which, as will be discussed, has had global economic impacts.

Western countries are perceived to be world leaders in recycling—with certain exceptions such as Japan and Korea. However, Western countries have been largely dependent on the non-Western world for recycling services—burden shifting again—and now many Western countries, such as the UK, France, and the US, are facing serious difficulty in recycling key waste products, such as plastics. This is because in July 2017, China enacted its National Sword policy, which cut plastic imports by 99 percent, a decision that has had global ramifications. Before this, China was one of the world's largest dumping grounds, for thirty years importing plastic to be recycled. The majority of this plastic waste came from the West, which often claimed that it was "reusing and recycling" the waste it was producing.

The reality is that much of Western waste is shipped to poorer countries that hope to claim economic gains from the global recycling industry. But this has almost never manifested so neatly. For example, the plastics China was receiving from the West pre–National Sword were not at a level of quality to *even be recycled*: much of the plastic was contaminated, not sorted into correct recycling variants, or not appropriate for recycling. In fact, the situation got so bad that China carried out the Green Fence Operation in 2013, to improve the quality of waste coming into China. But to no avail: plastics were simply not being properly sorted or cleaned sufficiently by Western countries and their green-conscious populations. So instead it was sorted into landfills or burned—clearly not very proenvironmental—which Western nations were very much aware of, but conveniently ignored while continuing their plastic export.

The flow of plastic waste from the West to the Rest is an expression of White privilege: that other nations *want* or *need* Western waste. This view shunts pollution problems onto non-Western nations, allowing Western governments to cite sustainability numbers that hide this truth while allowing Western populations to continue high-consumption lifestyles unhindered by the external costs of proper waste management.

This mindset of privilege has been on display even more in the years since National Sword was enacted. Faced with serious breaks in their waste disposal chain, Western countries have reacted by illegally dumping plastic waste in non-Western countries. This has occurred in several Southeast Asian countries, including Malaysia. In 2018, a total of 3,737 tons of waste illegally transported into Malaysia was sent back to thirteen countries, including 11 full shipping containers to Canada, 17 to the United States, 42 to the UK, and 43 to France.[17]

Meanwhile, in Western countries themselves, recyclable plastic waste is now being sent to landfills or burned like all other waste because very few Western nations have developed the infrastructure and capacity to deal with the sheer amount of waste being generated.

At this point, it is important to consider how countries such as China, Nigeria, Indonesia, and the Philippines are demonized for their plastic waste challenges, but Western countries are not. In fact, a study using World Bank data revealed that China is *not* the largest producer of plastic waste per capita: it is the US (105 kg per person, per year), followed by the UK (99 kg). Previously, the US stood at twentieth in the world—until researchers included its waste export to poorer countries and illegal waste dumping. With this new study, the US represents just 4 percent of the world's population, but produces 17 percent of its plastic waste.[18]

Again, it is the privilege embedded in the global waste management system that allows White Western countries not to be lambasted by the media. Here again it is critical that the nations of Asia and Africa learn from the fallacies of Western market-based prescriptions and take draconian measures to curb this scourge through strong state intervention.

The New Challenge of E-Waste

Plastic isn't the only example of burden shifting by Western governments in order to claim effectiveness of policies at home. Take e-waste, which is rising as electronic technology is adopted worldwide.[19] In 2017, more than forty-nine million tons of e-waste were generated globally, the majority of which was shipped to non-Western countries to recycle. This type of waste is often hazardous because of the presence of chemicals and heavy metals, and it is common practice for Western countries to exploit developing countries' lower labor costs and less stringent environmental regulations to deal with it. On the other end, developing countries accept this waste, as they believe they can benefit economically by selling recycled outputs back to the West. However, these countries also face a severe lack of facilities and resources to properly recycle and dispose of this waste (which is not surprising—remember that the West does not have these facilities either). These countries thus resort to rudimentary methods of disposal and recycling, such as the physical dismantling of e-waste with hammers, chisels, and screwdrivers. This is a very unsafe process. Countries such as Thailand have been quick to absorb the business of recycling that China no longer takes, and to bitter ends: workers are regularly exposed to toxins; unregulated waste management is contaminating fresh water supplies; and antiwaste, proenvironmental activists have even been murdered to keep the industry running.[20]

The higher levels of disposable income and higher levels of development in White Western countries enable many people to afford to consume goods that are "green"—made from recycled materials, or materials produced with processes that are incredibly resource efficient or don't produce toxins during the manufacturing stage. Although this may seem like a step in the right direction, these goods often represent a minute proportion of the total waste Westerners produce; not using a straw might make you feel good, but what about the amount of waste you produce when ordering from Amazon for the third time in one month? How much waste is generated in the manufacturing, transporting, packaging, and administrating of the products you get shipped to your door?

The ability to afford "green" goods does not preclude people from committing environmental damage, because a core issue remains: Westerners live in the most consumption-driven societies in the world, in which green products are a drop in the ocean of waste produced every day. Yet green products help maintain the moral high ground of the West nonetheless.

Taking a closer look at the way waste is managed in Western countries reveals how it has been structured to favor the West at the expense of the Rest. Although this is not universal across waste management systems, it represents a mindset of White privilege—that it is legitimate to exploit non-Western and non-White countries to deal with an unwanted environmental issue.

Conclusion: White Privilege in Sustainability and Environmentalism

In the case of climate change, conservation, and pollution, the West has exerted selective representation and selective addressing of one environmental issue over another. It has created narratives that are still driven by and understood through a Western economic, political, and moral framework. And although generally people understand that global action is needed to combat most environmental problems, many of the solutions or tactics proposed are still led by Western activists, policymakers, business leaders, and thought leaders. This not only reduces and oversimplifies the complexities of environmental challenges to fit the Western context, but also allows White power to manifest itself in these conversations. Hence, the issue of the environment is (like so many others discussed in this book) inseparable from issues of race and power.

Further, instead of accepting historical responsibility and addressing the core reasons for climate change and other environmental issues, Western countries seek solutions that do not compromise existing lifestyles. In fact, that is what much of sustainability, ESG (environmental, social, and corporate governance), and CSR (corporate social responsibility) are today—convenient and seemingly rigorously thought-through solutions, but which in reality hide the fact that leading Western countries are unable and unwilling to limit overconsumption or to price it appropriately and rein in unregulated business activity.

It is now even accepted as legitimate for companies to "make up" for the environmental degradation arising from their business models by funding "green" activities elsewhere. Many philanthropic activities of business leaders fall into the same category. Take Coca-Cola, which publicly announced in 2010 that seventy-five liters of water are required to make one liter of Coke.[21] The company vowed to be "water neutral" by 2020 and claims that it is now offsetting more than 100 percent of the water it uses—but in reality, this is just "operational" water, and does not include the water used along the entire supply chain; with this water included, the offset is just 1 percent.[22]

These kinds of "offsetting" approaches are not a solution. They enable the continuation of core problems, and what ties this issue to the racial power balance is the exportation of this approach to the rest of the world, which further enhances the dominance of White economic power under the namesake of sustainability.

Going forward, dismantling White power is paramount if we are to really combat climate change as a global problem rather than as a Western problem. This entails actually listening to what non-White countries really need. They do not need more technological gadgets that make consumption easier. They surely do not need yet another White hero icon. They need solutions that are applicable to their own cultures, development levels, and environments—solutions that can work alongside population growth, the limited number of resources, as well as the knowledge and expectations of the local, indigenous communities. This entails dismantling hierarchical racial relationships in the way that climate issues are reported and in the ways that solutions are presented.

CONCLUSION

How Change Happens: No Whitewash, Please!

> My very presence in the White House had triggered a deep-seated panic, a sense that the natural order had been disrupted. Millions of Americans spooked by a Black man in the White House.
>
> —President Barack Obama

Not Getting Spooked

The preceding chapters have attempted to outline how White privilege works, how its tentacles have spread far and wide across all corners of the world, and how it has infiltrated so many critical aspects of how societies are organized and function in an interconnected world.

But four to five centuries of White privilege in the pursuit of global economic dominance cannot be easily rectified, especially when it has been so actively cultivated and so astutely woven into the fabric of modern-day globalization and even the foreign policy of the collective West. White people accustomed to being at the top of the global pecking order are easily spooked by changes to the status quo. Some are not even aware of their privilege, and many are in denial.

Even White liberals comfortable with Barack Obama in the White House may be unnerved when confronted by other inconvenient truths about the privileges they have taken for granted. They may react by engaging in denial or resisting changes to share power with others.

I have experienced this when I have spoken at forums in Europe—even in Asia—to Americans and Europeans about the post-Western world and why such changes would be necessary for a fairer and more equal world. There is a real fear of losing power to others deemed unqualified to have a say in making the rules of a new world order and losing the privileges embedded in the current order. Almost unwittingly, people who one would think of as liberals and who should know better present views and arguments that betray deep-rooted prejudices. They are spooked by the idea of a world order in which the West is not at the top. In his book, *A Promised Land*, Barack Obama reflects on how in the American context he got a real dose of the anxiety so many White Americans feel about having a Black man in the White House. The response was the election of Trump. Now try to imagine how such a reaction would play out globally: the harm it would do and the expected resistance to change. Addressing the UN Human Rights Council in February 2021, Secretary General Antonio Guterres called White supremacy a "transnational" threat. I hope this book shows that White supremacy is the visible tip of the iceberg and that what lies underneath is as dangerous and a lot more insidious, and has been persistently harmful to the world.[1]

Therefore, if humanity is to fulfill the promise of its ingenuity and to leverage its rising collective social consciousness, then we must (among other things) tackle the insidious nature of global White privilege and supremacy, which this book argues and demonstrates is the cause of so much harm and injustice.

Overturning structural discrimination is a long and difficult process that needs to go through multiple stages. It can be complicated enough to unpack how domestic institutions and culture create and reinforce patterns of domination; doing the same for global institutions, social structures, norms, and cultures to tackle global patterns of domination creates an additional challenge. To dismantle White privilege and create a fairer world with less conflict, there is a need for the global community to know what White privilege is—its roots, its objectives, its sinister nature, where it lurks, and how it is perpetuated. This means that non-White people need to be aware of the unwelcome makeover of their economies, culture, and traditions that has taken place (and continues to take place), so that they can resist with positive action.

This global structural discrimination that upholds White privilege will not be achieved in merely a decade; at least a couple of generations are needed. To reverse the mind capture of entire societies is generational work. And let us be clear: the resistance to change will be strong and will come in many forms, both overt and subtle. Overt resistance will come from the White supremacist supporters of political leaders such as Donald Trump (as was on display for the world to see on January 6, 2021) and their kindred spirits across the Western world, as well as powerful businesses with significant vested interests in Asia and Africa. They will resort to violence. The more subtle response will come in the form of the unwillingness of global organizations and individuals in key positions of power to recognize that they are part of the architecture of upholding White privilege, that they are its key beneficiaries, and that they thereby help maintain global inequality. They will embrace cosmetic measures that will put them in a good light but avoid fundamental change, as that would challenge their economic interests and supremacy. Their powerful stakeholders will not tolerate any deviation from the plan.

A Time for Leadership That Matters

Those who are ready can start this process now. This chapter, together with suggestions made in earlier chapters, will provide some clear pathways to action.

There are even precedents. For example, if the women's equality movement in the West can create the "Lean In" and "Me Too" movements, then surely it is time for a global "Push In" or "Share Too" movement by all those who believe that White privilege has no place in a fair and progressive world. White people need to be willing to accept that others have a right to push for their rights and call for equal shares. For White people who are not in denial, it is a time to perhaps start a "Give In" movement—putting up less resistance to change and allowing others into their realms of power and influence, which they have been so steadfast in guarding for themselves. Whether they can do that will be the test of their belief in confronting White privilege.

If they want to live in peace and as equals with others in the coming post-Western world, Western societies must ask themselves if they are willing to reject the following:

- The subconscious sense of superiority born from centuries of dominance over others, and encouraging others to act in ways that reinforce their own inferiority

- Engineering and promoting all forms of economic activity in pursuit of wealth and power in order to build an unfair level of security for themselves at the expense of others, a sense of being distinct from others, and a global economic "Us and Them" syndrome
- The sense of righteous entitlement and their access to all forms of economic opportunity, advantages, and privileges across the world
- Their belief in models of wealth creation that turn a blind eye to the rights of "the other," and their singular pursuit of such dominance because it is even expected of them to adhere to such practices
- The norm that global domination of business is the prerogative of White people (Google not Huawei, Facebook not TikTok, Ford not Geely, Made in Japan/China)
- The notion of being more "civilized," which springs from a belief in their exceptionalism and thus the right to attain economic well-being through exerting power (economic and military) irrespective of the impact on non-White people
- The pretext of promoting liberal ideas about diversity and free speech yet being unwilling to embrace the diversity and voices of other societies, be they related to political systems, economic models, cultural norms, or even ways of behaving

Personal leadership is key and must be on full display at every level. Personal actions matter, perhaps even starting with raising children to detect and reject White privilege. Parents will need to learn and be taught. Honest conversations with children about White privilege will be difficult for White people. How should you deal with neighbors who are not like you? How will you live and assimilate into a different society that has been subject to centuries of White rule, and learn what it takes to ensure that you do not seek the privileges so often bestowed on White people and taken for granted? How will you respect people of other cultures who are economically disadvantaged? This has to be taught. It is much, much more than a simple and superficial smile with a handshake or a token donation. It takes courage, honesty, cultural awareness, and learning to change behaviors that are steeped in centuries of arrogance and a lack of empathy.

But all of this requires a certain level of consciousness and a wider worldview. This book seeks to ignite this in people who live lives that profit from White privilege. Many White people who are the beneficiaries of White privilege do not have a broad worldview, due to an upbringing that isolates them or actively denies and suppresses this very inconvenient truth. Some deflect this awkward realization and guilt trip into actions—the White savior mode—which often translates into acts of goodness or campaigns to confront others who perpetrate injustice on their own people. This is a perfect "win-win" situation from a denial mentality: benefiting from all the privileges of being White or having close proximity to White power, and then not giving up any of it while using those same privileges to be a savior, which in turn brings more prestige and reinforces that very same sense of superiority. Others engage in what can be called casual moral actions, thereby giving them a sense of achievement, association with a social movement, and relief from guilt, while they in no way let go of their privileges.

Rejecting the Three E's: Entitlement, Exclusivity, and Exceptionalism

If we are to dismantle White privilege, we will need a global rejection and dishonoring of the pursuit of entitlement, exclusivity, and exceptionalism for economic gain through the exploitation and promotion of the notion of White superiority.

What does this mean?

Centuries of power and economic dominance over others change the way any society evolves and thinks of itself in relation to others. Children are raised with odd views of the world and of other races and nationalities. This race-based conditioning stretches from what you are taught about history and economics to how you see others and a belief in your right and ability to call the shots. From childhood, this sort of conditioning distorts your understanding of the modern world, your nation's role in it, the harm felt by others, and even how you understand the notion of equality.

This sort of upbringing fosters a sense of great entitlement and superiority. When you travel, you should be granted a visa; if you are not, that country is backward or anti-Western. If you are a businessperson from a Western multinational, you expect access to markets and decision-makers; if you are not granted such access, that country is inefficient and must be required to undertake market-opening reforms and even deregulate. If you are a Western journalist, you must be able to write whatever you want, irrespective of what chaos it may trigger; if you are not, then the government is repressive. The list is long, but every example is rooted in this sense of White entitlement.

Exclusivity arises from entitlement. It comes in the form of "Whites-only clubs," seeking exclusive rights across the world, and building structures which ensure that Whites are separate from the rest and entitled to special perks. Even as these structures and special separateness have been challenged and diluted in some areas, they are still deeply rooted in the psyche of White societies. The most obvious example is the continued segregation in US cities—between wealthy White suburbs and poorer majority-minority neighborhoods—which is to some extent repeated in European cities. Across Asia, the Middle East, and Africa, this desire of Westerners for privilege is expressed in the form of exclusive housing areas, exaggerated pay scales, employment perks, exclusive shops catering to their needs, and private schools often supported by governments.

And then there is the sense of exceptionalism, which is synonymous with the American worldview. In the US, exceptionalism is sadly not confined only to White supremacists in the Republican Party but is instead a national belief system. Democrats and even some African Americans and Asian Americans in the US believe that America is a country that stands alone among the nations of the world, and thus has the right to impose itself on other regions and countries. This desire to dominate the world has its roots in White supremacy. It is ironic to me that many African Americans who know about their history of brutal subjugation due to White oppression are unable to see how American exceptionalism plays out globally as a manifestation of White racism, including in foreign policy.[2] Asian Americans who for decades tried so hard to assimilate, which even meant gaining closer proximity to Whiteness, now have to confront a new reality as racist attacks soar in 2021. This is emboldening many to speak out about identity more openly.[3]

But while the American version may be the most virulent, exceptionalism exists across the Western world, from Europe to Australia and Canada. The citizens of these Western nations are, to different degrees, immersed in a belief in their exceptionalism, and this is often expressed in their political views, steadfast defense of their own privileges, and even in blatantly racist behavior, all justified by their self-proclaimed moral authority.

To dismantle the three E's, we will need to pursue the following objectives:

1. *Raise awareness of the dynamics of White privilege and how those dynamics operate differently on different levels (i.e., individual, group, organizational, communal, national, and global).*

    The first step is raising awareness of the issue among the population. Due to the subtle nature of how privilege operates, it can be easy to accept it as the way that things "normally" work. It is only after questioning many of these accepted norms that the pervasiveness of privilege becomes clear. Let's start with education. In the West, schools and universities should offer courses that teach various aspects of how global White privilege works, why it exists, and what harms it causes. Business schools could do the same and begin to design new curriculum about business models that confront the issues of racism, do not further the idea of Western superiority, and call into question the perpetuation of White privilege. Businesses, especially MNCs, should introduce these concepts into their training and induction courses, and their onboarding processes for senior executives. They should invite people from within the company, especially those employees who have experienced the wrath of White power on a daily basis, to speak at these sessions to share their experience. Businesses should avoid leaving this training to academics and professional trainers, who are likely to sugarcoat their content to appease management.

2. *Form and popularize a new narrative that can grow over time.*

    It's one thing to criticize the mainstream narrative; it's another to propose an alternative to replace it. Only the latter will truly change people's minds, as people will gravitate back to mainstream narratives if they are provided nothing else with explanatory power.

    There is a real global need to build a body of work based both on research and storytelling about the issues related to White privilege and the harm it causes in its many manifestations. Universities across the world and especially in countries that experience the discriminatory power of White privilege should establish courses and begin the much needed and challenging task of developing this body of work based on facts and data. We need ten thousand books over the next ten years that capture the modern history of White privilege and power, ranging from business and investment decisions having to do with what books people read to the power of social media empires such as Facebook and Netflix.

These will not be published by Western publishers, who will be reluctant to work against a business model hardwired to promote Western authors and their worldviews. Thus we need publishers across Asia, Africa, and the Middle East. They should receive assistance from governments and even UN bodies such as UNESCO.

These books will become a treasured repository of information about the past century's events seen through the lens of "the others." These publishers will not be beholden to Western publishers and their tastes, which are often dictated to appeal to a Western instead of a global audience. The wealthy in these countries could easily support such an effort over a ten-year period.

Building this body of work is especially important so that we do not lose the stories that can be told by those who have experienced White privilege in the pre- and postcolonial eras, before the stories are lost as these generations pass on, and we are left only with Western versions. Governments should establish these national projects in this critical time, which will not only considerably add to the knowledge of the world but also be a very important legacy of this incredibly important period of human history as we move into a post-Western world.

3.   *Transform power structures to remove structural inequalities based on race and White superiority.*

As this new narrative is being established, the next step will be to look internally, dismantling power structures that are contingent on racial and White superiority. Power structures need to be transformed to remove the areas where communities that are discriminated against are denied opportunities and oppressed by dominant communities. In the West, doing this will not be easy, and will likely cause a pitched battle in the United States, as White privilege is even wedded to the justice system. This effort in the United States will require changes to the US Constitution and even the way the Supreme Court is configured.

Europe may find this process to be a tad easier, and the focus will need to be in four areas: foreign policy, trade, how businesses are run, and what is taught to children about global White privilege. At the geopolitical level, Europe will need to decide whether it still wants to be part of archaic Western structures that reek of imperial attitudes or whether it wants to be partners with the rest of the world—non-Western nations such as China, Nigeria, and Indonesia. *Partners* is the key word, and Europe needs to understand that this means shedding its notion of privilege in its dealings with these rising powers. One test will be the redefinition of its "White kin" special relationship with the US.

The UK in a post-Brexit world will have to adjust to being equal with others, which means not viewing the world through a lens of empire and White privilege or seeking relevance through its relationship with the United States. It should dismantle the Five Eyes Alliance, which, as has been pointed out, is well past its sell-by date, as it is essentially a White supremacist race-based club. Alternatively, the alliance can welcome non-White nations, even if it may think it an unwanted geopolitical complication. After all: What is the alliance's purpose in the twenty-first century?[4]

The World Bank and the IMF should send a strong signal to the world that they accept the need to move away from a world where White people and Western powers make the rules, toward a single global community based on meritocracy and inclusiveness. These entities must ensure that their next presidents are not from the West. Other international bodies should do the same; for too long, organizations such as the World Food Programme, various UN bodies, and the International Olympic Committee have been run like White boys' clubs.[5]

4.   *Change the rules and norms of relationships among and between White and non-White people (i.e., racist behaviors and willing subjugation).*

Institutional change is followed by behavioral change. New rules in the form of laws and regulations will help determine how different communities will relate to each other and build bridges while dismantling discrimination. This will help discourage acts of racism on the part of formerly dominant classes and reduce any willing subservience on the part of formerly oppressed classes.

For example, in countries like the United States, The use of Whiteness to intimidate Black people through law enforcement and the threat of arrest should be punishable by law. Clubs/associations in fields such as sports and business with unsaid rules about race and Whiteness should be carefully scrutinized by members and executives, especially in former colonies where they are still so very prevalent. Perks that are specific to White bosses in MNCs operating in the non-White world should also be carefully scrutinized by boards, as these benefits perpetuate White privilege and the belief in White superiority. Use of the terms *Sir* and *Madam* for expatriates should be strongly discouraged. Perks for Western journalists should not be taken for granted, as recipients may become arrogant and racist (even inadvertently). And it would be good to see international conferences in Asia and the Middle East stop allowing White executives to dominate their platforms, which elevate them and grant them advantages others do not receive.

5. *Restore the damage caused by White privilege, starting with apologies and even leading to reparations.*
    When a new baseline has been established, societies can then start to repair the damage caused by centuries of oppression. This could begin with truth commissions in such places as Australia, France, and Belgium. The postwar generation was reluctant to do this, but one hopes that young people will lead this effort. Many countries in Africa and Asia are owed apologies, and there should be clear-cut statements about the nature of the damage done. This could be overseen by the UN, or by the EU in the case of European nations.
    Apologies are a good start as a symbolic appreciation of the harm that has been done. Many Western governments have issued such apologies regarding their treatment of indigenous communities. But apologies should be backed by action, whether through monetary reparations or active efforts to ensure that oppressed communities have access to economic opportunities. Targets can be set for compensation of specific damages and monitored by an international body.
    It should also be made clear that while there is a growing call for reparations in different parts of the world that were subject to White exploitation, such as in the US, and although these discussions are critically important,[6] reparations should not be seen as a solution or panacea. Reparations, though vital to the debate, are not going to dismantle global White privilege, and thus it is crucial not to be seduced by suggestions that they serve as the solutions. Even if paid, reparations can flow right back into the existing structures that maintain White privilege. It is for this reason that I have not focused on reparations extensively in this book.

6. *Create new international institutions to reflect a more equal global society.*

Once change is achieved domestically, societies can then work to push for change internationally. A coalition of antiracist societies can work to build a truly antiracist system of global governance. This could take the form of a global postcolonial council or Office of the Ombudsman that would listen to complaints and decide on a course of action. This entity would not be based in the West but elsewhere, in, say, Africa (Johannesburg) or Asia (Singapore), with a global council of advisors not dominated by White people. It would work similarly to how the WTO works with regard to trade disputes, but would instead be focused on issues where White privilege has allowed or continues to allow Western organizations to gain controlling stakes within international political and business systems (e.g., the cartel of accounting firms and rating agencies).

Changing Societies: Dishonoring Privilege at All Levels of Society

White privilege is pervasive both within countries and globally, affecting all levels of society. It therefore needs to be fought at all levels if we are truly to create a better world not plagued by privilege. Those involved in these different levels of society can use their positions to help combat global White privilege, in addition to pushing against domestic White privilege. These actions too will differ for White societies and for non-White societies. For example, how a society such as France looks at its history and continuing influence in Francophone Africa and thus how the country takes steps to reverse the most adverse aspects of White privilege will be very different from how one of France's former colonies such as Senegal or Burkina Faso decides to teach its history or reject all manifestations of White privilege.

Dismantle, Don't Destroy: Act Now

The next several sections will outline examples of the actions that can be taken at all layers of society, starting with the family.

The Family

The core of the family relationship is between parents and their children: parents in Western societies have a responsibility to guide their children away from global White privilege and toward a broader understanding of global cultures. Depending on their economic status, parents may start with making their children acutely aware of their privileged circumstances. This requires a shift away from addressing just the standard symbols of privilege normally pursued by parents. The responsibility is on parents to know what narratives they teach and to ensure that their children are exposed to the breadth of cultures out there; parents need to scrutinize everything, ranging from the movies their children watch to the books they read, from the friends they have to the role models they follow.

Parents will even have to question the schools their children attend if these schools do not allow them to grow up with kids of other races, nationalities, and religions. It is not good enough just to enroll kids in elite liberal arts classes and proudly call them citizens of the world.

In the non-Western world, elites will need to confront their desire to Westernize their kids at all costs because they see Westernization as the passport to a better university and thus better prospects. They need to strike a balance so that their kids can have the best of both worlds—easier said than done given the well-entrenched structures for upward mobility. In the world of social media, families can be strong anchors, offering support to children so that they do not become victims of mind capture and are not overwhelmed by the tsunami of Westernization and the desire to seek Whiteness for success.

The Neighborhood

Neighborhoods—in Western societies—have long been a vehicle for discrimination and segregation, as whole demographics, whether defined by race, religion, culture, or wealth, are excluded from more well off communities with better access to public services. As every disenfranchised person knows: your address matters and it can shape your life. Similar patterns, though on a different scale, persist in former colonies, seen in the way expatriates are treated and where they live in their exclusive neighborhoods. The same symbols of cultural capital that protect domestic White privilege also protect global White privilege: a neighborhood that rejects these symbols would be doing its part to help undo global structural discrimination. City planners have a very important role to play in not allowing forms of apartheid to persist. These city planning efforts will take different forms in Western nations such as the UK, the US, or Germany, where persistent ghettoes need to be reshaped and integrated into predominantly White communities.

In the developing world, planners need to ensure that market forces are not allowed to shape the sorts of outcomes that encourage segregation and the reinforcement of privilege.

In both the Western and the non-Western worlds, people make decisions that shape racial and class divides, the perpetuation of segregation, and the economic ripple effects these create. Thus everyone, including city planners and policymakers, should provide encouragement to people who consciously decide to integrate by making the choice to live with others and learn from them in a multicultural society. These individual decisions shape neighborhoods, and if people are serious about dismantling racial divides, then they need to make conscious choices around these issues and not just be swayed by decades-old biases and prejudices.

We all have a responsibility to build the neighborhoods we desire rather than be observers or tenants willing only to indulge in the privileges we "purchase" to protect ourselves from fears about others.

Schools and Education Institutions

Education at all levels enables the reproduction of White privilege by prioritizing Western and White history and schools of thought, while actively omitting the dark side of Western and White history, as well as silencing or diminishing the viewpoints and achievements of non-Whites and their cultures and traditions.

Western education institutions need to recognize the role they play in shaping contemporary White privilege and must be required to deeply scrutinize curriculums and education practices to determine what areas can be improved on to better represent non-Whites and the ugly truths of White history.

In the non-Western world, there is a more careful balancing act to be performed. The aspects of Western education that have contributed to human progress should not be rejected in some naïve approach to dismantling White privilege or thwarting Westernization. That is not what this book is calling for. The key areas where there is a need for a complete review and the inculcating of local knowledge and building of local approaches are in such spheres as the teaching of history, economics, culture, business education, development, and foreign policy.

Western universities and business schools should begin to understand that the very economics and business ideas they teach perpetuate institutionalized White privilege at a global scale, enabling domination through the furthering of old and out-of-date economic theories that have relied on the exploitation of "developing" (i.e. non-White, non-Western) countries.

The Workplace

Global businesses, by virtue of being predominantly from the West, have often acted as the vanguard of global White privilege. Some have operated in regions such as Asia and Africa for a century, yet still have management teams dominated by White people. Having diversity and inclusion teams headed by "natives" seems to be as far as many are willing to go. I remember running a two-day workshop in London for one of the world's leading advisory firms; even though this firm offers diversity and inclusion services globally, the entire group of twenty workshop participants was made up of White men from Europe and the United States.

Western global businesses need to take real action to eradicate these archaic attitudes and structures that favor White people from the home country, which in turn preserves and reinforces White privilege within their organization. They will need to move beyond token changes and lip service to true diversity and inclusion, which has become an industry in itself.

I would argue that this drive for diversity needs to be perhaps strengthened and that a board member should be given the responsibility for transitioning the company away from exercising White privilege in international promotions and career advancements as well as in the bestowing of perks and privileges. International businesses need to look at who runs their overseas operations: White managers should not be managing overseas offices outside the West if there are better-qualified locals. And asking an international Western headhunting firms with close relationships to senior management to do the recruiting is often not the answer as they often share the same worldview, move in the same circles, and rarely push the case for change. International businesses in the non-Western world should also stop the discriminatory policy of paying White professionals a premium to perform jobs others can.

Further, these companies should examine their products: Do their goods and services promote Western and White privilege or cause cultural harm? They should also examine their frame of reference: Do they expect their diverse and international stakeholders to think and act like Westerners?

In the midst of all of this soul searching in the wake of the George Floyd murder and the Black Lives Matter movement it was reassuring to see the launch in March 2021 of the World Economic Forum's Partnering for Racial Justice in Business initiative. It is a coalition of organizations and their C-suite leaders committed to leveraging their collective power to build equitable and just workplaces for professionals with underrepresented racial and ethnic identities. Here too the challenge will be to avoid the trap of simply focusing on the issue of racism—important as it is—and actions that are easy to take, but to actually address racism along with the issue of White privilege and its harm. That will be the mark of real change.[7]

Professional Bodies

International professional bodies such as those that represent influential trades—accounting, medicine, architecture and planning, writers, and various sports (to name a few)—also help solidify White privilege at both the local and global levels, by determining which people and ideas are worth listening to. White and Western experts are presented as the best sources of expertise and insight compared to their non-Western counterparts in many of these bodies. Bodies need to question whom they consider valuable sources of expertise, especially if they purport to be global.

If these organizations are committed to building a fairer and more equitable world, they need to have an honest conversation about their makeup and leadership. Their governing bodies should begin a conversation to address the issues raised in this book. They could ask an independent advisor to examine whether they are guilty, even unwittingly, of perpetuating White privilege. Recommendations, including some made in this book, can easily be assembled for all members to vote on, thereby democratizing the process of dismantling White privilege in international professional bodies.

Another clear area for professional bodies to send signals about change is in the way they seek expert opinions from external sources. The leading consultants are often the usual suspects in Western and typically Anglo-Saxon firms. Irrespective of what the issues may be, the same consultants are sought to lend legitimacy to any given advice, even when it is obvious that local insights would be much more valuable. This is an area where White privilege is deeply entrenched and long overdue for an overhaul.

Conferences and panels need to give non-Whites equal status on the podium. Why do Asian conference organizers and leading speaker bureaus (usually Western) always feel obliged to overpopulate their keynote

speaker slots with Westerners? Local sponsors of the events run by professional organizations should challenge these racist views and cast side
their subservience.

The Media

The global Western media as described in this book helps disseminate narratives around the globe and also locally, helping solidify narratives of
White and Western supremacy. Even if on occasions unintentional or not
deliberate, the dominance of Western outlets such as the BBC and CNN
in global media coverage coupled with even unconscious biases will privilege a Western framing of world events, not to mention culture and value
systems.

Outlets need to look at what they promote: Are they promoting Western and White narratives over a more representative global discussion,
especially in such areas as geopolitics, economics, and business-related
news? What is the balance between Western and non-Western commentators? What books, stories, and ads do these outlets feature? Will they
allow a non-Western commentator to comment critically on a Western
story?

Although it will undoubtedly be difficult to transition to a post-
Western media landscape given the entrenched position of Western media, doing so is incumbent on business leaders, investors, and governments.
This will be an area of great interest to non-Western governments as they
seek to counter the power of the Western media and what they see as its
biases. However, they often fall into the trap of promoting anti-Western
rhetoric rather than produce content that reflects the reality in their countries or region or that shares the wealth of insights from their societies. It
should be made clear that there is great opportunity for investors in Asia
and elsewhere to tap into a growing market for non-Western narratives
essential to balancing Western dominance.

The good news is that there are now a number of non-Western media outlets that Westerners interested in different perspectives can tune
into. These non-Western sources include Al Jazeera, China Global TV,
Channel News Asia, and NHK from Tokyo, to name a few. But how many
audiences in the West are interested in the fascinating non-Western insights these outlets can provide? People in the US and Europe will need
to shed their insular and inward-looking attitudes with regard to learning about other societies. They will need to make an effort to be informed
about the global majority, and it will require them to fundamentally

overcome long-held biases and prejudices about these regions and countries and their media.

Civil Society

Civil society groups around the world are critical in the fight against injustice and White privilege. These groups can agitate for change and push leaders to make substantial reforms. But the global civil society landscape in terms of influence and coverage is dominated by international Western NGOs. Willing partners in the Western media are all too ready to believe the Western liberal version of the story and sensationalize issues rather than do the hard and less glamorous task of working with locals to find solutions to complex challenges which cannot be readily defined through their liberal ideological lens. This is White liberal power in action.[8]

International civil society groups should conduct complete reviews of how they operate in non-Western countries and question the positions they take, which are often imperial in nature, riddled with White savior attitudes, and counterproductive, but which are pursued because the groups garner financial support from Western sources. This funding helps pay for expatriate lifestyles for the Westerners who even to this day are the leaders of these organizations in Asia and Africa despite an abundance of talent in the two regions. If these organizations are truly committed to social justice, they need to be asking themselves some serious questions about how they play a part in promoting White privilege.

To local governments and civil society groups, these Western civil society groups and organizations are often viewed as unified by a wish to preserve the privileges they already possess, to the exclusion of others. Groups need to ask themselves whether their "moral authority" is a product of global White privilege. They will thus also need to combat discrimination within their international networks—something that many have found very difficult to confront—and ask for new rules and laws.

Non-Western governments should resist the temptation to curb and ban these groups' activities, as this ultimately plays into the hands of those who would seek to judge the governments as unworthy, corrupt, or undemocratic. Instead, they should be more strategic, seeking dialogue and finding ways to leverage the mission of these organizations and their considerable power to resolve issues of mutual interest. Local civil society organizations too need to break away from decades of adopting the positions and issues of Western organizations with no position of their own, thus stymieing the growth of local ideas and ecosystems. The same can be said of local public intellectuals and even academics who are all too ready to support Western positions without caring to scrutinize the validity and intentions of those positions.

National Governance

Western countries need to have a conversation about not just domestic White privilege but also global White privilege. Many Western countries have benefited, and continue to benefit, from global White privilege, in positioning themselves as role models for the rest of the world to follow. Changing this will be harder than imagined, as it is often intertwined with foreign policy. But if Western societies—where support for Black Lives Matter seemed to surge in the summer of 2020—are truly willing to adapt to the idea of sharing power in a post-Western world for the sake of global equality, then one has to hope that perhaps the millennials and Generation Z will make this their goal and demand this of their governments.

Non-Western countries, by contrast, need to determine where and how they can undo centuries of global White privilege. This should never be in the form of xenophobic anti-Western policies steeped in misplaced nationalism but instead as well-designed strategies and policies that help their societies adopt the best of both worlds, as mentioned before, yet be strong enough to withstand the assault of Westernization. Key areas will be certain aspects of education as described in this book, foreign policy, media and entertainment, and the nature of certain investments and rules of business.

Global Geopolitics

Global White privilege is institutionalized primarily in the systems of global governance, ranging from international institutions such as the IMF and the World Bank to the dominant players in critical economic sectors. These structures reinforce the prime placement of Western countries atop the rules-based global order.

Either the systems of global governance need to be radically reformed through international cooperation to allow for greater non-Western representation or alternatives need to be established by emerging non-Western powers to balance against a system that currently protects and preserves Western privilege. This means changing the leadership of groups such as the UN Security Council and breaking the de facto agreement that preserves Western leadership of the IMF and the World Bank.

Act Now!

This book has covered the key areas where I believe we can act, and where those with power and influence, especially political, business, and community leaders, can make a real difference in demanding and initiating change. It was not possible in just one short book to cover every facet of global White privilege. Additional areas that I hope others will examine in the future include religion, sexual politics, health care, and the role of technology, among others.

DISMANTLING GLOBAL WHITE PRIVILEGE

T he purpose of this book is to stimulate people around the world to
rethink the way they understand racism, White privilege, and White
superiority so that they can take specific positive actions. The objective is
to provide a framework for a constructive conversation, with a focus on
solutions.

The discussion points in the following lists are meant to serve as tools
to open a conversation. They cannot cover all aspects of what people want
to discuss after having read the book, but I hope they offer a safe framing
with which to begin long-overdue exchanges at various levels of society.

Being Me!
- What is your understanding of global White privilege as it affects
  your life?
- As a successful White person, do you understand that some of what
  you have achieved in life is due to the White privileges woven into
  the fabric of your society and into our globalized world? If you reject this idea, why?
- If you do accept this idea, then try to identify three areas that you
  can work on to change things. Have a discussion with friends and
  see where it leads.
- Are you willing to accept that non-White people in your community face more challenges if they have not sought the social, cultural,
  and economic behaviors associated with "Whiteness"? And even if

they have, that they do not receive the same privileges as you? How does that make you feel?

- As a non-White person, how has White privilege affected your life beyond typical acts of racism? Are you able to speak to White friends, family, or colleagues about your experiences?
- As a non-White person, do you accept that certain aspects of how you live and act are due to and framed by a desire to be closer to Whiteness and to seek the socioeconomic benefits of White privilege?
- Have you reached a certain status in your professional life by "playing White" in a White-dominated workplace or by living in a White neighborhood and acquiring White friends?
- As a White person, what does White privilege mean to you? Do you recoil when it is suggested that you may be a beneficiary? Or does it force you to confront some inconvenient truths and provide an opportunity to change your way of life?
- Does your recognition of White privilege make you reflect on the world? Does it prompt you to reframe your understanding of the world we live in and how it works?

Family Affair
- As a parent, do you think that it is important to raise your children to understand that White privilege exists and is unjust?
- What aspects of your children's being beneficiaries of White privilege do you think you are most concerned about? What actions would you take to get your children to understand these privileges, and how would you withhold these privileges from them? How old should they be when they are made aware?
- Assuming you know families who are non-White and are disadvantaged by not being White, how do you see yourself opening a conversation with them to learn and share? How do you get your children involved?
- If you are non-White and understand that seeking White privilege/proximity is a route to success, how do you get your kids not to seek Whiteness so as not to lose their culture and traditions? How would you engage them in an early discussion, and which aspects would be most important? What would the most difficult trade-offs be?
- How many of your conversations with your family about the injustice of White privilege turn into racist banter or anger and resent-

ment? What do you think can be done to get your family to understand what they can do to not perpetuate privileges (if they are White) or to not see themselves as victims and accept their treatment as the norm?

- If you are White and a privileged millennial, are you comfortable speaking about your privileges to your siblings and parents or even relatives? What safe topics would you use to start the conversation, and what actions would you take?

- If you are non-White and a privileged millennial, are you comfortable questioning how you have co-opted being White?

Team Work—See Nothing, Say Nothing?

- If you are a White person in a predominantly White society and workplace, are you aware of how White privilege works against non-Whites in the workplace, in ways that go beyond the company's best-laid plans to ensure diversity and inclusion?

- If you are a White person in a predominantly non-White society and workplace, are you aware of the privileges that come your way just by virtue of being White? What are the downsides? Are you conscious of how you rely on White privilege for its benefits?

- If you are non-White in a predominantly White society, how does it make you feel when White privilege hinders your career prospects? Do you just expect this to happen because you believe it is the norm? Or do you use a strategy of getting closer to Whiteness to achieve success? Think of some examples and speak to colleagues. Would your management entertain your viewpoints on this topic?

- Does your workplace have a forum for employees and managers to get together and discuss how White privilege manifests itself in the workplace? Have you or your team considered how White privilege affects corporate culture and the careers of non-White employees?

- If you are an executive, do you believe that some of your business decisions unintentionally or inadvertently promote White privilege? If you do, then give examples and consider actions that can be taken.

- From a gender point of view, what are similar and differing ways in which White men and women leverage White privilege?

- What are the similar and differing ways that non-White men and women seek Whiteness to succeed in a White-dominated environment, and why? Who typically succeeds, and why?

The Organization—Leadership in a Post-Western World

- As a leader of an international organization, are you able to list three areas where your organization perpetuates White privilege? If so, would you be willing to take these issues to your board? How open would they be to including this topic and your listed issues in the next meeting?
- How often have you discussed the issue of White privilege with your executive team? Are you comfortable doing so? Would they welcome it and be able to have a frank discussion?
- Do you think your diversity and inclusion strategy should start to address White privilege issues and how White privilege is often the elephant in the room?
- Assuming that White privilege is an issue you want to tackle, where would you start?
- If your organization or company has a history rooted in White privilege and supremacy, are you conscious of it, and is it a subject of discussion?

NOTES

Preface

1. Tarling, Nicholas. *Imperialism in Southeast Asia: "A Fleeting Passing Phase."* London: Routledge, 2006.
2. Tharoor, Shashi. *An Era of Darkness: The British Empire in India.* Melbourne, Australia: Scribe, 2016; Mishra, Pankaj. *From the Ruins of Empire: The Revolt against the West and the Remaking of Asia.* London: Penguin Books, 2015.
3. Simpson, Thula. *Umkhonto We Sizwe: The ANC's Armed Struggle.* Cape Town, South Africa: Penguin Random House South Africa, 2016; Chiwapu, Dhazi. *Struggle for Liberation in Zimbabwe: The Eye of War Collaborator (Mujibha).* Bloomington, IN: Trafford Publishing, 2013.
4. Baker, Paul, Costas Gabrielatos, Majid KhosraviNik, Michał Krzyżanowski, Tony McEnery, and Ruth Wodak. "A Useful Methodological Synergy? Combining Critical Discourse Analysis and Corpus Linguistics to Examine Discourses of Refugees and Asylum Seekers in the UK Press." *Discourse & Society* 19, no. 3 (2008): 273–306. https://doi.org/10.1177/0957926508088962.
5. Musa, M. Bakri. *The Malay Dilemma Revisited: Race Dynamics in Modern Malaysia.* North Charleston, SC: Create Space Independent Publishing Platform, 2017; Gidla, Sujatha. *Ants among Elephants: An Untouchable Family and the Making of Modern India.* Old Saybrook, CT: Tantor Media, 2018; Telles, Edward Eric. *Race in Another America: The Significance of Skin Color in Brazil.* Princeton, NJ: Princeton University Press, 2006.

Introduction

1. Wong, Alexandra. *Made in Malaysia: Stories of Hometown Heroes and Hidden Gems.* Petaling Jaya, Malaysia: MPH Group Publishing, 2014.

2. Çoban, Savaş. *Media, Ideology and Hegemony.* Chicago: Haymarket Books, 2019.

3. Zeilig, Leo. *Lumumba: Africa's Lost Leader.* London: Haus, 2015; X., Malcolm, and Alex Haley. *The Autobiography of Malcolm X.* New York: Ballantine Books, 2015.

4. Crothers, Lane. *Globalization and American Popular Culture.* Lanham, MD: Rowman & Littlefield, 2021.

5. Tambo, Oliver, and E. S. Reddy. *Oliver Tambo and the Struggle against Apartheid.* New Delhi: Sterling Publishers, in collaboration with Namedia Foundation, 1987.

6. "Covid 'Hate Crimes' against Asian Americans on Rise." *BBC News.* BBC, April 2, 2021. https://www.bbc.com/news/world-us-canada-56218684.

7. Prideaux, J. "Is America Irredeemably Racist?" *The Economist,* May 21, 2021, https://www.economist.com/podcasts/2021/05/21/is-america-irredeemably-racist.

8. DiAngelo, Robin J. *White Fragility: Why It's So Hard for White People to Talk about Racism.* Boston: Beacon Press, 2020.

9. Fanon, Frantz. *Black Skin, White Masks.* Trans. Richard Philcox. New York: Grove Press, 1952.

10. Hickel, Jason. "Apartheid in the World Bank and the IMF." *International Monetary Fund News.* Al Jazeera, November 30, 2020. https://www.aljazeera.com/opinions/2020/11/26/it-is-time-to-decolonise-the-world-bank-and-the-imf.

11. Flitter, Emily. "She Spent 16 Years as Morgan Stanley's Diversity Chief. Now She's Suing." *New York Times,* June 16, 2020. https://www.nytimes.com/2020/06/16/business/morgan-stanley-discrimination-lawsuit.html.

12. "Black Journalists Weigh In on a Newsroom Reckoning." NPR, July 2, 2020. https://www.npr.org/2020/07/02/886845421/Black-journalists-weigh-in-on-a-newsroom-reckoning.

13. Thiong'o, Ngũgĩ wa. *Decolonizing the Mind: The Politics of Language in African Literature.* London: J. Currey, 1986.

14. Carmichael, Stokely, and Charles V. Hamilton. *Black Power: The Politics of Liberation.* New York: Random House, 1967.

15. Frantz, *Black Skin.*

16. Fanon, Frantz. *The Wretched of the Earth.* New York: Grove Press, 2004.

17. Pailey, Robtel Neajai. "De-Centring the 'White Gaze' of Development." *Development and Change* 51, no. 3 (2019): 729–45. https://doi.org/10.1111/dech.12550.

18. Appiah, Kwame Anthony. "There Is No Such Thing as Western Civilisation." *Guardian,* November 28, 2017. https://www.theguardian.com/world/2016/nov/09/Western-civilisation-appiah-reith-lecture.

19. Bhambra, Gurminder K. "Postcolonial and Decolonial Reconstructions." In *Connected Sociologies*, 117–40. Bloomsbury Collections. London: Bloomsbury Academic, 2014.

20. Nair, Chandran. *The Sustainable State: The Future of Government, Economy, and Society.* Oakland, CA: Berrett-Koehler, 2018.

21. Hoffman, Philip T. *Why Did Europe Conquer the World?* Princeton, NJ: Princeton University Press.

22. Robinson, Cedric J. *Black Marxism, Revised and Updated Third Edition: The Making of the Black Radical Tradition.* Chapel Hill: University of North Carolina Press, 1983.

Chapter 1: Geopolitics of Dominance

1. Wright, Thomas. "The Return to Great-Power Rivalry Was Inevitable." *Atlantic*, September 12, 2018. https://www.theatlantic.com/international/archive/2018/09/liberal-international-order-free-world-trump-authoritarianism/569881/.

2. Kozloff, Nikolas. "Geopolitics of Racism: The NSA and the 'Five Eyes' Network." *HuffPost*, January 23, 2014. https://www.huffpost.com/entry/geopolitics-of-racism-nsa_b_4206263?ncid=engmodushpmg00000006.

3. Jacques, Martin. *When China Rules the World: The End of the Western World and the Birth of a New Global Order.* London: Penguin, 2012; Ayres, Alyssa. *Our Time Has Come: How India Is Making Its Place in the World.* New York: Oxford University Press, 2020.

4. Dole, Charles F. "The Right and Wrong of the Monroe Doctrine." *Atlantic*, June 19, 2017. https://www.theatlantic.com/magazine/archive/1905/04/the-right-and-wrong-of-the-monroe-doctrine/530856/.

5. Bevins, Vincent. *The Jakarta Method: Washington's Anticommunist Crusade and the Mass Murder Program That Shaped Our World.* New York: Public Affairs, 2021.

6. Adomaitis, Nerijus, and Stephanie Nebehay. "U.N. Food Agency WFP Hails Peace Nobel as Call to Action against Hunger." *Reuters*, October 9, 2020. https://www.reuters.com/article/us-nobel-prize-peace-idUSKBN26U0UO.

7. Lopes, Carlos. "Economic Growth and Inequality: The New Post-Washington Consensus." *RCCS Annual Review*, no. 4 (2012). https://doi.org/10.4000/rccsar.426.

8. "RCEP: Asia-Pacific Countries Form World's Largest Trading Bloc." *BBC News*. BBC, November 16, 2020. https://www.bbc.com/news/world-asia-54949260.

9. United Nations Digital Library. "A Global Call for Concrete Action for the Elimination of Racism, Racial Discrimination, Xenophobia and Related Intolerance and the Comprehensive Implementation of and Follow-up

to the Durban Declaration and Programme of Action." United Nations. https://digitallibrary.un.org/record/3896183?ln=en.

10. Mahbubani, Kishore, Jeffery Sng, and Hidayati Kasuma Abdul Hadi. *The ASEAN Miracle: A Catalyst for Peace*. Ipoh, Malaysia: Media Masters Publishing, 2017.

11. Dollar, David. "The AIIB and the 'One Belt, One Road.'" Brookings, September 7, 2017. https://www.brookings.edu/opinions/the-aiib-and-the-one-belt-one-road/.

12. Zoellick, Robert B. "Whither China: From Membership to Responsibility?" Archive, US Department of State, September 21, 2005. https://2001-2009.state.gov/s/d/former/zoellick/rem/53682.htm.

Chapter 2: The Retelling of History

1. National Geographic Society. "Taj Mahal." *National Geographic*, November 9, 2012. https://www.nationalgeographic.org/media/taj-basics/.

2. Safi, Michael. "Churchill's Policies Contributed to 1943 Bengal Famine—Study." *Guardian*, March 29, 2019. https://www.theguardian.com/world/2019/mar/29/winston-churchill-policies-contributed-to-1943-bengal-famine-study.

3. Dahlgreen, Will. "The British Empire Is 'Something to Be Proud Of.'" *YouGov*, July 26, 2014. https://yougov.co.uk/topics/politics/articles-reports/2014/07/26/britain-proud-its-empire.

4. Tunzelmann, Alex von. "The Imperial Myths Driving Brexit." *Atlantic*, August 12, 2019. https://www.theatlantic.com/international/archive/2019/08/imperial-myths-behind-brexit/595813/.

5. Andersen, Kurt. "How the U.S. Lost Its Mind." *Atlantic*, April 3, 2020. https://www.theatlantic.com/magazine/archive/2017/09/how-america-lost-its-mind/534231/.

6. Tharoor, Shashi. "'But What about the Railways . . . ?' The Myth of Britain's Gifts to India." *Guardian*, March 8, 2017. https://www.theguardian.com/world/2017/mar/08/india-britain-empire-railways-myths-gifts.

7. Maynard, John. *Fight for Liberty and Freedom: The Origins of Australian Aboriginal Activism*. Canberra, Australia: Aboriginal Studies Press, 2007.

8. *Acknowledging Genocide* (HRW Report—Leave None to Tell the Story: Genocide in Rwanda, March 1999). Human Rights Watch. https://www.hrw.org/reports/1999/rwanda/Geno15-8-02.htm.

9. Wheatcroft, Geoffrey. "The Myth of the Good War." *Guardian*, December 9, 2014. https://www.theguardian.com/news/2014/dec/09/-sp-myth-of-the-good-war.

10. Wingfield-Hayes, Rupert. "Hiroshima Bomb: Japan Marks 75 Years since Nuclear Attack." *BBC News.* BBC, August 6, 2020. https://www.bbc.com /news/world-asia-53660059.

11. "Was the US Justified in Dropping Atomic Bombs on Hiroshima and Nagasaki during the Second World War?" *HistoryExtra*, November 26, 2020. https://www.historyextra.com/period/second-world-war/atomic-bomb -hiroshima-nagasaki-justified-us-debate-bombs-death-toll-japan-how-many -died-nuclear/.

12. "Secret War in Laos." Legacies of War. http://legaciesofwar.org/about-laos /secret-war-laos/.

13. "Agent Orange Still Linked to Hormone Imbalances in Babies in Vietnam." *ScienceDaily*, September 26, 2017. https://www.sciencedaily.com/releases /2017/09/170926091427.htm.

14. "The Vietnamese Lawsuit." *Agent Orange Record*, December 4, 2020. https:// agentorangerecord.com/the-vietnamese-lawsuit/.

15. Goodwin, Gerald F. "Black and White in Vietnam." *New York Times*, July 18, 2017. https://www.nytimes.com/2017/07/18/opinion/racism-vietnam-war .html.

16. Mahajan, Rahul, Tari Tessier, Derrick Michael, Rob Hurley, and Jo Cummings. "'We Think the Price Is Worth It.'" FAIR, February 8, 2016. https:// fair.org/extra/we-think-the-price-is-worth-it/.

17. Mitter, Rana. "Forgotten Ally? China's Unsung Role in World War II." CNN, September 1, 2015. https://www.cnn.com/2015/08/31/opinions/china-wwii -forgotten-ally-rana-mitter/index.html.

18. Syed, Hassan. "Arabic Literature's Influence on Renaissance Europe: Beyond Bias," May 2019. https://www.researchgate.net/publication/333516912 _Arabic_Literature's_influence_on_Renaissance_Europe_Beyond_Bias.

19. Lee, Jun Jie. "Colonialism and ASEAN Identity: Inherited 'Mental Barriers' Hindering the Formation of a Collective ASEAN Identity." *Kyoto Review of Southeast Asia*, January 4, 2019. https://kyotoreview.org/trendsetters /colonialism-asean-identity/.

20. Mancini, Donato Paolo. "Pfizer and BioNTech's COVID-19 Vaccine Found to Be 90% Effective." *Financial Times*, November 9, 2020. https://www.ft.com /content/9bde4bff-acf0-4c2a-a0d0-5ed597186496.

21. Barrington, Lisa, and Alexander Cornwell. "China's Sinopharm Begins Late Stage Trial of COVID-19 Vaccine in UAE." *Reuters*, July 16, 2020. https:// www.reuters.com/article/us-health-coronavirus-emirates-vaccine-idUSKCN 24H14T.

22. Glenza, Jessica. "Coronavirus: How Wealthy Nations Are Creating a 'Vaccine Apartheid.'" *Guardian*, March 31, 2021. https://www.theguardian

.com/world/2021/mar/30/coronavirus-vaccine-distribution-global-disparity.

23. Bump, Philip. "15 Years after the Iraq War Began, the Death Toll Is Still Murky." *Washington Post*, March 29, 2019. https://www.washingtonpost.com/news/politics/wp/2018/03/20/15-years-after-it-began-the-death-toll-from-the-iraq-war-is-still-murky/.

Chapter 3: The World of Business

1. Chang, Ha-Joon, J. Gabriel Palma, and D. H. Whittaker. *Financial Liberalization and the Asian Crisis*. London: Palgrave Macmillan, 2001.

2. PricewaterhouseCoopers. "Global Top 100 Companies—June 2020 Update." PwC. https://www.pwc.com/gx/en/services/audit-assurance/publications/global-top-100-companies.html.

3. "Business Roundtable Redefines the Purpose of a Corporation to Promote 'An Economy That Serves All Americans': Updated Statement Moves away from Shareholder Primacy, Includes Commitment to All Stakeholders." Business Roundtable, August 19, 2019. https://www.businessroundtable.org/business-roundtable-redefines-the-purpose-of-a-corporation-to-promote-an-economy-that-serves-all-americans.

4. Wright, Tom, and Bradley Hope. *Billion Dollar Whale: The Man Who Fooled Wall Street, Hollywood, and the World*. London: Scribe, 2019.

5. Parker, Martin. "Why We Should Bulldoze the Business School." *Guardian*, April 27, 2018. https://www.theguardian.com/news/2018/apr/27/bulldoze-the-business-school.

6. Sheppard, Emma. "'You're Buying into an Incredibly Smart Group of People': The Enduring Pull of the MBA." *Guardian*, January 28, 2020. https://www.theguardian.com/education/2020/jan/28/youre-buying-into-an-incredibly-smart-group-of-people-the-enduring-pull-of-the-mba.

7. Sorkin, Andrew Ross. *Too Big to Fail: The Inside Story of How Wall Street and Washington Fought to Save the Financial System—and Themselves*. New York: Penguin Books, 2018.

8. McCrum, Dan. "Executive at Wirecard Suspected of Using Forged Contracts." *Financial Times*, January 30, 2019. https://www.ft.com/content/03a5e318-2479-11e9-8ce6-5db4543da632.

9. Palma, Stefania, and Dan McCrum. "Police Raid Wirecard's Singapore Offices." *Financial Times*, February 8, 2019. https://www.ft.com/content/f6e8a58a-2b93-11e9-88a4-c32129756dd8.

10. Kollewe, Julia. "Watchdog Investigates EY Audit of Scandal-Hit NMC Health." *Guardian*, May 4, 2020. https://www.theguardian.com/business/2020/may/04/watchdog-investigates-ey-audit-of-scandal-hit-nmc-health.

11. Sender, Henry. "The Luckin Scandal: Fake Sales, Power Struggles and a 'Broken Model.'" *Nikkei Asian Review*, July 8, 2020. https://asia.nikkei.com/Spotlight/The-Big-Story/The-Luckin-scandal-fake-sales-power-struggles-and-a-broken-model.

12. Lewis, Michael. *The Big Short: Inside the Doomsday Machine*. Melbourne, Australia: Penguin, 2016.

13. International Monetary Fund Research Department. "Global Prospects and Policies." In *World Economic Outlook, April 2011: Tensions from the Two-Speed Recovery: Unemployment, Commodities, and Capital Flows*. International Monetary Fund, 2011. https://doi.org/10.5089/9781616350598.081.

Chapter 4: Media and Publishing

1. Gathara, Patrick. "The Problem Is Not 'Negative' Western Media Coverage of Africa." *Freedom of the Press News*. Al Jazeera, July 9, 2019. https://www.aljazeera.com/opinions/2019/7/9/the-problem-is-not-negative-Western-media-coverage-of-africa.

2. Nakamura, David. "Beyond the Pandemic, Asian American Leaders Fear U.S. Conflict with China Will Fan Racist Backlash." *Washington Post*, March 18, 2021. https://www.washingtonpost.com/national-security/biden-china-asian-american-racism/2021/03/17/69eb4bc6-873d-11eb-82bc-e58213caa38e_story.html.

3. Menadue, John. "Why Has There Been a Spike in Anti-Asian Hate? The NY Times Answers Their Own Questions." Pearls and Irritations, March 23, 2021. https://johnmenadue.com/why-has-there-been-a-spike-in-anti-asian-hate-the-ny-times-answers-their-own-questions/.

4. Sullivan, Margaret. "The Media Loved Trump's Show of Military Might. Are We Really Doing This Again?" *Washington Post*, April 8, 2017. https://www.washingtonpost.com/lifestyle/style/the-media-loved-trumps-show-of-military-might-are-we-really-doing-this-again/2017/04/07/01348256-1ba2-11e7-9887-1a5314b56a08_story.html.

5. Borpujari, Priyanka. "The Problem with 'Fixers.'" *Columbia Journalism Review*. https://www.cjr.org/special_report/fixers.php.

6. Borpujari, "Problem with 'Fixers.'"

7. Perkins, John. *Confessions of an Economic Hit Man*. New York: Plume, 2006.

Chapter 5: Education

1. Raikhan, Sadykova, Myrzabekov Moldakhmet, Myrzabekova Ryskeldy, and Moldakhmetkyzy Alua. "The Interaction of Globalization and Culture in the Modern World." *Procedia—Social and Behavioral Sciences* 122 (2014): 8–12. https://doi.org/10.1016/j.sbspro.2014.01.1294.

2. Lo, Alex. "Why the West Is So Focused on Hong Kong." *South China Morning Post*, May 26, 2020. https://www.scmp.com/comment/opinion/article /3086203/why-West-so-focused-hong-kong.

3. Akhtar, Allana. "The 15 Biggest Private Donations to Universities by the Ultra Rich." *Business Insider*, May 21, 2019. https://www.businessinsider.in /the-15-biggest-private-donations-to-universities-by-the-ultra-rich /articleshow/69435257.cms.

4. Chow, Jason. "Hong Kong Tops List of Foreign Donors to U.S. Schools." *Wall Street Journal*, September 22, 2014. https://www.wsj.com/articles/hong-kong -tops-list-of-donors-to-u-s-schools-1411401637.

5. Wu, Hantian, and Qiang Zha. "Chinese Higher Education, History Of." *Encyclopedia of Educational Philosophy and Theory*, 2018, 1–7. https://doi.org /10.1007/978-981-287-532-7_598-1.

6. Sterns, Olivia. "Muslim Inventions That Shaped the Modern World." CNN, July 22, 2015. https://www.cnn.com/2015/07/22/world/muslim-inventions /index.html.

7. Reardon, Sara. "'Elite' Researchers Dominate Citation Space." *Nature News*, March 1, 2021. https://www.nature.com/articles/d41586-021-00553-7.

8. Tagore, Rabindranath, and G. M. Muncker. *Gitanjali*. Simbach am Inn, Germany: Hyperion-Verlag, 2013.

9. Nair, Chandran. "Developed World Missing the Point on Modern Slavery." *Time*, June 20, 2016. https://time.com/4374377/slavery-developed -developing-world-index-slave-labor/.

10. Samuelson, Paul A., William D. Nordhaus, Sudip Chaudhuri, and Anindya Sen. *Economics*. Boston: McGraw-Hill, 2020.

11. Parker, Martin. "Why We Should Bulldoze the Business School." *Guardian*, April 27, 2018. https://www.theguardian.com/news/2018/apr/27/bulldoze -the-business-school.

Chapter 6: Culture and Entertainment

1. Greenburg, Zack O'Malley. "The World's Top-Earning Musicians of 2019." *Forbes*, December 6, 2019. https://www.forbes.com/sites/zackomalley greenburg/2019/12/06/the-worlds-top-earning-musicians-of-2019/.

2. Dearling, Robert. *Non-Western & Obsolete Instruments*. Philadelphia: Chelsea House, 2001.

3. Hills, Rodney C., and Paul W. B. Atkins. "Cultural Identity and Convergence on Western Attitudes and Beliefs in the United Arab Emirates." *International Journal of Cross Cultural Management* 13, no. 2 (2013): 193–213. https:// doi.org/10.1177/1470595813485380.

4. Yuen, Nancy Wang. *Reel Inequality: Hollywood Actors and Racism*. New Brunswick, NJ: Rutgers University Press, 2017.

5. Rose, Steve. "From Tarzan to Avatar: The Problem with 'the White Man in the Jungle.'" *Guardian*, July 6, 2016. https://www.theguardian.com/film /2016/jul/06/why-the-white-man-in-the-jungle-film-wont-die.

6. Woodard, Laurie A. "Black Dancers, White Ballets." *New York Times*, July 15, 2015. https://www.nytimes.com/2015/07/15/opinion/Black-dancers-White -ballets.html.

7. Tyler, Royall. *Japanese Nō Dramas*. London: Penguin Books, 2004; And, Metin. *Karagöz: Turkish Shadow Theatre*. İstanbul: Yapı Kredi Yayınları, 2019; Gopalakrishnan, K. K. *Kathakali Dance-Theatre: A Visual Narrative of Indian Sacred Mime*. New Delhi: Niyogi Books, 2016.

8. Crane, Diana. "Cultural Globalization and the Dominance of the American Film Industry: Cultural Policies, National Film Industries, and Transnational Film." *Semantic Scholar*, September 2014. https://www .semanticscholar.org/paper/Cultural-globalization-and-the-dominance -of-the-and-Crane/82f1024c9a6946a183d502fae7b94deb94f86036.

Chapter 7: Sports

1. Davey, Melissa. "Adam Goodes Should Apologise, Says Mother of Girl Who Called Him an Ape." *Guardian*, July 30, 2015. https://www.theguardian.com /sport/2015/jul/30/adam-goodes-should-apologise-says-mother-of-girl -who-called-him-an-ape.

2. Torrens University. "Why the Sports Industry Is Booming in 2020 (and Which Key Players Are Driving Growth)." *Torrens Blog*, February 10, 2020. https://www.torrens.edu.au/blog/why-sports-industry-is-booming-in -2020-which-key-players-driving-growth.

3. McLoughlin, Danny. "Racial Bias in Football Commentary (Study): The Pace and Power Effect." RunRepeat, March 2, 2012. https://runrepeat.com /racial-bias-study-soccer.

4. Gilmour, Rod, and Alan Thatcher. *Jahangir Khan 555: The Untold Story behind Squash's Invincible Champion and Sport's Greatest Unbeaten Run*. Sussex, United Kingdom: Pitch, 2016.

5. Tendulkar, Sachin, and Boria Majumdar. *Playing It My Way: My Autobiography*. London: Hodder & Stoughton, 2015.

6. Lee, Amran Abdullah, and P. Sundaralingam. *Sepak Takraw*. Petaling Jaya, Malaysia: Sutrapadu, 2007.

Chapter 8: Fashion

1. Moulds, Josephine. "Child Labour in the Fashion Supply Chain." *Guardian*. https://labs.theguardian.com/unicef-child-labour/.

2. "Global Apparel and Footwear Valued at US$ 1.7 Trillion in 2017, Yet Used Clothing Worth Millions Disposed of Every Year." *Business Wire*,

May 4, 2018. https://www.businesswire.com/news/home/20180504005285/en/Global-Apparel-and-Footwear-Valued-at-US-1.7-Trillion-in-2017-Yet-Used-Clothing-Worth-Millions-Disposed of Every Year.

3. Racinet, Auguste. *The Complete Costume History.* Cologne, Germany: Taschen, 2012.

4. Ray, Shantanu Guha. "India's Unbearable Lightness of Being." *BBC News.* BBC, March 23, 2010. http://news.bbc.co.uk/2/hi/south_asia/8546183.stm.

5. "Skin Lightening Products Market Size Worth $13.7 Billion by 2025." Grand View Research, August 2019. https://www.grandviewresearch.com/press-release/global-skin-lightening-products-market.

6. Adow, Mohammed. "Nigeria Skin Whitening." *Health News.* Al Jazeera, April 6, 2013. https://www.aljazeera.com/features/2013/4/6/nigerias-dangerous-skin-Whitening-obsession.

7. Illmer, Andreas, Nanchanok Wongsamuth, and Thanyarat Doksone. "Thai Penis Whitening Trend Raises Eyebrows." *BBC News.* BBC, January 5, 2018. https://www.bbc.com/news/world-asia-42575155.

8. Park, Patricia. "TV Host Julie Chen Reveals She's Had Plastic Surgery and We're Supposed to Cheer?" *The Guardian*, September 15, 2013. https://www.theguardian.com/commentisfree/2013/sep/15/julie-chen-asian-eye-surgery.

9. Eckardt, Stephanie. "Beverly Johnson Recalls Racism On Set: 'They Drained the Pool.'" *W Magazine,* July 20, 2020. https://www.wmagazine.com/story/beverly-johnson-racism-fashion-industry.

10. X., Malcolm, and Alex Haley. *The Autobiography of Malcolm X.* New York: Ballantine Books, 2015, p. 138.

11. Rosenstein, Jenna. "Michelle Obama's Bouncy Inauguration Hair Started Trending on Twitter." *Harper's Bazaar*, January 20, 2021. https://www.harpersbazaar.com/beauty/hair/a35267021/michelle-obama-hair-curls-biden-inauguration-2021/.

12. Kumar, Rashmee. "Marketing the Muslim Woman: Hijabs and Modest Fashion Are the New Corporate Trend in the Trump Era." *Intercept*, December 29, 2018. https://theintercept.com/2018/12/29/muslim-women-hijab-fashion-capitalism/.

13. Murphy, Simon, and Redwan Ahmed. "'Girl Power' Charity T-Shirts Made at Exploitative Bangladeshi Factory." *Guardian*, March 1, 2019. https://www.theguardian.com/business/2019/mar/01/charity-t-shirts-made-at-exploitative-bangladeshi-factory.

14. Sabanoglu, Tugba. "Fast Fashion Market Value Forecast Worldwide 2009–2029." *Statista*, November 27, 2020. https://www.statista.com/statistics/1008241/fast-fashion-market-value-forecast-worldwide/.

15. Sabanoglu, "Fast Fashion."

16. Hossain, Akbar. "Coronavirus: Two Million Bangladesh Jobs 'at Risk' as Clothes Orders Dry Up." *BBC News*. BBC, April 28, 2020. https://www.bbc .com/news/world-asia-52417822.

17. Mirdha, Refayet Ullah. "Coronavirus Outbreak: Rights Bodies Express Concern over '10,000 RMG Workers Laid Off.'" *Daily Star*, April 13, 2020. https://www.thedailystar.net/online/news/coronavirus-outbreak-rights -bodies-express-concern-over-10000-rmg-workers-laid-1892860.

18. "Covid: Denmark to Dig Up Millions of Mink Culled over Virus." *BBC News*. BBC, December 21, 2020. https://www.bbc.com/news/world-europe -55391272.

19. Chan, Emily. "Outrage Isn't Enough: 7 Years on from the Rana Plaza Disaster, Here's How We Can Protect the People Who Make Our Clothes." *Vogue India*, April 23, 2020. https://www.vogue.in/fashion/content/7-years-on -from-the-rana-plaza-disaster-heres-how-we-can-protect-the-people -who-make-our-clothes.

20. Nair, Chandran. "Developed World Missing the Point on Modern Slavery." *Time*, June 20, 2016. https://time.com/4374377/slavery-developed -developing-world-index-slave-labor/.

21. Chan, Emily. "The Fast-Fashion System Is Broken—So What Happens Next?" *Vogue India*, July 8, 2020. https://www.vogue.in/fashion/content/the -fast-fashion-system-is-broken-so-what-happens-next.

22. Tai, Cordelia. "Report: Racial, Size and Gender Diversity Get a Boost at New York Fashion Week Spring 2020." *TheFashionSpot*, September 30, 2019. https://www.thefashionspot.com/runway-news/846053-diversity-report -new-york-fashion-week-spring-2020/.

23. Segran, Elizabeth. "The Fashion Industry Is Notoriously Racist. Here's How to Make It More Inclusive." *Fast Company*, June 10, 2020. https://www .fastcompany.com/90514039/the-fashion-industry-is-notoriously-racist -heres-how-to-make-it-more-inclusive.

24. Wagner, Lindsay Peoples, and Delphine Diallo. "What It's Really Like to Be Black and Work in Fashion." *Cut*, August 23, 2018. https://www.thecut.com /2018/08/what-its-really-like-to-be-Black-and-work-in-fashion.html.

25. Nelson, Karin. "Anok Yai Leads Fashion's New Wave of Style Rebels." *W Magazine*, September 9, 2019. https://www.wmagazine.com/gallery /anok-yai-fashion-shoot-mert-marcus.

26. Tai, Cordelia. "Report: Racial, Size and Gender Diversity Get a Boost at New York Fashion Week Spring 2020." TheFashionSpot, September 30, 2019. https://www.thefashionspot.com/runway-news/846053-diversity-report -new-york-fashion-week-spring-2020/.

27. Young, Sarah. "New York Fashion Week Show Only Features Immigrants in Hijabs." *Independent*, February 16, 2017. https://www.independent.co.uk/life

-style/fashion/new-york-fashion-week-hijabs-islam-immigrant-fashion
-show-anniesa-hasibuan-a7583321.html.

Chapter 9: Environment, Sustainability, and Climate Change

1. Global Footprint Network. [Map of biocapacity and ecological footprint]. Accessed May 3, 2021. https://data.footprintnetwork.org/.
2. "Renewable Capacity Statistics 2020." IRENA—International Renewable Energy Agency, March 2020. https://www.irena.org/-/media/Files/IRENA /Agency/Publication/2020/Mar/IRENA_RE_Capacity_Statistics_2020.pdf.
3. "Ahead of Biodiversity Summit, UN Officials Call for Action to Preserve the Natural World." *UN News.* United Nations, September 28, 2020. https://news .un.org/en/story/2020/09/1074002.
4. Savolainen, Anna. "One in Four Species in France Is Endangered, Despite Biodiversity Protection Efforts." Climate Scorecard, June 15, 2020. https:// www.climatescorecard.org/2020/06/one-in-four-species-in-france-is -endangered-despite-biodiversity-protection-efforts/.
5. Sánchez, Silvia, Andrea Pino del Carpio, Ana Nieto, and Melanie Bilz. "Italy's Biodiversity at Risk." International Union for Conservation of Nature, May 2013. https://www.iucn.org/sites/dev/files/content/documents/italy_s _biodiversity_at_risk_fact_sheet_may_2013.pdf.
6. Arvin, Jariel. "The World's Biggest Banks Have Pumped Trillions into Fossil Fuel Projects in the Past 5 Years." *Vox,* March 26, 2021. https://www.vox .com/22349601/banks-fossil-fuels-finance-trillions-climate-change.
7. "Each Country's Share of CO_2 Emissions." Union of Concerned Scientists, August 12, 2020. https://www.ucsusa.org/resources/each-countrys-share -co2-emissions.
8. "Compilation and Synthesis of Fourth Biennial Reports of Parties Included in Annex I to the Convention." United Nations Framework Convention on Climate Change, November 12, 2020. https://unfccc.int/documents /266353.
9. Stern, Nicholas. *The Economics of Climate Change: The Stern Review.* Cambridge, United Kingdom: Cambridge University Press, 2011.
10. Unigwe, Chika. "It's Not Just Greta Thunberg: Why Are We Ignoring the Developing World's Inspiring Activists?" *Guardian,* October 5, 2019. https:// www.theguardian.com/commentisfree/2019/oct/05/greta-thunberg -developing-world-activists.
11. Elks, Sonia. "Factbox: In Greta's Footsteps: 10 Young Climate Activists Fighting for Change." *Reuters,* September 27, 2019. https://www.reuters.com /article/us-climate-change-youth-factbox-idUSKBN1WC1ZA.
12. Phippen, J. Weston. "'Kill Every Buffalo You Can! Every Buffalo Dead Is an Indian Gone.'" *Atlantic,* November 18, 2019. https://www.theatlantic.com /national/archive/2016/05/the-buffalo-killers/482349/.

13. Press, Hannah. "News: Norway Now Kills More Whales Than Japan." International Marine Mammal Project, July 19, 2019. http://savedolphins.eii .org/news/entry/norway-now-kills-more-whales-than-japan.

14. Hoyte, Simon, and Catherine Clark. "Violence, Corruption, and False Promises: Conservation and the Baka in Cameroon." International Work Group for Indigenous Affairs, June 26, 2020. https://www.iwgia.org/en/cameroon /3791-violence,-corruption,-and-false-promises-conservation-and-the -baka-in-cameroon.html.

15. Vidal, John. "'Large-Scale Human Rights Violations' Taint Congo National Park Project." *Guardian*, November 26, 2020. https://www.theguardian.com /world/2020/nov/26/you-have-stolen-our-forest-rights-of-baka-people-in -the-congo-ignored.

16. Greenfield, Patrick. "World Fails to Meet a Single Target to Stop Destruction of Nature—UN Report." *Guardian*, September 15, 2020. https://www .theguardian.com/environment/2020/sep/15/every-global-target-to-stem -destruction-of-nature-by-2020-missed-un-report-aoe.

17. "Malaysia Returns 42 Containers of 'Illegal' Plastic Waste to UK." *BBC News*, January 20, 2020. https://www.bbc.com/news/uk-51176312.

18. Law, Kara Lavender, Natalie Starr, Theodore R. Siegler, Jenna R. Jambeck, Nicholas J. Mallos, and George H. Leonard. "The United States' Contribution of Plastic Waste to Land and Ocean." *Science Advances*. American Association for the Advancement of Science, October 1, 2020. https://advances .sciencemag.org/content/6/44/eabd0288.

19. Lewis, Tanya. "World's E-Waste to Grow 33% by 2017, Says Global Report." *LiveScience*, December 15, 2013. https://www.livescience.com/41967-world -e-waste-to-grow-33-percent-2017.html.

20. Hodal, Kate. "Murder of Environmentalist 'Highlights Thailand's Failure to Protect Activists.'" *Guardian*, February 27, 2013. https://www.theguardian .com/world/2013/feb/27/murder-environmentalist-thailand-failure.

21. MacDonald, Christine. "Coke Claims to Give Back as Much Water as It Uses. An Investigation Shows It Isn't Even Close." *Verge*, May 31, 2018. https:// www.theverge.com/2018/5/31/17377964/coca-cola-water-sustainability -recycling-controversy-investigation.

22. MacDonald, "Coke Claims."

Conclusion

1. "White Supremacy a Global Threat, Says UN Chief." *Independent*, February 22, 2021. https://www.independent.co.uk/news/world/White-supremacy -threat-neo-nazi-un-b1805547.html?utm_source=reddit.com.

2. Nair, Chandran. "Foreign Lives Matter." *Foreign Policy*, April 30, 2015. https://foreignpolicy.com/2015/04/30/foreign-lives-matter-american -racism-foreign-policy-baltimore-ferguson/.

3.   Grady, Constance. "A Reading List to Understand Anti-Asian Racism in America." *Vox*, March 18, 2021. https://www.vox.com/culture/22336712 /anti-asian-racism-reading-list.

4.   Mitcham, John. "Jan Smuts and the Racial Origins of Five Eyes." Centre for International Policy Studies, October 8, 2020. https://www.cips-cepi.ca/2020 /10/08/jan-smuts-and-the-racial-origins-of-five-eyes/.

5.   Rachman, Gideon. "Race Is Also a Geopolitical Issue." *Financial Times*, April 5, 2021. https://www.ft.com/content/d99b84e4-0bf2-47c1-9270-c82aecd0e8dd.

6.   Agence France-Presse. "UN Human Rights Chief Calls for Reparations to Make Amends for Slavery." *Guardian*, June 17, 2020. https://www .theguardian.com/world/2020/jun/17/un-human-rights-chief-calls-for -reparations-to-make-amends-for-slavery.

7.   "World Economic Forum Launches Coalition to Tackle Racism in the Work-place." World Economic Forum, January 25, 2021. https://www.weforum .org/press/2021/01/world-economic-forum-launches-coalition-to-tackle -racism-in-the-workplace/.

8.   Nair, Chandran. "NGOs Should Re-Think Activism Strategies in Develop-ing World." *Financial Times,* June 9, 2016. https://www.ft.com/content /1a7357f7-abf9-3359-a29e-cc60097d23b.

ACKNOWLEDGMENTS

This book owes a debt to two people. The first is Zuraidah Ibrahim, the editor of *This Week in Asia*, a weekly publication of the *South China Morning Post* in Hong Kong. She was courageous enough to publish an article of mine about global White privilege in June 2020 and give it the headline "Fifty Shades of White." I did not send this article to the editors of Western publications I know, as I was almost certain they would cringe and not run the piece. I was also afraid of burning bridges with them.

However, the piece did very well, and I shared it with my publisher, Steve Piersanti, simply as a matter of interest. He immediately came back and said that if I wanted to turn it into a book, he would consider publishing it. I was rather surprised and thought about it for a day before saying I would be interested. The rest, as they say, is history, but what was most surprising to me was how engaged and curious he was in every aspect of the various arguments I was making. In addition he provided me with invaluable guidance, but never told me what to write. I had never met a White man who was so comfortable with and committed to the core thesis: that White privilege is a global challenge and must be dismantled for the world to progress. He was eager to support me in reaching a global audience with the ideas in this book.

But writing a book while holding a full-time job running the Global Institute for Tomorrow during the pandemic meant I needed the support, help, patience, and tolerance of many. They are far too many to mention here, but I must acknowledge a few.

First, I thank all my colleagues at GIFT who tolerated my constant interruptions in the office. In particular, I thank two colleagues, Rohan Hazell and Nicholas Gordon, who supported me throughout the entire process. They helped with conducting the research, framing the arguments, and writing the book. I am extremely indebted to them. They provided a sounding board for some of my ideas and pulled me back when I went off on a tangent.

I also thank Mikhail Petra for assisting with the research, and my very capable colleague Mei Cheung, who helped with ensuring the manuscript was always in order and stitched it together.

Three interns helped with the internal research and drafting. It was also fun to work with them, given their very different cultural and educational backgrounds, not to mention their growing awareness of various contemporary issues. The first was Ali Taha Brown, who has Palestinian roots; Charlotte Cheang, who is Hong Kong Chinese; and Keshav Menon, who is of Indian descent. It was interesting to see how young students responded when allowed to engage in this topic—they expressed that they learned so much about issues they had never thought about, given their immersion in Western-centric education. They committed themselves to learning a great deal and providing good research material in the process.

Then there are others who by just being there and providing encouragement gave me the strength to take on these issues in the manner I have. For this I first thank my dear friend and former band member Dumasani Kambishama, who is American and lives in New York City. In the wake of the race protests across the US in 2020, he continually kept me fired up with insights about the struggles of Black people in America. His short essays sent on WhatsApp convinced me that I should write this book.

My American colleague in Hong Kong, Eric Stryson, expressed great interest and support, sharing with me interesting articles about White privilege; he also never once denied that he was a beneficiary of White privilege at various points in his life. It was most useful to have a White American colleague with whom I could openly discuss sensitive topics and test my ideas. And then there is my colleague Karim Rushdy, a UK citizen, who had much to share, given his acute awareness of the harm of White privilege.

Finally, I thank the entire Berrett-Koehler team for their support despite what I assume was some level of discomfort with the arguments in the book. I thank in particular Jeevan Sivasubramaniam for his no-nonsense approach to feedback and keeping me on track. I also thank the three reviewers for their invaluable feedback: Dr. Shonali Banerjee, Shabnam McFarland, and Terri Frick.

INDEX

Page numbers in italics refer to figures.

A

AC Milan, 113
academia, discourse in, xii, 6, 13
Academic Ranking for World
   Universities, 88
Academy Awards/Oscars, 104, 105
accounting firms, 57, 58, 62, 63, 67, 68, 164
accreditation, 20
acculturation, 85, 97, 100, 106, 108
Acosta, Carlos, 105
Adhanom, Tedros, 31
Adidas, 92, 124
advertising. *See* marketing/advertising
Afghanistan war, 24, 46, 48
Agence France-Presse, 72
Agent Orange, 47–48
Airbus, 67
Al Jazeera, 79, 80, 169
Al Maktoum, Mohammed bin Rashid, 51
Aladdin story, 91
Albright, Madeleine, 48
Ali, Muhammad, 2, 22, 111, 117
All-England Championship, 115
"alternative facts," subscribing to, 43
American Revolution, 70
amnesia, historical, 42, 43, 45
Ancient Greece, 41, 50
Ancient Rome, 50
Ant Group, 64
antiapartheid movement, ix, 3
anti-Communism, 29, 46, 48, 87
antidoping system, 112, 116, 121
antiracist system, building, 164

apartheid system: economic basis for,
   xiii; forms of, in neighborhoods,
   dismantling, suggestions for, 165–166;
   impact of, 45–46
apologies, 34, 43, 163
Apple iPhones, 92
appropriation, 98, 125, 128, 133, 135
Aquino, Francisco, 30
Aristotle, 50
ASEAN Miracle, The (Mahbubani), 35
Asian Development Bank, 36
Asian financial crisis, reaction to, 55
Asian Infrastructure Investment Bank
   (AIIB), 36–37
assimilation, 157, 159
Associated Press, 72
Association of Southeast Asian Nations
   (ASEAN), 35–36, 68
AT&T, 72
atomic bombing, 47
Attenborough, David, 137
authority/legitimacy, described, *16,*
   17, 20
Avatar (film), 104
Avengers: Endgame (film), 103–104

B

Bach, 102
Back to the Future II (film), 65
Bain, 60
Baldwin, James, 100
Bandung Conference, ix
Banks, Tyra, 123, 124–125

Baudhayana Sutra, 50
BBC, 72, 73, 80, 126, 169
BCG, 60
Beasley, David, 30
Beatles music, 98
Beauty without Borders, 128
Beckham, David, 115
best practices, setting, 60–61
Beyoncé, 127, 133
Biden, Joe, 140, 141
"Big Four," 58, 62, 63, 68
"Big Three," 63–64
biodiversity: and conservation efforts, 146–149, 152; loss of, 139, 145–146, 149
Black Lives Matter: creation of, catalyst for, xiii; impact of, ix, 4, 167–168, 171; viewed as tip of the iceberg, ix, xiii, 4, *5*, 6
Blade Runner (film), 65
Blair, Tony, 31
blind patriotism, 48, 76
Bloomberg, Michael, 87
Bloomberg TV, 69, 73
Boateng, Kevin-Prince, 113
Body Snatcher, The (film), 103
Boeing, 67
Bollywood, 106, 109
Bombardier, 67
Bong Joon Ho, 104
Borpuhjari, Priyanka, 76–77
Bose, Jagadish, 50
brain drain, 89
Buddhist literature, 83
Bush, George W., 31
business: adherence to standards in, 20; competition in, reactions to, 65–66, 66–67; conclusions on, 67–68; costs of, 59; enforcement authority in, 58, 65–66; and the environment, 59, 140, 145, 153; expressions of White privilege in, 19; fighting White privilege in, suggestions for, xv–xvi, 68–69, 160, 161, 162–163, 167–168; gatekeepers in, 57, 58, 61–65, 68; legitimacy/authority and privilege in, 67–68; and media, 58, 60, 64, 69; personal story involving, 55–56; relationship of, to White privilege, *18*; and resistance to change, 156; rules of, and their significance, 58–59; setting the standards in, 60–61, 69; success in, determination of, 56–58. *See also* business schools

Business Roundtable, 56–57
business schools, 58, 60, 61, 87–88, 94–95, 96, 160, 166–167

C

Cambridge, 87
capital, global, access to, guarding, 57, 58, 61–65
capitalism, 58, 60, 92–93, 94
capturing minds. *See* "mind capture"
Carmichael, Stokely (Kwame Ture), 12
Chanel, 128
change: at all levels of society, 164–171; in business, xv–xvi, 68–69, 167–168; and a call for action, 172; in civil society, 170–171; in education, 96, 166–167; in entertainment, 108–109; in environmental protection, 153; in families, 157, 164–165; in fashion, 135, 136; in geopolitics, 37–38, 171; and leadership that matters, 156–158; in media, 81–82, 169–170; in national governance, 170, 171; in neighborhoods, 157, 165–166; in professional bodies, 168–169; rejecting the three E's for, 158–164; resistance to, overcoming, 154–156; in sports, 122; in the telling of history, 53–54; willingness to, assessing, 156–157
Channel News Asia, 169
Chen, Julie, 126
"chic" fashion, 20
China Global TV, 169
Christian schools, 87
Churchill, Winston, 42
civil rights movements, 40
civil society, change in, suggestions for, 170–171
"civilization," idea of, 15, 40, 41, 42
"civilized" state, idea of, 15, 27–28, 147
Climate Action Network, 139
climate change, *18*, 19, 74, 137, 139, 141–145, 152, 153
Clinton, Bill, 141
CNBC, 69, 73
CNN, 69, 72, 73, 79, 169
Coca-Cola, 153
Cold War, 22–24, 29, 53
Cole, Teju, 137
colonization: atrocities of, 42, 52–53; combined with globalization, and erosion of history, 50–51; and culture, 97, 98; and education, 83, 84, 90, 93,

95; limited explanations of, 40, 52–53; media coverage and residual effects of, 73, 75; motives behind, full awareness of, 3; period of, lasting effect of, 4–5; selective perceptions of, maintaining, effect of, 40, 42–46; and sports, 117; studies of, 12; subversive, 10, *16*, 17; trigger of, xii; vestiges of, alliances comprising, 24–25; whitewashing of, 43–44, 45

colonizing minds, 3, 10, *16*, 17, 40–42, 44, 45, 83, 84–85, 89–91, 100, 106, 119. *See also* decolonizing minds; "mind capture"

Columbia Journalism Review (magazine), 76–77

Comme des Garçons, 133

Confucius, 83, 87, 90

Confucius Institutes, 87

conservation, 146–149, 152

consultants, 57, 58, 60–61, 168

conversations: in academia, xii, 6, 13; following decolonization, ix–x; global, about White privilege, benefit of, 9–10; inclusion in, addressing, 6–7; involving race on a global level, lack of, 13; mainstream, shift in, limitations of, 4–6; nonacademic, 6; silenced, x; taboo, ix, 8

COVID-19, 51–52, 71. *See also* pandemic

crimes against humanity, 34, 47

critical race theory, 13, 14–15

critical theory, 12–13

cultural capital, 12, 19, 88, 89, 165

cultural control, *5*

cultural imperialism, *16*, 17, 97

cultural priorities, sphere of, 18. *See also* entertainment; fashion; sports

cultural traditions, ignorance and disrespect of, pattern of, 21

"culture clashes," 50–51

D

Daei, Ali, 115

dance and theater (performing arts), 100, 104–105

Darwin, Charles, 50

David, Nicol, 115, 116

debt, 13, 63

decolonization: catastrophes that followed, narratives on, 44–46; conversations following, ix–x; and economic power, 8–9; and education,

93; ending the process of, effect of, 10; era of, start of, 8; and the idea of the "civilized" state, 28; limited explanations of, 40; success of, 27

decolonizing minds, x, 2–3, 53, 99–100, 160

Deloitte, 62

democracy: claims about, 15, 139; focus on, as solution to environmental issues, critique of, 139–140; and a post-Western world, 9; proclamations about spreading, 10, 28

deregulation/laissez-faire system, 59, 92, 93, 96

Diesel, 128

diplomacy, 21, 52, 66, 75

Disney, 91, 124

disrespect and ignorance, pattern of, 21

Dolce & Gabbana, 129

dominance: architecture of, establishing and maintaining, 8–9; global, descriptor of, ix; historical, 10, *16*; new realities challenging, 9; period of, rooted in racism, xiv; as the principal objective, xii; superstructure that perpetuates, dismantling, need for, 9; understanding, means of, 6. *See also* economic power; military power; White privilege

double standards, pattern of, 21

Dow Jones, 72

E

East India Trading Company, 43–44

ecological footprints, 138, 143

economic policies, sphere of, 18. *See also* business

economic power: centuries of, impact of, and change, 154, 158; and decolonization, 8–9; expressions of White privilege through, 9; fetish of dominance and, 15–17; military power and, xii, 9, 13, 15, *16*; as the objective, 5–6, 10; prerequisite for maintaining, 10; rising, of non-Western countries, reactions to, 5, 23, 24, 25, 26, 30, 31, 37; understanding privilege and, 10–11; visibility of structures enabling dominance and, *5*; Western domination based on, xiv

Economist (newspaper/magazine), 73, 91

education: adherence to standards in, 20; conclusions on, 95–96; as a contributor to delegitimizing non-Western innovation, 91–94; diversity of thought in, need for, 96; emulation of, 84; expressions of White privilege in, 19; fighting White privilege in, suggestions for, 96, 160, 161, 166–167; and geopolitics, 85; and history, 39, 40, 42, 43, 44, 50, 51, 52, 53–54, 85, 87, 91, 96, 166; as a means for capturing the mind, 84–86, 95; and media, 88, 91; personal story involving, 83–84; and prestige, 86–89, 94, 95; profitability of, 86, 95; questioning, suggestions for, 165; relationship of, to White privilege, 18; selective curriculums in, 89–91, 94, 95, 96; and Whiteness, 10–11; and world order, 85. *See also* business schools

Einstein, Albert, 91

Embraer, 67

"emerging market," using, as a term, critique of, xv

emulation, role of, described, *16*, 17

Enlightenment, 41, 70

Enninful, Edward, 135

entertainment: conclusions on, 108; cultural impact of, 102–103; expressions of White privilege in, 19; and fashion, 99, 106; fighting White privilege in, suggestions for, 108–109; and globalization of Western culture, 99–100; and history, 103; personal story involving, 1, 2–3, 98–99; popularity and prestige in, and impacts, 101–102, 103–105; profitability of, 101, 103; race and representation in, 105–107; relationship of, to White privilege, 18; Western culture and, seduction of, 97–99; whitewashing in, 105

entitlement, exclusivity, and exceptionalism (three E's): described, 158–159; dismantling, objectives and steps toward, 159–164; pursuit of, rejecting, need for, 158

environment: and biodiversity loss, 139, 145–146; and business, 59, 140, 145, 153; and climate change, *18*, 19, 74, 137, 139, 141–145, 152, 153; conclusions on, 152–153; and conservation, 146–149, 152; dispersal of responsibility for, concentration of power and, 139–141; and e-waste, 151–152; and expressions of White privilege, 19; and fighting White privilege, suggestions for, 153; and history, 146; and media, 74, 137, 144, 145; and plastic waste, 149–151; and pollution, 138, 139, 140, 149–152; relationship of, to White privilege, *18*; and sustainability, *18*, 19, 131, 137, 138, 140, 144, 148, 150, 152–153; and the whitewashed environmental movement, 137–139

environmental agendas, sphere of, 18. *See also* environment

Ernst and Young (EY), 62, 63

ethnicity, described, 11

European Union (EU), 34, 35, 36, 43, 68, 142, 143, 163

expatriates, xiii, 42, 84, 111, 163, 165, 170

explicit racism, described, 11

F

Facebook, 67, 100, 160

fairness: global call for, 8; and a post-Western world, 8, 9; proclamations about spreading, xii

families, change within, suggestions for, 157, 164–165

Fanon, Frantz, 12, 13, 40, 45, 97

fashion: adherence to standards in, 20; clothing, and the fashion police, 128–129; conclusions on, 135–136; and cultural identity, 98; emulation of, 126; and entertainment, 99, 106; expressions of White privilege in, 19; fast, economics of, and exploitation, 124, 130–132; fighting White privilege in, suggestions for, 135, 136; gatekeepers in, 133–134; and the high entry barrier for non-Whites, 134–135; high-end, racism in, 125, 132–134; and media, 74, 127, 131–132; naked, and body modification, 125–127; profitability of, 124, 126, 131; relationship of, to White privilege, *18*; representation in, 129–130; and the stripping of identity, 124–125, 126; and trends, influence of, 123–124

Fashion Week shows, 132, 133, 135

Fauci, Anthony, 88

Federer, Roger, 115

FIFA, 112

film and television shows, 65, 97, 98, 100, 101, 103–104, 105–107, 109

financial crises, 55, 64
financial system, global, power of, 17, 55–56, 58, 67–68. *See also* business
Financial Times (newspaper), 51–52, 62, 69, 72, 73, 80, 82, 89, 91, 94, 131
Fitch, 59, 63
Five Eyes Intelligence Alliance, 24–25, 33, 162
Floyd, George, 4, *5*, 167
Foreign Correspondence Clubs, 77
Forever 21, 124
fortress conservation, 146–148, 149
Fortune (magazine), 69
Fox News, 72, 74
free press, idea of, 70–71, 73, 74
free trade, 61, 131, 132
freedom: calling out others on, hypocrisy in, 33; preaching, xv; proclamations about spreading, 10, 46, 49
Freeman, R. Edward, 56
free-market system, 21, 61, 87, 92–93, 94, 96, 143
Freire, Paulo, 45
French Revolution, 70
Friedman, Milton, 61
Frontline States movements, ix
fur trade, 132

G

Gandhi, Indira, 87
Gap, 124, 128, 130
garment factories, 131, 132, 135
gated sports, 112–113
gatekeepers, 57, 58, 61–65, 68, 133–134
gender: and gender politics, effect of, addressing, need for, xvi; injustices based on, awareness of, xiv
generation gap, 107
genocide, 45
geopolitics: adherence to standards in, 20; and the "civilized" state, 27–28; in the Cold War and post-Cold War eras, 23–24; and colonization, 4–5, 46; conclusions on, 35; and decolonization, 8–9; and education, 85; expressions of White privilege in, 19; fighting White privilege in, suggestions for, 37–38, 161–162, 171; and history, 22, 23, 46; and international leadership issues, 30–32; lessons on, from other models, 35–37; and media, 22, 23, 31, 74, 75; personal story involving, 22–23; relationship of, to White privilege, *18*; removing structural inequalities in, 161–162; and the "rogue" state, 28–30; role of White privilege in, 24–25; significance of, 25–26; and sovereign equality, 26–28; and sports, 112; and violating the rules-based order, 25, 32–35
Gibson, Althea, 111
Giselle (ballet), 104
global governance: change in, suggestions for, 171; and critical race theory, 14; mainstream discussions of race and, 13; new systems of, creating, suggestions for, 164. *See also* geopolitics
Global Institute for Tomorrow, 1
global order. *See* world order
"Global South," using, as a term, critique of, xv
globalization, xiii, 3, 4–5, 9, 10, 12, 15, 23, 50–51, 72, 99–100, 103, 123, 124, 132, 154
Goldman Sachs, 59, 64
Goodes, Adam, 111
Google, 67
Gore, Al, 141, 145
governance. *See* global governance; national governance
Grand Slams, 112–113, 119, 133
Great Depression, 32
Great Leap Forward, 42
"greed is good" mantra, 94
Green Fence Operation, 150
"green" movement, 139, 151–152, 153
Greenpeace, 139
Group of 7 (G7), 31
Group of 8 (G8), 68
Group of 20 (G20), 68
Guardian (newspaper), 46
Gulf War. *See* Iraq War
Guterres, Antonio, 155

H

H&M, 124, 129, 130
Haley, Nikki, 30
Hansel and Gretel story, 91
hard power. *See* economic power; military power
HarperCollins, 72
Harper's Bazaar (magazine), 133
Harrow School, 86, 87
Harry Potter story, 91
Hartono, Rudy, 115, 116
Harvard, 60, 87
Hasibuan, Anniesa, 135

Hawking, Stephen, 91
Hei An Zuhan story, 91
heroes, 2, 41, 49, 103, 104, 107, 114–116,
   119, 144, 145, 153. *See also* White
   savior model
Heron, Gil-Scott, 39
history: colonizing minds through,
   40–42, 85; conclusions on, 52–53;
   controlling the narratives of, science
   of, 51–52; and education, 39, 40, 42,
   43, 44, 50, 51, 52, 53–54, 85, 87, 91, 96,
   166; and entertainment, 103; and the
   environment, 146; exporting, 42;
   expressions of White privilege in, 19;
   fighting White privilege in the telling
   of, suggestions for, 53–54; framing of,
   critique of, 15; and geopolitics, 22, 23,
   46; and the glorification of war and
   liberal interventionism, 46–48; of
   human progress, 41, 49–51, 52, 53, 91;
   legacy of, as being in the past, lie of,
   xii, 40; and media, xii, 43, 48, 51–52,
   70–71; modern, of White privilege,
   capturing, 160–161; personal story
   involving, 39–40; relationship of, to
   White privilege, *18*; selective perceptions of, maintaining, effect of, 40,
   42–46; silenced, impacts of, 44–46;
   whitewashing of, 43–44
Hollywood, 103, 104, 106, 127. *See also*
   film and television shows
Homer, 90
How Europe Underdeveloped Africa
   (Rodney), 39
HR Ratings de México, 63
Huawei, 66–67
Hugo Boss, 128
human progress, framing of, in history,
   41, 49–51, 52, 53, 91
human rights, xiii, xv, 28, 29, 33, 48
Huntington, Samuel P., 22

I

"ideal" model, 20
identity: and colonization, 40–41, 45, 46,
   50; and entertainment, 97–98, 100,
   103, 107, 109; and fashion, 98,
   124–125, 126; impact of White
   privilege on, ix; speaking out about,
   159; and sports, 98
ignorance and disrespect, pattern of, 21
immigration/immigrants, 44, 75, 78
imperialism, xii, 3, 9, *16*, 17, 22, 24, 40, 41,
   42, 43, 73, 77, 85, 97, 99, 148, 161, 170

implicit racism, described, 11, 12
Imru' al-Qays, 90
Independent (newspaper), 113
initial public offering (IPO), 64
injustices: documenting, xii; global, root
   cause of, 3; oppression and, 1; other
   forms of, xiv; visible and invisible,
   5, 6
institutional power, leveraging, 10
institutions, role of, 4, 9, 10, 11, 12, 14,
   15, 17, 20
integration, 35, 44, 66, 102, 165, 166
Intergovernmental Panel on Climate
   Change, 139
International Cricket Council, 119
International Declaration of Human
   Rights, 71
International Monetary Fund (IMF), 8,
   13, 30–31, 31–32, 46, 162, 171
International Olympic Committee, 118,
   162
international order. *See* world order
international relations: histories of, 23;
   main objective of, 26; race and
   discussions of, 13; rules of, concept
   used to determine, 15, 27; and setting
   terms of engagement, pattern
   involving, 21. *See also* geopolitics;
   US-China relations
International Tennis Federation, 112
International Union for Conservation of
   Nature, 139
internet, 17, 100
Iraq War, 24, 43, 46, 48, 53
Ivy League, 10, 12, 87

J

Jagger, Mick, 99
Jahiz, al-, 50, 83
James Bond character, 106
Japan Credit Rating Agency, 63
Japanese car companies, rise of, 65–66
John, Elton, 99
John Hopkins University, 87
Johnson, Beverly, 133
Johnson, Boris, 43
Jordan, Michael, 115, 117
JP Morgan, 141
justice. *See* injustices; social justice

K

Kaepernick, Colin, 117
Kagame, Paul, 31
Kant, Immanuel, 90

Kean, Moise, 113
Kenzo, 135
Khan, Bismillah, 102
Khan, Jahangir, 115, 116
Khan, Shahid, 117
Khayyam, Omar, 83
Khwārizmī, Muhammad ibn Mūsā al-, 50
Korean War, 46
Kozloff, Nikolas, 25
KPMG, 62, 63
Kyoto Protocol, 139, 141

L

Lagarde, Christine, 30–31
Lahouri, Ahmad, 41
laissez-faire system/deregulation, 59, 92, 93, 96
Lamarck, Jean-Baptiste, 50
Laozi, 83
Last Samurai, The (film), 104
Lauv, 103
Lawrence of Arabia (film), 104
leadership: conversations about White privilege and, need for, 168; discussion questions for, 176; key areas for, to begin the process of change, xv–xvi; personal, as key, 157–158; positions of, selection of, 13, 25, 30–31, 66, 104; taboo subject among, 8; Western-dominated, consequences of, 31–32
Lee Kuan Yew, 31
legitimacy/authority, described, *16*, 17, 20, 21
Leon, 135
Leonardo da Vinci, 41, 50, 91
Life and Works of Jahiz, The (Jahiz), 83
Lim, 135
literature: delegitimizing non-Western, 84, 93; and selective curriculums, 83, 90–91
lobbying, 29
London Stock Exchange, 64
Lord of the Rings (Tolkien), 91
Louis Vuitton, 135
Luckin Coffee, 63
Lukaku, Romelu, 113

M

Machiavelli, Niccolò, 41
Macron, Emmanuel, 51–52
Madonna, 128
magazines/newspapers. *See* media
Mahbubani, Kishore, 35

Major League Baseball, 118
Malcolm X, 2, 70, 127
management consultants, 57, 58, 60–61
MANGO, 129
Mao Zedung, 42
Marconi, Guglielmo, 50
Marie Claire (magazine), 128
marketing/advertising, 53, 93, 99, 108, 127, 128, 129, 130, 131
Marley, Bob, x, xi, 2
McKinset, 60
media: aiding in narratives about success, 21; and business, 58, 60, 64, 69; and commercial television, 71; conclusions on, 82; diversity in, in terms of writing and reporting, 74, 76–78; and education, 88, 91; emulation of, 77; and environment, 74, 137, 144, 145; expressions of White privilege in, 19; and fashion, 74, 127, 131–132; fighting White privilege in, suggestions for, 81–82, 163, 169–170; and geopolitics, 22, 23, 31, 74, 75; global vs. Western, distinguishing between, 74–76; and history, xii, 43, 48, 51–52, 70–71; lack of context in, 75, 170; major global newspapers and news networks in, 72; and primary concerns of Western outlets, 74–76; relationship of, to White privilege, *18*; role of, 70–72; significance of, that is global, 72–73; social, 100, 160, 165; and sports, 112, 114, 117, 118, 119, 120, 121; tone in, dictating, 72, 73, 78–79; and the treatment of non-Western outlets, 79–80; truly global, lack of, 72, 73–74
Messi, Lionel, 115
Michelangelo, 50
military power: acceptance of, 28, 33, 46, 47, 48, 49; displaying, media and, 75–76; and economic power, xii, 9, 13, 15, *16*; expressions of White privilege through, 9; shift away from using, as a punitive action, 33–34. *See also* war
"mind capture," 40, 60, 73, 84–86, 93, 95, 156, 165. *See also* colonizing minds
modernity/modernization: contributors to, history and, 49–51; conversations about, 3; embarking on, to be a "civilized" state, 27–28; embracing, 123, 128; ongoing assault of, 100; spreading, 11, 40; Western standard of, xv
Monroe, Marilyn, 106, 127
Monroe Doctrine, 27

Moody's, 55–56, 63
Morales, Evo, 78–79
Morgan Stanley, 8, 64
Mowgli story, 91
Mozart, 102
Mulan story, 91
Muralitharan, Muttiah, 120
music, 1, 2–3, 97, 98–99, 101–103
Musk, Elon, 145

N
Nasdaq, 64
national anthem, "taking a knee" during, 111–112, 117
National Basketball Association (NBA), 116, 117
National Football League (NFL), 114, 116, 117, 119
national governance: change in, suggestions for, 170, 171; and critical race theory, 14; and education, 85
national pride, 43, 51, 53
National Sword policy, 149, 150
nationalism, 53, 111, 171
natural resources, abuse of, 59, 139, 145, 147–148, 149
neighborhoods, change within, suggestions for, 157, 165–166
neocolonialism, 99
neoliberalism, x, 92
Netflix, 100, 160
New York Times (newspaper), 72, 73, 74, 79, 80, 82, 91, 131
News Corporation, 72
newspapers/magazines. *See* media
Newton, Isaac, 91
Ngöugöi wa Thiong'o, 83
NHK, 169
Nike, 92, 124, 128
NMC Health, 63
Nobel Prize, 30, 81, 87, 92, 145
norms, role of, 4, 9, 10, 12, 14, 15, *16*, 17, 20
nostalgia, 42–43
nuclear weapons, 47
NYSE, 64

O
Obama, Barack, 154, 155
Obama, Michelle, 127
Office of the Ombudsman, creation of, 164
"offsetting" approaches, 139, 143, 153
Olympics, 118, 120

1MDB, 59
Onuora, Iffy, 110
Operation Ranch Hand, 47
Opium Wars, 27
oppression: centuries of, repairing the damage done by, 163; expanding understanding of, need for, xii; and geopolitics, 26, 27; persistence of, 24; understanding, means of, 6; visibility of structures enabling dominance and, 5. *See also* colonization; White privilege
Organization for Economic Co-operation and Development (OECD), 31
Organization of American States (OAS), 78–79
Oscars/Academy Awards, 104, 105
outsourcing, 59, 131, 132, 143
overt racism, described, 11
Owens, Jesse, 111
Oxford, 87

P
pan-Africanist movements, ix
pandemic, 4, 20, 31, 51–52, 71, 88, 131, 132, 141
Parasite (film), 104
Paris Agreement, 143
Parker, Martin, 94
Partnering for Racial Justice in Business, 168
patriotism, 48, 76
peace, maintaining: ASEAN's success in, 35–36; claims of, issues with, 23, 24, 25, 28, 46; success of other regions in, recognizing, need for, 37
pecking order, 4, 17, 154. *See also* world order
Pegula, Kim, 117
performing arts (dance and theater), 100, 104–105
Pfizer, 51–52
philosophy, history of, 41, 49–51
Plato, 50, 90
Plaza Accord, 66
political systems, sphere of, 18. *See also* geopolitics; world order
pollution, 138, 139, 140, 149–152
post-Cold War era, 23–24
postcolonial council, creation of, 164
postcolonial studies/discussions, 12–13, 15
post-Western world: consensus for, issue of, 14; creating, benefits of, 7, 9; meaning of, defining, 8–9

post-World War II, 8–9, 23, 27, 32, 33, 70–71, 101, 107
power, leveraging, 10
power shift, determination for, x
Prada, 124
Premier League, 114, 116, 118
PricewaterhouseCoopers (PwC), 56, 62
Pro Patria, 113, 114
professional bodies, change in, suggestions for, 168–169
Professional Footballers' Association (PFA), 114
Promised Land, A (Obama), 155
propaganda, 42, 80, 107
publishing: conclusions on, 81–82; and fashion, 127; fighting White privilege in, suggestions for, 54, 160–161; and the global market, 80–81; mainstream, critique of, xii, xiv. *See also* media
Pythagoras, 50

Q

Qarawiyyin, al-, 87

R

race, described, 11
Rachmaninoff, 102
racial discrimination, described, 11
racial prejudice, described, 11
racial privilege, described, 11
racism: current debate about, primary concern in, 12; fighting, posturing about, xii, 4, 8, 167, 168; forms of, described, 11; persistence of, xiv; shifting discussions of, from domestic to global, 12–15; trigger for shift in conversations about, 4; Western domination rooted in, xiv
radio, 98, 99, 101
Ramayana story, 91
ranking systems, 55, 87, 88–89, 130, 148, 149
rating systems, 55, 57, 59, 63–64, 67, 68, 164
Reagan, Ronald, 66
recycling, 149–150, 151
Reebok, 92
Regional Comprehensive Economic Partnership (RCEP), 32
regulations. *See* rules and standards, setting, role of
relationships, rules of, creating new, 162–163

religion, xiii, xiv, xvi, 27
Renaissance, 41, 50
reparations, 163
"responsible" stakeholders, 29–30, 36–37
Reuters, 72
Revolution! South America and the Rise of the New Left (Kozloff), 25
Rihanna, 128
Roda, James, 114
Rodney, Walter, 39–40
"rogue" state, idea of the, 28–30
Rolling Stones, 98
Ronaldo, Cristiano, 115
Rose, Axel, 99
Rudolph, Wilma, 111
rules and standards, setting, role of, 15, *16*, 17, 20, 21
Run-Repeat, 114
Russo-Japanese War, 28

S

Sachs, Jeffrey, 137
Samuelson, Paul, 92
sanctions, 20, 28, 34–35, 46, 48, 67
Sankara, Thomas, x
Sarr, Yero, 144
schools. *See* business schools; education; universities
science: of controlling narratives, 51–52; delegitimizing non-Western, education as a contributor to, 88, 91–92, 93; history of, 49–51; and selective curriculums, 91
segregation, 159, 165–166
self-hate, 100
Shakespeare, 83–84, 90, 104–105
Shankar, Ravi, 102
shareholder value, 56–57, 60, 61
Singh Munda, Jaipal, 111
Sinopharm, 52
Smith, Adam, 51, 90, 92
Smith, Tommy, 111
social foundations, sphere of, 18. *See also* education; history; media
social justice: global call for, and a post-Western world, 8; proclamations about spreading, xii, 10
social media, 100, 160, 165
social responsibility, claims of, 59, 131, 152–153
soft power, leveraging, 10
South China Morning Post (SCMP), 80
sovereign equality, 15, 26–28

sports: changing arena of, and race, 111–113; conclusions on, 121–122; and cultural identity, 98; exception to the Western-centered focus in, 119–120; expressions of White privilege in, 19; fighting White privilege in, suggestions for, 122, 162; and geopolitics, 112; and the impacts of Western control in, 118–119; major, 112, 117; managerial control in, on a global level, 116–121; and media, 112, 114, 117, 118, 119, 120, 121; and non-Western sporting heroes, 114–116; personal story involving, 110–111; popularity and prestige in, 114–116, 118, 121; profitability of, 112, 117–118, 121; racism and adoration in, 113–114; relationship of, to White privilege, *18*
stakeholder value, 56
stakeholders, "responsible," 29–30, 36–37
Standard and Poor's, 63
standards. *See* rules and standards, setting, role of
Stanford, 60
status quo, 8, 29, 62, 65, 108, 154
stereotyping, 73, 105–106, 106, 107, 109, 116, 130
Stern Review (report), 143
stock markets, 64
Strategic Management: A Stakeholder Approach (Freeman), 56
Structural Assistance Programmes, 32
structural racism: addressing, difficulties in, 14; described, 11, 12; visibility and invisibility of, 5
structures, role of, 4, 9, 10, 11, 12, 14, 15–17, 20
success, spread and celebration of, disparity in, 21
Sukhoi, 67
Sunday Times (newspaper), 72
superficial representation. *See* tokenism
sustainability, *18*, 19, 131, 137, 138, 140, 144, 148, 150, 152–153
Sustainable State, The (Nair), 14
Swan Lake (ballet), 104

T

taboo subject: impact of Black Lives Matter on, ix; tackling a, 8
Taghribat Bani Hilal story, 91
Tagore, Rabindranath, 90

Taj Mahal, 41
Tambo, Oliver, 3
Tarzan (film/television show), 104
technology: competition over, reaction to, 66–67; delegitimizing non-Western, education as a contributor to, 91–92; focus on, as solution to environmental issues, critique of, 139–140, 143; and selective curriculums, 91
television news networks. *See* media
television shows. *See* film and television shows
Tendulkar, Sachin, 120
Tharoor, Shashi, 44
theater and dance (performing arts), 100, 104–105
think tanks, 1, 35, 79
Thunberg, Greta, 137, 144, 145
Tik Tok, 67
Time Person of the Year, 145
tokenism, 11, 59, 105, 123, 125, 129–130, 135, 167
Tolkien, J.R.R., 51, 90
Tosh, Peter, 2
trade, free, 61, 131, 132
trade agreements, 32
trade barriers, 66
Trans-Pacific Partnership (TPP), 32
Trump, Donald, 7, 8, 44, 66–67, 75, 141, 155, 156
truth commissions, 163
Ture, Kwame (Stokely Carmichael), 12
Tutu, Desmond, 1

U

UN Human Rights Council, 155
UN Security Council, 33, 171
UNESCO, 161
Unigwe, Chika, 144
Uniqlo, 129
United Nations Framework Convention on Climate Change, 143
United Nations (UN), 27, 28, 30, 33, 37, 46, 162, 163
unity/unifying, 8, 35, 111
universities: change within, suggestions for, 166–167; difference between business schools and, 94; establishing courses at, to study issues related to White privilege, 160; and prestige, 86–87, 88, 89; ranking, 87, 88, 89. *See also* education
University of Bologna, 87

Upanishads, 83
US Capitol attack, 4, 8, 156
US Constitution, 161
US Government Accountability Office, 87
US National Institute of Allergy and
    Infectious Disease (NIAD), 88
US Securities and Exchange Commis-
    sion, 63
US Supreme Court, 161
US-China relations, 4, 5, 23, 29, 36–37,
    66–67, 71, 106

V

vaccines, 17, 20, 51–52. *See also*
    pandemic
Victoria's Secret, 124
Vietnam War, 2, 22, 24, 46, 47–48, 107
visas, 78, 158
Vogue (magazine), 133, 135

W

Wall Street Journal (newspaper), 72,
    73, 80
Wang, Alexander, 134
war: atrocities of, 47, 48, 49, 53; avoiding,
    26; films depicting, 107; glorification
    of, and liberal interventionism, 41,
    46–48, 49; lives that matter in, Western
    narrative of, 48–49, 76; media
    coverage of, 75–76; using hunger as a
    tool of, efforts to prevent, 30. *See also*
    military power
war crimes, 33, 43, 48
War on Terror, 128
Washington Consensus, 32
waste management, 149–152
Wealth of Nations (Smith), 92
Welch, Jack, 61
Western civilization, contributions of,
    xiv, 8
Western enlightenment, as a lie, xii
Western hegemony: confronting, after
    decolonization, ix; current explana-
    tions of, critique of, xii. *See also*
    dominance
Western privilege/superiority. *See* White
    privilege
Westernization, 1, 2, 11, 40, 84, 85, 89,
    91, 100, 103, 106, 107, 108, 123, 130,
    133, 135, 165, 166, 171
Wharton, 60
Wheatcroft, Geoffrey, 46
White, using, as a term, significance of, 7
White populism, rise of, 76

White privilege: circular mechanism
    behind, and its perpetuation, 16–17;
    concept of, understanding, 10–11; as a
    descriptor, ix, 1; dismantling, need for,
    7, 9, 15; early awareness of, xi;
    examining, purpose of, 6; expanding
    the conversation about, reasons for,
    3–7; global dimension of, 4–5, 6;
    global expressions of, 9–10; greater
    awareness of, need for, xi–xii, 15; key
    to dismantling, 10; mainstreaming of,
    xii–xiii; objective of, 5–6; origins of,
    xiv; patterns reinforcing, 4, 15, 19–21;
    profound and insidious impact of, xi,
    xiii–xiv, 1, 3, 4–5; spheres of, 18; as a
    taboo subject, ix, 8; unmasking,
    importance of, 7–8; various pathways
    to dismantling, 21. *See also* business;
    change; education; entertainment;
    environment; fashion; geopolitics;
    history; media; sports
White savior model, 19, 21, 75, 137,
    144–145, 148, 149, 158, 170. *See also*
    heroes
White supremacy: and the attack on the
    US Capitol, 4, 8, 156; domination
    rooted in, 159; in film and television,
    104; mainstreaming of, xii–xiii;
    race-based clubs of, 162; and religion,
    xiii; sharp rise of, xii; system built to
    perpetuate, camouflaging, 3; as a
    threat, 155
White Zombie (film), 103
Whiteness: access to power afforded by,
    determining, 20; connection of
    capitalism and, 60; craving, in sports
    heroes, 119; described, 10–11;
    discouraging the use of race and,
    creating new rules for, 162–163;
    dominant belief about, reinforcing, 17;
    exposing the nature of, in fashion,
    135–136; messaging in music and
    promotion of, 103; promoting, as an
    issue with products and services, xv–
    xvi; seeking, phenomenon of, xi, 126,
    159, 165; status symbols of, spreading,
    71–72
Whitewashing, 41, 43–44, 45, 105,
    137–139
Williams, Serena, 115
Wimbledon Tennis Championship, 115
Wirecard, 62–63
World Anti-Doping Agency (WADA),
    112

World Bank, 8, 13, 30, 31–32, 36–37, 46, 142, 150, 162, 171
World Cups: field hockey, 110; soccer, 120–121
World Economic Forum, 168
World Food Programme (WFP), 30, 162
World Health Organization (WHO), 31, 37
world order: bipolar, shift from, to unipolar, 23; building of, 9; contemporary, 4; disrupting, reaction to, 154–155; and education, 85; expressions of White privilege in, 19; fraying of, 9; managing, 24–25; and the pecking order, 4, 17, 154; relationship of, to White privilege, *18*; and "responsible" stakeholders, 29, 36; significance of, 23; sustaining, 29, 171; violating, 20, 25, 32–35. *See also* geopolitics
"world police," 37, 47
World Rugby, 112
World Trade Organization (WTO), 36, 66, 164
World War I, 28, 41, 107

World War II: and culture, 101, 107; and education, 96; and geopolitics, 8–9, 23, 24, 26, 27, 28, 32, 33; and history, 41, 46, 47, 49, 53, 96; and the media, 70–71
World Wide Fund for Nature (WWF), 148
Wretched of the Earth, The (Fanon), 12, 40

X
Xakriaba, Artemisa, 144
xenophobia, 23, 33

Y
Yai, Anok, 133
Yosemite National Park, 147
younger generation: involvement of, in change, suggestions for, 171; need for, to study White privilege, xi
YouTube, 100
Yo-Yo Ma, 102

Z
Zara, 124
Zhengfei, Ren, 55
Zhong Nanshan, 88

C handran Nair grew up in postcolonial Malaysia, amid the nation's diverse racial and cultural composition. After attending university in the UK, he moved to southern Africa to do volunteer work on development issues. It was during this time that he became very interested in the nature of economic development, its relationship with geopolitics, and the nature of institutionalized racism.

He returned to Asia to pursue a career in environmental consulting, during which time he built Asia's largest environmental consulting group. Twenty years in consulting offered him an opportunity to work with many from all parts of the world, both in government and the private sector. His experience led to an acute understanding of the norms and tensions of conducting business between the West and the Rest.

In particular, his firsthand experience of the inequalities of this relationship led him to the belief that the non-Western world should not be reliant on Western models of political and economic development, which have been designed in favor of a Western agenda. This belief prompted him to start a pan-Asian think tank in 2006 called the Global Institute for Tomorrow (GIFT), which promotes a deeper understanding of the shift of influence from the West to Asia and focuses on what the needs of the post-Western world will be.

His views on issues in Asia and the developing world have been featured in the print media, ranging from the *Financial Times*, the *Wall Street Journal* and the *New York Times* to *HuffPost*, the *Guardian*, and *China Daily*. His opinions have been sought by an array of media outlets, including the BBC, CNN, NHK, Al Jazeera, CCTV, Bloomberg, and Channel News Asia, among others.

He sits on the executive committee of the Club of Rome, one of the world's premier scientific think tanks, and was one of the founding members of the Club of Rome China. He is an advisor to the Royal Cambodian government and is a fellow of the Royal Society of the Arts.

He is a keen sportsman and managed the Hong Kong field hockey team to two Asian Games. He plays the saxophone and used to be a member of an Afro-Jazz-Reggae band called *Imphandze* during his time in Africa; one of their albums, *Mlabalaba*, can be found on Spotify.

WORKING ON EQUITY: THE GLOBAL INSTITUTE FOR TOMORROW

In 2004, I left my position as Asia-Pacific chairman for Environmental Resource Management (ERM), the international consultancy firm that advises global companies and governments on environmental management and sustainability.

I spent many enjoyable years there, growing the company from a single office in Hong Kong to twenty-two offices in twelve countries, making it the leading environmental consultancy in the Asia Pacific. However, as the only non-White board member and the only one with a non-Western worldview, I came to understand over time that my presence was causing discomfort among the other board members.

This coincided with my growing appreciation of how entrenched Western viewpoints are in so many global businesses and the widespread unwillingness to adopt non-Western ideas and practices. In the United States, ERM did not, at that time, have even a single Black partner.

That motivated me to leave and set up the Global Institute for Tomorrow (GIFT) in Hong Kong in 2006 as a pan-Asian think tank, with the hope of developing and promoting new ideas about the future, rooted in a non-Western experience. It had always struck me as odd that the most prominent think tanks in the region were from the West and that most of the others were state or industry funded and thus not truly independent.

GIFT is now an independent and internationally recognized think tank, with offices in Hong Kong and Kuala Lumpur and with partner organizations across the world, from Europe to Africa and the Middle East. GIFT is committed to promoting a deeper understanding of the shift of influence from the West to Asia; the dynamic relationships among business, society, and the state; and the reshaping of the rules of global capitalism in order to create a more just and sustainable world. A key goal is to prepare the next generation of leaders with insights, mindsets, and behaviors to navigate the coming post-Western world.

We developed our own operating model to ensure our independence—experiential programs for young leaders from across Asia and beyond, which expose them to new ideas and new thinking.

For over a decade, we have been on the front lines of cultivating ideas around economic development, sustainability, and the world's neglect of biological systems—a position now bearing fruit with the new normal created in the wake of the pandemic.

The 2020 pandemic has helped further validate many of the ideas we have been developing, such as the need for food self-sufficiency, massive investments in local health care industries to build self-reliance, the concept of moderate prosperity, an emphasis on collective welfare rather than individual rights, and the primary role of the state.

Finally, we are seeking to frame the very inconvenient truths/answers to and search for unanswered economic questions within the business models of today: How do we price externalities and redesign our economies so that we are not reliant on relentless underpricing of resources and the externalization of true costs as our main pathway to create prosperity as we currently understand it? Within that context and in the face of the harsh realities of a constrained planet, what are our rights and freedoms?

Berrett–Koehler
Publishers

Berrett-Koehler is an independent publisher dedicated to an ambitious mission: *Connecting people and ideas to create a world that works for all.*

We believe that the solutions to the world's problems will come from all of us, working at all levels: in our organizations, in our society, and in our own lives. Our BK Business books help people make their organizations more humane, democratic, diverse, and effective (we don't think there's any contradiction there). Our BK Currents books offer pathways to creating a more just, equitable, and sustainable society. Our BK Life books help people create positive change in their lives and align their personal practices with their aspirations for a better world.

All of our books are designed to bring people seeking positive change together around the ideas that empower them to see and shape the world in a new way.

And we strive to practice what we preach. At the core of our approach is Stewardship, a deep sense of responsibility to administer the company for the benefit of all of our stakeholder groups including authors, customers, employees, investors, service providers, and the communities and environment around us. Everything we do is built around this and our other key values of quality, partnership, inclusion, and sustainability.

This is why we are both a B-Corporation and a California Benefit Corporation—a certification and a for-profit legal status that require us to adhere to the highest standards for corporate, social, and environmental performance.

We are grateful to our readers, authors, and other friends of the company who consider themselves to be part of the BK Community. We hope that you, too, will join us in our mission.

We hope you enjoy this BK Currents book.

A BK Currents Book

BK Currents books bring people together to advance social and economic justice, shared prosperity, sustainability, and new solutions for national and global issues. They advocate for systemic change and provide the ideas and tools to solve social problems at their root. So get to it!

To find out more, visit **www.bkconnection.com.**

Berrett–Koehler
Publishers

Connecting people and ideas
to create a world that works for all

Dear Reader,

Thank you for picking up this book and joining our worldwide community of Berrett-Koehler readers. We share ideas that bring positive change into people's lives, organizations, and society.

To welcome you, we'd like to offer you a free e-book. You can pick from among twelve of our bestselling books by entering the promotional code **BKP92E** here: http://www.bkconnection.com/welcome.

When you claim your free e-book, we'll also send you a copy of our e-newsletter, the *BK Communiqué*. Although you're free to unsubscribe, there are many benefits to sticking around. In every issue of our newsletter you'll find

- A free e-book
- Tips from famous authors
- Discounts on spotlight titles
- Hilarious insider publishing news
- A chance to win a prize for answering a riddle

Best of all, our readers tell us, "Your newsletter is the only one I actually read." So claim your gift today, and please stay in touch!

Sincerely,

Charlotte Ashlock
Steward of the BK Website

Questions? Comments? Contact me at bkcommunity@bkpub.com.